The Word of the Lord –
Special Occasions

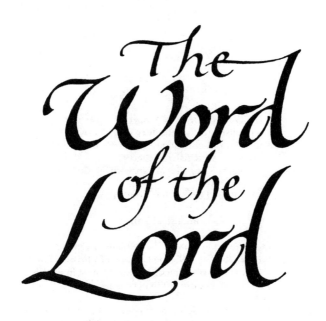

The Word of the Lord

Special Occasions

Collects, Post-Communion Prayers
& Scripture Readings
for use with

Common Worship

Services
in The Church of England

CANTERBURY
PRESS
Norwich

The Word of the Lord - Special Occasions
is published by **Canterbury Press Norwich**
a publishing imprint of Hymns Ancient & Modern Limited,
a registered charity,
St Mary's Works, St Mary's Plain, Norwich, Norfolk, NR3 3BH

Edited by Brother Tristam SSF

Published 2001

Bible Readings are from the *New Revised Standard Version* of the Bible,
Anglicized Edition, © 1989, 1995, the Division of Christian Education
of the National Council of the Churches of Christ in the USA
and are used with permission.

Ordination Services' lectionaries, collects and post-communion prayers used are from:
The Alternative Service Book 1980,
© The Central Board of Finance of the Church of England, 1980, 1985;
and are used with permission;
and the Ordination Services' lectionaries from:
The Book of Common Prayer,
the rights in which are vested in the Crown,
and used by permission of the Crown's Patentee, Cambridge University Press.

Other services' lectionaries, collects and post-communion prayers used are from:
Common Worship: Services and Prayers for the Church of England,
© The Archbishops' Council, 2000;
Common Worship: Pastoral Services, © The Archbishops' Council, 2000;
Common Worship: Initiation Services,
© The Central Board of Finance of the Church of England, 1997, 1998
and are used with permission.

A catalogue record for this book is available
from the British Library.

ISBN 1-85311-355-7

Printed and bound in Great Britain by Biddles Ltd, *www.biddles.co.uk*

Contents

Notes

The Word of the Lord - Special Occasions is intended primarily for use at public, corporate worship, though some of the pastoral offices are rightly used often with simply the minister and one or two other persons present. Generally, however, the book is intended to be used at a lectern or on a minister's stall, and not for direct congregational use.

ORDERING THE SERVICE
Notes for ordering the particular service can be found in the series of books which make up *Common Worship*, published by Church House Publishing.

COLLECTS & POST-COMMUNION PRAYERS
No provision is made in *Common Worship* 'For those taking vows'; the Collect provision from *The Alternative Service Book 1980* has been used and a Post-Communion Prayer added.
For services of *Ordination*, see the notes on pages 77 and 86.

THE LECTIONARY
The portions from Scripture are printed in order: **Old Testament** (including Apocrypha), **Psalmody**, **Epistle** (including Acts and Revelation) and **Gospel**, so as to facilitate their use at the Eucharist. In no way is this intended to inhibit their use at services in a different context.

The printed introduction to **the Gospel reading** is that for normative use at non-eucharistic worship (except at ordinations, where the service is always in the context of the eucharist, and at *A Celebration of Wholeness and Healing* and at services of *Baptism and Confirmation*, where clear guidelines are given).
If the service is in the context of a eucharist, the introduction should be changed to: 'Hear the Gospel of our Lord Jesus Christ according to N.'and the Gospel reading should be completed with the words: 'This is the Gospel of the Lord'. This introduction and ending may also be used at non-eucharistic services.

Similarly, **other scriptural readings** may end with: 'This is the word of the Lord' and these words may be used at any service, be it eucharistic or non-eucharistic worship.

The **references** give book, chapter and verse, in that order, and if chapter and verse are being announced (which is not a requirement), they should be stated in that order.

The text of **The Psalms** is not printed out, as it is expected that psalms and other hymns will normally be sung by the whole congregation, either fully or responsorially, and this book will not meet that need.

ROUND BRACKETS ( ) which are included in the Biblical text are repeated here. Such texts should always be read.

SQUARE BRACKETS [ ] indicate that the text within them may be omitted, as suggested by the compilers of the various lectionaries.

SUPERSCRIPT VERSE NUMBERS
Where some verses have been omitted, the verse number at which the text resumes is noted in superscript. This may be quietly announced if others are following the text in their own Bibles. Otherwise, no announcement is necessary.

SISTER VOLUMES
Three books, entitled *The Word of the Lord – Year A*, *The Word of the Lord – Year B* and The *Word of the Lord – Year C* complement this book.

A book containing the **Gospel readings** for use at the Principal Service is called *The Gospel of The Lord.*

The final sister volume to this series of books is *Exciting Holiness.* It contains the readings necessary for use at the Principal Service on **Festivals and Lesser Festivals**.

All these books follow the Church of England lectionaries, chiefly for use with *Common Worship,* and also include some readings included in *The Book of Common Prayer* and in *The Alternative Service Book 1980* not specifically referenced in *Common Worship.*

Two books of non-Scriptural spiritual readings complement the Calendar of *Common Worship*: these are *Celebrating the Saints* and *Celebrating the Seasons,* edited by the Revd Robert Atwell.

All these books are published by The Canterbury Press Norwich.

Welcome

Welcome

Thanksgiving for the Gift of a Child

Collect
Loving God,
you hold all things in life
and call us into your kingdom of peace:
help us to walk the path of your truth
and fill our lives with gratitude and faith;
through Jesus Christ our Lord.

A reading from the Book of the Exodus. (20.12)
God spoke these words: Honour your father and your mother, so that
your days may be long in the land that the Lord your God is giving
you.

A reading from the prophecy of Isaiah. (9.2,6-7)
The people who walked in darkness
   have seen a great light;
those who lived in a land of deep darkness –
   on them light has shined.
6 For a child has been born for us,
   a son given to us;
authority rests upon his shoulders;
   and he is named
Wonderful Counsellor, Mighty God,
   Everlasting Father, Prince of Peace.
His authority shall grow continually,
   and there shall be endless peace
for the throne of David and his kingdom.
   He will establish and uphold it
with justice and with righteousness
   from this time onward and for evermore.
The zeal of the Lord of hosts will do this.

Psalm 20; Psalm 128; Psalm 139.7-18

A reading from the Letter of Paul to the Ephesians. (3.14-end)
I bow my knees before the Father, from whom every family in heaven and on earth takes its name. I pray that, according to the riches of his glory, he may grant that you may be strengthened in your inner being with power through his Spirit, and that Christ may dwell in your hearts through faith, as you are being rooted and grounded in love. I pray that you may have the power to comprehend, with all the saints, what is the breadth and length and height and depth, and to know the love of Christ that surpasses knowledge, so that you may be filled with all the fullness of God.

Now to him who by the power at work within us is able to accomplish abundantly far more than all we can ask or imagine, to him be glory in the church and in Christ Jesus to all generations, for ever and ever. Amen.

A reading from the Letter of Paul to the Ephesians. (6.1-4)
Children, obey your parents in the Lord, for this is right. 'Honour your father and mother' – this is the first commandment with a promise: 'so that it may be well with you and you may live long on the earth.'

And, fathers, do not provoke your children to anger, but bring them up in the discipline and instruction of the Lord.

A reading from the First Letter of John. (2.12-14)
I am writing to you, little children,
because your sins are forgiven on account of Christ's name.
I am writing to you, fathers,
because you know him who is from the beginning.
I am writing to you, young people,
because you have conquered the evil one.
I write to you, children,
because you know the Father.
I write to you, fathers,
because you know him who is from the beginning.
I write to you, young people,
because you are strong
and the word of God abides in you,
and you have overcome the evil one.

A reading from the Gospel according to Matthew. (1.18-end)
The birth of Jesus the Messiah took place in this way. When his mother Mary had been engaged to Joseph, but before they lived together, she was found to be with child from the Holy Spirit. Her husband Joseph, being a righteous man and unwilling to expose her to public disgrace, planned to dismiss her quietly. But just when he had resolved to do this, an angel of the Lord appeared to him in a dream and said, 'Joseph, son of David, do not be afraid to take Mary as your wife, for the child conceived in her is from the Holy Spirit. She will bear a son, and you are to name him Jesus, for he will save his people from their sins.' All this took place to fulfil what had been spoken by the Lord through the prophet:
    'Look, the virgin shall conceive and bear a son,
        and they shall name him Emmanuel,'
which means, 'God is with us.' When Joseph awoke from sleep, he did as the angel of the Lord commanded him; he took her as his wife, but had no marital relations with her until she had borne a son; and he named him Jesus.

A reading from the Gospel according to Matthew. (7.24-27)
Jesus said to his disciples, 'Everyone who hears these words of mine and acts on them will be like a wise man who built his house on rock. The rain fell, the floods came, and the winds blew and beat on that house, but it did not fall, because it had been founded on rock. And everyone who hears these words of mine and does not act on them will be like a foolish man who built his house on sand. The rain fell, and the floods came, and the winds blew and beat against that house, and it fell – and great was its fall!'

A reading from the Gospel according to Matthew. (18.1-5)
The disciples came to Jesus and asked, 'Who is the greatest in the kingdom of heaven?' He called a child, whom he put among them, and said, 'Truly I tell you, unless you change and become like children, you will never enter the kingdom of heaven. Whoever becomes humble like this child is the greatest in the kingdom of heaven. Whoever welcomes one such child in my name welcomes me.'

A reading from the Gospel according to Matthew. (18.10-14)
Having called a child to him, Jesus said to his disciples, 'Take care that you do not despise one of these little ones; for, I tell you, in heaven their angels continually see the face of my Father in heaven. What do you think? If a shepherd has a hundred sheep, and one of them

has gone astray, does he not leave the ninety-nine on the mountains and go in search of the one that went astray? And if he finds it, truly I tell you, he rejoices over it more than over the ninety-nine that never went astray. So it is not the will of your Father in heaven that one of these little ones should be lost.'

A reading from the Gospel according to Mark. *(10.13-16)*
People were bringing little children to Jesus in order that he might touch them; and the disciples spoke sternly to them. But when Jesus saw this, he was indignant and said to them, 'Let the little children come to me; do not stop them; for it is to such as these that the kingdom of God belongs. Truly I tell you, whoever does not receive the kingdom of God as a little child will never enter it.' And he took them up in his arms, laid his hands on them, and blessed them.

A reading from the Gospel according to Luke. *(1.39-45)*
Mary set out and went with haste to a Judean town in the hill country, where she entered the house of Zechariah and greeted Elizabeth. When Elizabeth heard Mary's greeting, the child leapt in her womb. And Elizabeth was filled with the Holy Spirit and exclaimed with a loud cry, 'Blessèd are you among women, and blessèd is the fruit of your womb. And why has this happened to me, that the mother of my Lord comes to me? For as soon as I heard the sound of your greeting, the child in my womb leapt for joy. And blessèd is she who believed that there would be a fulfilment of what was spoken to her by the Lord.'

A reading from the Gospel according to Luke. *(2.22-24)*
When the time came for their purification according to to the law of Moses, Mary and Joseph brought Jesus up to Jerusalem to present him to the Lord (as it is written in the law of the Lord, 'Every first-born male shall be designated as holy to the Lord'), and they offered a sacrifice according to what is stated in the law of the Lord, 'a pair of turtledoves or two young pigeons.'

A reading from the Gospel according to Luke. *(2.33-40)*
Jesus' father and mother were amazed at what was being said about him. Then Simeon blessed them and said to his mother Mary, 'This child is destined for the falling and the rising of many in Israel, and to be a sign that will be opposed so that the inner thoughts of many will be revealed – and a sword will pierce your own soul too.'

There was also a prophet, Anna the daughter of Phanuel, of the tribe of Asher. She was of a great age, having lived with her husband seven years after her marriage, then as a widow to the age of eighty-four. She never left the temple but worshipped there with fasting and prayer night and day. At that moment she came, and began to praise God and to speak about the child to all who were looking for the redemption of Jerusalem.

When they had finished everything required by the law of the Lord, they returned to Galilee, to their own town of Nazareth. The child grew and became strong, filled with wisdom; and the favour of God was upon him.

A reading from the Gospel according to John. (1.9-14)
The true light, which enlightens everyone, was coming into the world.

He was in the world, and the world came into being through him; yet the world did not know him. He came to what was his own, and his own people did not accept him. But to all who received him, who believed in his name, he gave power to become children of God, who were born, not of blood or of the will of the flesh or of the will of man, but of God.

And the Word became flesh and lived among us, and we have seen his glory, the glory as of a father's only son, full of grace and truth.

Initiation

Initiation

Holy Baptism

The Collect, Post-Communion Prayer and readings 'of Sunday' are normally used; otherwise they are either 'of the day' or the following, which may also be used at Baptism with Confirmation, or Affirmation of Baptismal Faith or Reception into the Communion of the Church of England:

Collect
Heavenly Father,
by the power of your Holy Spirit
you give to your faithful people
  new life in the water of baptism;
guide and strengthen us by the same Spirit
that we, who are born again,
may serve you in faith and love
and grow into the full stature of your Son, Jesus Christ,
who is alive and reigns with you
in the unity of the Holy Spirit,
one God, now and for ever.

Post Communion
Eternal God, our beginning and our end,
preserve in your people the new life of baptism;
as Christ receives us on earth,
so may he guide us through the trials of this world
and enfold us in the joy of heaven,
where you live and reign,
one God, for ever and ever.

The following Post-Communion Prayer may be used at Baptism with Confirmation, or Affirmation of Baptismal Faith or Reception into the Communion of the Church of England:

God of mercy,
by whose grace alone
we are accepted and equipped for your service:
stir up in us the gifts of your Holy Spirit
and make us worthy of our calling,
that we may bring forth the fruit of the Spirit
in love and joy and peace;
through Jesus Christ our Lord.

General – Set I

A reading from the prophecy of Isaiah. (43.1-7)
> Thus says the Lord,
>> he who created you, O Jacob,
>> he who formed you, O Israel:
> Do not fear, for I have redeemed you;
>> I have called you by name, you are mine.
> When you pass through the waters, I will be with you;
>> and through the rivers, they shall not overwhelm you;
> when you walk through fire you shall not be burned,
>> and the flame shall not consume you.
> For I am the Lord your God,
>> the Holy One of Israel, your Saviour.
> I give Egypt as your ransom,
>> Ethiopia and Seba in exchange for you.
> Because you are precious in my sight,
>> and honoured, and I love you,
> I give people in return for you,
>> nations in exchange for your life.
> Do not fear, for I am with you;
>> I will bring your offspring from the east,
>> and from the west I will gather you;
> I will say to the north, 'Give them up,'
>> and to the south, 'Do not withhold;
> bring my sons from far away
>> and my daughters from the end of the earth –
> everyone who is called by my name,
>> whom I created for my glory,
>> whom I formed and made.'

Psalm 66.5-12

A reading from the Letter of Paul to the Romans. (5.6-11)
While we were still weak, at the right time Christ died for the ungodly. Indeed, rarely will anyone die for a righteous person – though perhaps for a good person someone might actually dare to die. But God proves his love for us in that while we still were sinners Christ died for us. Much more surely then, now that we have been justified by his blood, will we be saved through him from the wrath of God. For if while we were enemies, we were reconciled to God through the death of his Son, much more surely, having been reconciled, will we

be saved by his life. But more than that, we even boast in God through our Lord Jesus Christ, through whom we have now received reconciliation.

Hear the Gospel of our Lord Jesus Christ according to Mark.
(1.1-11 or 9-11)

[The beginning of the good news of Jesus Christ, the Son of God.
  As it is written in the prophet Isaiah,
    'See, I am sending my messenger ahead of you,
      who will prepare your way;
    the voice of one crying out in the wilderness:
      "Prepare the way of the Lord,
      make his paths straight,"'
John the baptizer appeared in the wilderness, proclaiming a baptism of repentance for the forgiveness of sins. And people from the whole Judean countryside and all the people of Jerusalem were going out to him, and were baptized by him in the river Jordan, confessing their sins. Now John was clothed with camel's hair, with a leather belt around his waist, and he ate locusts and wild honey. He proclaimed, 'The one who is more powerful than I is coming after me; I am not worthy to stoop down and untie the thong of his sandals. I have baptized you with water; but he will baptize you with the Holy Spirit.'
⁹ In those days] Jesus came from Nazareth of Galilee and was baptized by John in the Jordan. And just as he was coming up out of the water, he saw the heavens torn apart and the Spirit descending like a dove on him. And a voice came from heaven, 'You are my Son, the Belovèd; with you I am well pleased.'

This is the Gospel of Christ.

General – Set II

A reading from the book Genesis. (17.1-8)

When Abram was ninety-nine years old, the Lord appeared to Abram, and said to him, 'I am God Almighty; walk before me, and be blameless. And I will make my covenant between me and you, and will make you exceedingly numerous.' Then Abram fell on his face; and God said to him, 'As for me, this is my covenant with you: You shall be the ancestor of a multitude of nations. No longer shall your name be Abram, but your name shall be Abraham; for I have made you the ancestor of a multitude of nations. I will make you exceedingly fruitful; and I will make nations of you, and kings shall come from you. I will establish my covenant between me and you, and your offspring after you throughout their generations, for an everlasting covenant, to be God to you and to your offspring after you. And I will give to you, and to your offspring after you, the land where you are now an alien, all the land of Canaan, for a perpetual holding; and I will be their God.'

Or:

A reading from the book Genesis. (22.15-18)

The angel of the Lord called to Abraham a second time from heaven, and said, 'By myself I have sworn, says the Lord: Because you have done this, and have not withheld your son, your only son, I will indeed bless you, and I will make your offspring as numerous as the stars of heaven and as the sand that is on the seashore. And your offspring shall possess the gate of their enemies, and by your offspring shall all the nations of the earth gain blessing for themselves, because you have obeyed my voice.'

Psalm 89.21,22,25-29

A reading from the Letter of Paul to the Galatians. (3.27 – 4.7)

As many of you as were baptized into Christ have clothed yourselves with Christ. There is no longer Jew or Greek, there is no longer slave or free, there is no longer male and female; for all of you are one in Christ Jesus. And if you belong to Christ, then you are Abraham's offspring, heirs according to the promise.

My point is this: heirs, as long as they are minors, are no better than slaves, though they are the owners of all the property; but they remain under guardians and trustees until the date set by the father. So with us; while we were minors, we were enslaved to the elemental spirits of the world. But when the fullness of time had come, God sent his Son, born of a woman, born under the law, in order to redeem those who were under the law, so that we might receive adoption as children. And because you are children, God has sent the Spirit of his Son into our hearts, crying, 'Abba! Father!' So you are no longer a slave but a child, and if a child then also an heir, through God.

Hear the Gospel of our Lord Jesus Christ according to John. (15.1-11)
Jesus said to his disciples, 'I am the true vine, and my Father is the vinegrower. He removes every branch in me that bears no fruit. Every branch that bears fruit he prunes to make it bear more fruit. You have already been cleansed by the word that I have spoken to you. Abide in me as I abide in you. Just as the branch cannot bear fruit by itself unless it abides in the vine, neither can you unless you abide in me. I am the vine, you are the branches. Those who abide in me and I in them bear much fruit, because apart from me you can do nothing. Whoever does not abide in me is thrown away like a branch and withers; such branches are gathered, thrown into the fire, and burned. If you abide in me, and my words abide in you, ask for whatever you wish, and it will be done for you. My Father is glorified by this, that you bear much fruit and become my disciples. As the Father has loved me, so I have loved you; abide in my love. If you keep my commandments, you will abide in my love, just as I have kept my Father's commandments and abide in his love. I have said these things to you so that my joy may be in you, and that your joy may be complete.'

This is the Gospel of Christ.

General – Set III

A reading from the Second Book of the Kings. (5.1-15a)

Naaman, commander of the army of the king of Aram, was a great man and in high favour with his master, because by him the Lord had given victory to Aram. The man, though a mighty warrior, suffered from leprosy. Now the Arameans on one of their raids had taken a young girl captive from the land of Israel, and she served Naaman's wife. She said to her mistress, 'If only my lord were with the prophet who is in Samaria! He would cure him of his leprosy.' So Naaman went in and told his lord just what the girl from the land of Israel had said. And the king of Aram said, 'Go then, and I will send along a letter to the king of Israel.'

He went, taking with him ten talents of silver, six thousand shekels of gold, and ten sets of garments. He brought the letter to the king of Israel, which read, 'When this letter reaches you, know that I have sent to you my servant Naaman, that you may cure him of his leprosy.' When the king of Israel read the letter, he tore his clothes and said, 'Am I God, to give death or life, that this man sends word to me to cure a man of his leprosy? Just look and see how he is trying to pick a quarrel with me.'

But when Elisha the man of God heard that the king of Israel had torn his clothes, he sent a message to the king, 'Why have you torn your clothes? Let him come to me, that he may learn that there is a prophet in Israel.' So Naaman came with his horses and chariots, and halted at the entrance of Elisha's house. Elisha sent a messenger to him, saying, 'Go, wash in the Jordan seven times, and your flesh shall be restored and you shall be clean.' But Naaman became angry and went away, saying, 'I thought that for me he would surely come out, and stand and call on the name of the Lord his God, and would wave his hand over the spot, and cure the leprosy! Are not Abana and Pharpar, the rivers of Damascus, better than all the waters of Israel? Could I not wash in them, and be clean?' He turned and went away in a rage. But his servants approached and said to him, 'Father, if the prophet had commanded you to do something difficult, would you not have done it? How much more, when all he said to you was, "Wash, and be clean"?' So he went down and immersed himself seven times in the Jordan, according to the word of the man of God; his flesh was restored like the flesh of a young boy, and he was clean.

Then he returned to the man of God, he and all his company; he came and stood before him and said, 'Now I know that there is no God in all the earth except in Israel.'

Psalm 51.1-6

A reading from the Letter of Paul to Titus. *(3.3-7)*
We ourselves were once foolish, disobedient, led astray, slaves to various passions and pleasures, passing our days in malice and envy, despicable, hating one another. But when the goodness and loving kindness of God our Saviour appeared, he saved us, not because of any works of righteousness that we had done, but according to his mercy, through the water of rebirth and renewal by the Holy Spirit. This Spirit he poured out on us richly through Jesus Christ our Saviour, so that, having been justified by his grace, we might become heirs according to the hope of eternal life.

Hear the Gospel of our Lord Jesus Christ according to John. *(3.1-8)*
There was a Pharisee named Nicodemus, a leader of the Jews. He came to Jesus by night and said to him, 'Rabbi, we know that you are a teacher who has come from God; for no one can do these signs that you do apart from the presence of God.' Jesus answered him, 'Very truly, I tell you, no one can see the kingdom of God without being born from above.' Nicodemus said to him, 'How can anyone be born after having grown old? Can one enter a second time into the mother's womb and be born?' Jesus answered, 'Very truly, I tell you, no one can enter the kingdom of God without being born of water and Spirit. What is born of the flesh is flesh, and what is born of the Spirit is spirit. Do not be astonished that I said to you, "You must be born from above." The wind blows where it chooses, and you hear the sound of it, but you do not know where it comes from or where it goes. So it is with everyone who is born of the Spirit.'

This is the Gospel of Christ.

General – Set IV

A reading from the book Genesis. *(7.1,7-16)*
The Lord said to Noah, 'Go into the ark, you and all your household, for I have seen that you alone are righteous before me in this
generation.'
⁷ And Noah with his sons and his wife and his sons' wives went into
the ark to escape the waters of the flood. Of clean animals, and of
animals that are not clean, and of birds, and of everything that creeps
on the ground, two and two, male and female, went into the ark with
Noah, as God had commanded Noah. And after seven days the
waters of the flood came on the earth.
  In the six hundredth year of Noah's life, in the second month, on the
seventeenth day of the month, on that day all the fountains of the
great deep burst forth, and the windows of the heavens were opened.
The rain fell on the earth forty days and forty nights. On the very
same day Noah with his sons, Shem and Ham and Japheth, and
Noah's wife and the three wives of his sons entered the ark, they and
every wild animal of every kind, and all domestic animals of every
kind, and every creeping thing that creeps on the earth, and every
bird of every kind – every bird, every winged creature. They went
into the ark with Noah, two and two of all flesh in which there was
the breath of life. And those that entered, male and female of all
flesh, went in as God had commanded him; and the Lord shut him in.

Psalm 46.1-7

A reading from the First Letter of Peter. *(3.18-end)*
Christ suffered for sins once for all, the righteous for the unrighteous,
in order to bring you to God. He was put to death in the flesh, but
made alive in the spirit, in which also he went and made a proclamation to the spirits in prison, who in former times did not obey,
when God waited patiently in the days of Noah, during the building
of the ark, in which a few, that is, eight persons, were saved through
water. And baptism, which this prefigured, now saves you – not as
a removal of dirt from the body, but as an appeal to God for a good
conscience, through the resurrection of Jesus Christ, who has gone
into heaven and is at the right hand of God, with angels, authorities,
and powers made subject to him.

Hear the Gospel of our Lord Jesus Christ according to Matthew.

(28.16-end)

The eleven disciples went to Galilee, to the mountain to which Jesus had directed them. When they saw him, they worshipped him; but some doubted. And Jesus came and said to them, 'All authority in heaven and on earth has been given to me. Go therefore and make disciples of all nations, baptizing them in the name of the Father and of the Son and of the Holy Spirit, and teaching them to obey everything that I have commanded you. And remember, I am with you always, to the end of the age.'

This is the Gospel of Christ.

Epiphany / Baptism of Christ / Trinity – Set I

The Collect, Post-Communion Prayer and readings 'of Sunday' are normally used; otherwise they are either 'of the day' or the following:

Collect
Lord of all time and eternity,
you opened heaven's gate and revealed yourself as Father
by the voice that called Jesus your belovèd Son,
baptizing him in the power of the Spirit:
reveal yourself to us now, to claim us as your children,
and so complete the heavenly work of our rebirth
in the waters of the new creation;
through Jesus Christ your Son our Lord,
who is alive and reigns with you
in the unity of the Holy Spirit,
one God, now and for ever.

Post Communion
God of glory,
you inspire us with the breath of life
which brought to birth a new world in Christ:
may we who are reborn in him
be transformed by the renewal of our lives,
that the light of your new creation
may flood the world with your abundant grace;
through Christ our Lord.

A reading from the Book of the Exodus. (33.12-20)
Moses said to the Lord, 'See, you have said to me, "Bring up this people"; but you have not let me know whom you will send with me. Yet you have said, "I know you by name, and you have also found favour in my sight." Now if I have found favour in your sight, show me your ways, so that I may know you and find favour in your sight. Consider too that this nation is your people.' He said, 'My presence will go with you, and I will give you rest.' And he said to him, 'If your presence will not go, do not carry us up from here. For how shall it be known that I have found favour in your sight, I and your people, unless you go with us? In this way, we shall be distinct, I and your people, from every people on the face of the earth.'

The Lord said to Moses, 'I will do the very thing that you have asked; for you have found favour in my sight, and I know you by name.' Moses said, 'Show me your glory, I pray.' And he said, 'I will make all my goodness pass before you, and will proclaim before you the name, "The Lord"; and I will be gracious to whom I will be gracious, and will show mercy on whom I will show mercy. But,' he said, 'you cannot see my face; for no one shall see me and live.'

Or:

A reading from the prophecy of Isaiah. *(9.2-3,6-7)*
>The people who walked in darkness
>>have seen a great light;
>those who lived in a land of deep darkness –
>>on them light has shined.
>You have multiplied the nation,
>>you have increased its joy;
>they rejoice before you
>>as with joy at the harvest,
>>as people exult when dividing plunder.

6   For a child has been born for us,
>>a son given to us;
>authority rests upon his shoulders;
>>and he is named
>Wonderful Counsellor, Mighty God,
>>Everlasting Father, Prince of Peace.
>His authority shall grow continually,
>>and there shall be endless peace
>for the throne of David and his kingdom.
>>He will establish and uphold it
>with justice and with righteousness
>>from this time onward and for evermore.
>The zeal of the Lord of hosts will do this.

Psalm 67

A reading from the Second Letter of Paul to the Corinthians. *(3.12 – 4.6)*
Since we have such a hope, we act with great boldness, not like Moses, who put a veil over his face to keep the people of Israel from gazing at the end of the glory that was being set aside. But their minds were hardened. Indeed, to this very day, when they hear the reading of the old covenant, that same veil is still there, since only in Christ is it set aside. Indeed, to this very day whenever Moses is read, a veil lies over their minds; but when one turns to the Lord, the veil is removed. Now the Lord is the Spirit, and where the Spirit of the Lord is, there is freedom. And all of us, with unveiled faces,

seeing the glory of the Lord as though reflected in a mirror, are being transformed into the same image from one degree of glory to another; for this comes from the Lord, the Spirit.

Therefore, since it is by God's mercy that we are engaged in this ministry, we do not lose heart. We have renounced the shameful things that one hides; we refuse to practise cunning or to falsify God's word; but by the open statement of the truth we commend ourselves to the conscience of everyone in the sight of God. And even if our gospel is veiled, it is veiled to those who are perishing. In their case the god of this world has blinded the minds of the unbelievers, to keep them from seeing the light of the gospel of the glory of Christ, who is the image of God. For we do not proclaim ourselves; we proclaim Jesus Christ as Lord and ourselves as your slaves for Jesus' sake. For it is the God who said, 'Let light shine out of darkness,' who has shone in our hearts to give the light of the knowledge of the glory of God in the face of Jesus Christ.

Hear the Gospel of our Lord Jesus Christ according to John. (1.14-18)
The Word became flesh and lived among us, and we have seen his glory, the glory as of a father's only son, full of grace and truth. (John testified to him and cried out, 'This was he of whom I said, "He who comes after me ranks ahead of me because he was before me."') From his fullness we have all received, grace upon grace. The law indeed was given through Moses; grace and truth came through Jesus Christ. No one has ever seen God. It is God the only Son, who is close to the Father's heart, who has made him known.

This is the Gospel of Christ.

Epiphany / Baptism of Christ / Trinity – Set II

For Collect and Post-Communion Prayer, see page 20.

A reading from the prophecy of Isaiah. (42.5-8)

> Thus says God, the Lord,
>> who created the heavens and stretched them out,
>> who spread out the earth and what comes from it,
> who gives breath to the people upon it
>> and spirit to those who walk in it:
> I am the Lord, I have called you in righteousness,
>> I have taken you by the hand and kept you;
> I have given you as a covenant to the people,
>> a light to the nations,
>>> to open the eyes that are blind,
> to bring out the prisoners from the dungeon,
>> from the prison those who sit in darkness.
> I am the Lord, that is my name;
>> my glory I give to no other,
>> nor my praise to idols.

Psalm 146.5-9

A reading from the Acts of the Apostles. (9.1-20 or 10-20)

[Saul, still breathing threats and murder against the disciples of the Lord, went to the high priest and asked him for letters to the synagogues at Damascus, so that if he found any who belonged to the Way, men or women, he might bring them bound to Jerusalem. Now as he was going along and approaching Damascus, suddenly a light from heaven flashed around him. He fell to the ground and heard a voice saying to him, 'Saul, Saul, why do you persecute me?' He asked, 'Who are you, Lord?' The reply came, 'I am Jesus, whom you are persecuting. But get up and enter the city, and you will be told what you are to do.' The men who were travelling with him stood speechless because they heard the voice but saw no one. Saul got up from the ground, and though his eyes were open, he could see nothing; so they led him by the hand and brought him into Damascus. For three days he was without sight, and neither ate nor drank.]

[10] Now there was a disciple in Damascus named Ananias. The Lord said to him in a vision, 'Ananias.' He answered, 'Here I am, Lord.' The Lord said to him, 'Get up and go to the street called Straight, and at the house of Judas look for a man of Tarsus named Saul. At this

moment he is praying, and he has seen in a vision a man named Ananias come in and lay his hands on him so that he might regain his sight.' But Ananias answered, 'Lord, I have heard from many about this man, how much evil he has done to your saints in Jerusalem; and here he has authority from the chief priests to bind all who invoke your name.' But the Lord said to him, 'Go, for he is an instrument whom I have chosen to bring my name before Gentiles and kings and before the people of Israel; I myself will show him how much he must suffer for the sake of my name.' So Ananias went and entered the house. He laid his hands on Saul and said, 'Brother Saul, the Lord Jesus, who appeared to you on your way here, has sent me so that you may regain your sight and be filled with the Holy Spirit.' And immediately something like scales fell from his eyes, and his sight was restored. Then he got up and was baptized, and after taking some food, he regained his strength.

For several days he was with the disciples in Damascus, and immediately he began to proclaim Jesus in the synagogues, saying, 'He is the Son of God.'

Hear the Gospel of our Lord Jesus Christ according to Luke.

(3.15-17,21-22)

As the people were filled with expectation, and all were questioning in their hearts concerning John, whether he might be the Messiah, John answered all of them by saying, 'I baptize you with water; but one who is more powerful than I is coming; I am not worthy to untie the thong of his sandals. He will baptize you with the Holy Spirit and fire. His winnowing fork is in his hand, to clear his threshing floor and to gather the wheat into his granary; but the chaff he will burn with unquenchable fire.'

[21] Now when all the people were baptized, and when Jesus also had been baptized and was praying, the heaven was opened, and the Holy Spirit descended upon him in bodily form like a dove. And a voice came from heaven, 'You are my Son, the Belovèd; with you I am well pleased.'

This is the Gospel of Christ.

Epiphany / Baptism of Christ / Trinity – Set III

For Collect and Post-Communion Prayer, see page 20.

A reading from the prophecy of Isaiah. *(63.15-16 & 64.1-4)*
> Look down from heaven and see,
>> from your holy and glorious habitation.
>
> Where are your zeal and your might?
>> The yearning of your heart and your compassion?
>> They are withheld from me.
>
> For you are our father,
>> though Abraham does not know us
>> and Israel does not acknowledge us;
>
> you, O Lord, are our father;
>> our Redeemer from of old is your name.

[64.1] O that you would tear open the heavens and come down,
>> so that the mountains would quake at your presence –
>
> as when fire kindles brushwood
>> and the fire causes water to boil –
>
> to make your name known to your adversaries,
>> so that the nations might tremble at your presence!
>
> When you did awesome deeds that we did not expect,
>> you came down, the mountains quaked at your presence.
>
> From ages past no one has heard,
>> no ear has perceived,
>
> no eye has seen any God besides you,
>> who works for those who wait for him.

Psalm 50.1-6

A reading from the First Letter of Paul to the Corinthians. *(10.1-4)*
I do not want you to be unaware, brothers and sisters, that our ancestors were all under the cloud, and all passed through the sea, and all were baptized into Moses in the cloud and in the sea, and all ate the same spiritual food, and all drank the same spiritual drink. For they drank from the spiritual rock that followed them, and the rock was Christ.

Hear the Gospel of our Lord Jesus Christ according to Mark. *(1.1-11)*
The beginning of the good news of Jesus Christ, the Son of God.
> As it is written in the prophet Isaiah,
>> 'See, I am sending my messenger ahead of you,

who will prepare your way;
the voice of one crying out in the wilderness:
"Prepare the way of the Lord,
make his paths straight,"'

John the baptizer appeared in the wilderness, proclaiming a baptism of repentance for the forgiveness of sins. And people from the whole Judean countryside and all the people of Jerusalem were going out to him, and were baptized by him in the river Jordan, confessing their sins. Now John was clothed with camel's hair, with a leather belt around his waist, and he ate locusts and wild honey. He proclaimed, 'The one who is more powerful than I is coming after me; I am not worthy to stoop down and untie the thong of his sandals. I have baptized you with water; but he will baptize you with the Holy Spirit.'

In those days Jesus came from Nazareth of Galilee and was baptized by John in the Jordan. And just as he was coming up out of the water, he saw the heavens torn apart and the Spirit descending like a dove on him. And a voice came from heaven, 'You are my Son, the Belovèd; with you I am well pleased.'

This is the Gospel of Christ.

Easter / Pentecost – Set I

The Collect, Post-Communion Prayer and readings 'of Sunday' are normally used; otherwise they are either 'of the day' or the following:

Collect
Father of our Lord Jesus Christ,
from whose wounded side flowed life for the world:
raise your people from sin and death
and build them as living stones
into the spiritual temple of your Church;
through Jesus Christ your Son our Lord,
who is alive and reigns with you
in the unity of the Holy Spirit,
one God, now and for ever.

Post Communion
Author of life divine,
in the resurrection of your Son
you set before us the mystery
  of his triumph over sin and death:
may all who are washed in the waters of rebirth
rise to newness of life
and find the promised presence of your abundant grace;
through Jesus Christ our Lord.

A reading from the prophecy of Ezekiel. *(37.1-14)*
The hand of the Lord came upon me, and he brought me out by the spirit of the Lord and set me down in the middle of a valley; it was full of bones. He led me all around them; there were very many lying in the valley, and they were very dry. He said to me, 'Mortal, can these bones live?' I answered, 'O Lord God, you know.' Then he said to me, 'Prophesy to these bones, and say to them: O dry bones, hear the word of the Lord. Thus says the Lord God to these bones: I will cause breath to enter you, and you shall live. I will lay sinews on you, and will cause flesh to come upon you, and cover you with skin, and put breath in you, and you shall live; and you shall know that I am the Lord.'

So I prophesied as I had been commanded; and as I prophesied, suddenly there was a noise, a rattling, and the bones came together, bone to its bone. I looked, and there were sinews on them, and flesh had come upon them, and skin had covered them; but there was no breath in them. Then he said to me, 'Prophesy to the breath, prophesy, mortal, and say to the breath: Thus says the Lord God: Come from the four winds, O breath, and breathe upon these slain, that they may live.' I prophesied as he commanded me, and the breath came into them, and they lived, and stood on their feet, a vast multitude.

Then he said to me, 'Mortal, these bones are the whole house of Israel. They say, "Our bones are dried up, and our hope is lost; we are cut off completely." Therefore prophesy, and say to them, Thus says the Lord God: I am going to open your graves, and bring you up from your graves, O my people; and I will bring you back to the land of Israel. And you shall know that I am the Lord, when I open your graves, and bring you up from your graves, O my people. I will put my spirit within you, and you shall live, and I will place you on your own soil; then you shall know that I, the Lord, have spoken and will act, says the Lord.'

Psalm 118.19-24

A reading from the Letter of Paul to the Romans. *(6.3-11)*
Do you not know that all of us who have been baptized into Christ Jesus were baptized into his death? Therefore we have been buried with him by baptism into death, so that, just as Christ was raised from the dead by the glory of the Father, so we too might walk in newness of life.

For if we have been united with him in a death like his, we will certainly be united with him in a resurrection like his. We know that our old self was crucified with him so that the body of sin might be destroyed, and we might no longer be enslaved to sin. For whoever has died is freed from sin. But if we have died with Christ, we believe that we will also live with him. We know that Christ, being raised from the dead, will never die again; death no longer has dominion over him. The death he died, he died to sin, once for all; but the life he lives, he lives to God. So you also must consider yourselves dead to sin and alive to God in Christ Jesus.

Hear the Gospel of our Lord Jesus Christ according to Matthew.
(28.16-end)
The eleven disciples went to Galilee, to the mountain to which Jesus had directed them. When they saw him, they worshipped him; but some doubted. And Jesus came and said to them, 'All authority in heaven and on earth has been given to me. Go therefore and make disciples of all nations, baptizing them in the name of the Father and of the Son and of the Holy Spirit, and teaching them to obey everything that I have commanded you. And remember, I am with you always, to the end of the age.'

This is the Gospel of Christ.

Easter / Pentecost – Set II

For Collect and Post-Communion Prayer, see page 27.

A reading from the prophecy of Ezekiel. (36.24-28)
I will take you from the nations, and gather you from all the countries, and bring you into your own land. I will sprinkle clean water upon you, and you shall be clean from all your uncleannesses, and from all your idols I will cleanse you. A new heart I will give you, and a new spirit I will put within you; and I will remove from your body the heart of stone and give you a heart of flesh. I will put my spirit within you, and make you follow my statutes and be careful to observe my ordinances. Then you shall live in the land that I gave to your ancestors; and you shall be my people, and I will be your God.

Psalm 51.6-13

A reading from the Letter of Paul to Titus. (3.3-7)
We ourselves were once foolish, disobedient, led astray, slaves to various passions and pleasures, passing our days in malice and envy, despicable, hating one another. But when the goodness and loving kindness of God our Saviour appeared, he saved us, not because of any works of righteousness that we had done, but according to his mercy, through the water of rebirth and renewal by the Holy Spirit. This Spirit he poured out on us richly through Jesus Christ our Saviour, so that, having been justified by his grace, we might become heirs according to the hope of eternal life.

Hear the Gospel of our Lord Jesus Christ according to John.
(20.19-23)
When it was evening on that day, the first day of the week, and the doors of the house where the disciples had met were locked for fear of the Jews, Jesus came and stood among them and said, 'Peace be with you.' After he said this, he showed them his hands and his side. Then the disciples rejoiced when they saw the Lord. Jesus said to them again, 'Peace be with you. As the Father has sent me, so I send you.' When he had said this, he breathed on them and said to them, 'Receive the Holy Spirit. If you forgive the sins of any, they are forgiven them; if you retain the sins of any, they are retained.'

This is the Gospel of Christ.

Easter / Pentecost – Set III

For Collect and Post-Communion Prayer, see page 27.

A reading from the prophecy of Ezekiel. (47.1-12)

The hand of the Lord came upon me, and he brought me back to the entrance of the temple; there, water was flowing from below the threshold of the temple toward the east (for the temple faced east); and the water was flowing down from below the south end of the threshold of the temple, south of the altar. Then he brought me out by way of the north gate, and led me around on the outside to the outer gate that faces toward the east; and the water was coming out on the south side.

Going on eastward with a cord in his hand, the man measured one thousand cubits, and then led me through the water; and it was ankle-deep. Again he measured one thousand, and led me through the water; and it was knee-deep. Again he measured one thousand, and led me through the water; and it was up to the waist. Again he measured one thousand, and it was a river that I could not cross, for the water had risen; it was deep enough to swim in, a river that could not be crossed. He said to me, 'Mortal, have you seen this?'

Then he led me back along the bank of the river. As I came back, I saw on the bank of the river a great many trees on the one side and on the other. He said to me, 'This water flows toward the eastern region and goes down into the Arabah; and when it enters the sea, the sea of stagnant waters, the water will become fresh. Wherever the river goes, every living creature that swarms will live, and there will be very many fish, once these waters reach there. It will become fresh; and everything will live where the river goes. People will stand fishing beside the sea from En-gedi to En-eglaim; it will be a place for the spreading of nets; its fish will be of a great many kinds, like the fish of the Great Sea. But its swamps and marshes will not become fresh; they are to be left for salt. On the banks, on both sides of the river, there will grow all kinds of trees for food. Their leaves will not wither nor their fruit fail, but they will bear fresh fruit every month, because the water for them flows from the sanctuary. Their fruit will be for food, and their leaves for healing.'

Psalm 46.1-7

A reading from the Revelation to John. (22.1-5)
The angel showed me the river of the water of life, bright as crystal, flowing from the throne of God and of the Lamb through the middle of the street of the city. On either side of the river is the tree of life with its twelve kinds of fruit, producing its fruit each month; and the leaves of the tree are for the healing of the nations. Nothing accursed will be found there any more. But the throne of God and of the Lamb will be in it, and his servants will worship him; they will see his face, and his name will be on their foreheads. And there will be no more night; they need no light of lamp or sun, for the Lord God will be their light, and they will reign for ever and ever.

Hear the Gospel of our Lord Jesus Christ according to John. (7.37-39)
On the last day of the festival, the great day, while Jesus was standing there, he cried out, 'Let anyone who is thirsty come to me, and let the one who believes in me drink. As the scripture has said, "Out of the believer's heart shall flow rivers of living water."' Now he said this about the Spirit, which believers in him were to receive; for as yet there was no Spirit, because Jesus was not yet glorified.

This is the Gospel of Christ.

All Saints – Set I

The Collect, Post-Communion Prayer and readings 'of Sunday' are normally used; otherwise they are either 'of the day' or the following:

Collect
Almighty Father,
you have made us heirs through hope of your everlasting kingdom
and in the waters of baptism
you have promised a measure of grace overflowing to all eternity:
take our sins and guilt away
and so inflame us with the life of your Spirit
that we may know your favour and goodness towards us
and walk in newness of life, both now and for ever;
through Jesus Christ your Son our Lord,
who is alive and reigns with you
in the unity of the Holy Spirit,
one God, now and for ever.

Post Communion
Lord,
in the vision of your heavenly kingdom
you reveal among us the promise of your glory:
may that glory be ours
as we claim our citizenship in the kingdom
where you are alive and reign, one God,
for ever and ever.

A reading from the Book of the Exodus. *(19.3-8)*
Moses went up to God; the Lord called to him from the mountain, saying, 'Thus you shall say to the house of Jacob, and tell the Israelites: You have seen what I did to the Egyptians, and how I bore you on eagles' wings and brought you to myself. Now therefore, if you obey my voice and keep my covenant, you shall be my treasured possession out of all the peoples. Indeed, the whole earth is mine, but you shall be for me a priestly kingdom and a holy nation. These are the words that you shall speak to the Israelites.'
So Moses came, summoned the elders of the people, and set before them all these words that the Lord had commanded him. The people all answered as one: 'Everything that the Lord has spoken we will do.' Moses reported the words of the people to the Lord.

Psalm 98.1-4

A reading from the Revelation to John. (5.6-10)

I saw between the throne and the four living creatures and among the elders a Lamb standing as if it had been slaughtered, having seven horns and seven eyes, which are the seven spirits of God sent out into all the earth. He went and took the scroll from the right hand of the one who was seated on the throne. When he had taken the scroll, the four living creatures and the twenty-four elders fell before the Lamb, each holding a harp and golden bowls full of incense, which are the prayers of the saints. They sing a new song:

'You are worthy to take the scroll
　and to open its seals,
for you were slaughtered
　and by your blood you ransomed for God
saints from every tribe and language and people and nation;
you have made them to be a kingdom and priests
　　serving our God,
and they will reign on earth.'

Hear the Gospel of our Lord Jesus Christ according to Matthew.

(28.16-end)

The eleven disciples went to Galilee, to the mountain to which Jesus had directed them. When they saw him, they worshipped him; but some doubted. And Jesus came and said to them, 'All authority in heaven and on earth has been given to me. Go therefore and make disciples of all nations, baptizing them in the name of the Father and of the Son and of the Holy Spirit, and teaching them to obey every-thing that I have commanded you. And remember, I am with you always, to the end of the age.'

This is the Gospel of Christ.

All Saints – Set II

For Collect and Post-Communion Prayer, see page 32.

A reading from the prophecy of Isaiah. (44.1-5)
> Hear, O Jacob my servant,
>> Israel whom I have chosen!
> Thus says the Lord who made you,
>> who formed you in the womb and will help you:
> Do not fear, O Jacob my servant,
>> Jeshurun whom I have chosen.
> For I will pour water on the thirsty land,
>> and streams on the dry ground;
> I will pour my spirit upon your descendants,
>> and my blessing on your offspring.
> They shall spring up like a green tamarisk,
>> like willows by flowing streams.
> This one will say, 'I am the Lord's,'
>> another will be called by the name of Jacob,
> yet another will write on the hand, 'The Lord's,'
>> and adopt the name of Israel.

Psalm 63.1-6

A reading from the Letter to the Hebrews. (11.32 – 12.2)
What more should I say? For time would fail me to tell of Gideon, Barak, Samson, Jephthah, of David and Samuel and the prophets – who through faith conquered kingdoms, administered justice, obtained promises, shut the mouths of lions, quenched raging fire, escaped the edge of the sword, won strength out of weakness, became mighty in war, put foreign armies to flight. Women received their dead by resurrection. Others were tortured, refusing to accept release, in order to obtain a better resurrection. Others suffered mocking and flogging, and even chains and imprisonment. They were stoned to death, they were sawn in two, they were killed by the sword; they went about in skins of sheep and goats, destitute, persecuted, tormented – of whom the world was not worthy. They wandered in deserts and mountains, and in caves and holes in the ground.

Yet all these, though they were commended for their faith, did not receive what was promised, since God had provided something better so that they would not, apart from us, be made perfect.

Therefore, since we are surrounded by so great a cloud of witnesses, let us also lay aside every weight and the sin that clings so closely, and let us run with perseverance the race that is set before us, looking to Jesus the pioneer and perfecter of our faith, who for the sake of the joy that was set before him endured the cross, disregarding its shame, and has taken his seat at the right hand of the throne of God.

Hear the Gospel of our Lord Jesus Christ according to Matthew.

(5.1-12[13-16])

When Jesus saw the crowds, he went up the mountain; and after he sat down, his disciples came to him. Then he began to speak, and taught them, saying:

'Blessèd are the poor in spirit, for theirs is the kingdom of heaven.

'Blessèd are those who mourn, for they will be comforted.

'Blessèd are the meek, for they will inherit the earth.

'Blessèd are those who hunger and thirst for righteousness, for they will be filled.

'Blessèd are the merciful, for they will receive mercy.

'Blessèd are the pure in heart, for they will see God.

'Blessèd are the peacemakers, for they will be called children of God.

'Blessèd are those who are persecuted for righteousness' sake, for theirs is the kingdom of heaven.

'Blessèd are you when people revile you and persecute you and utter all kinds of evil against you falsely on my account. Rejoice and be glad, for your reward is great in heaven, for in the same way they persecuted the prophets who were before you.

[13 'You are the salt of the earth; but if salt has lost its taste, how can its saltiness be restored? It is no longer good for anything, but is thrown out and trampled under foot.

'You are the light of the world. A city built on a hill cannot be hid. No one after lighting a lamp puts it under the bushel basket, but on the lampstand, and it gives light to all in the house. In the same way, let your light shine before others, so that they may see your good works and give glory to your Father in heaven.']

This is the Gospel of Christ.

All Saints – Set III

For Collect and Post-Communion Prayer, see page 32.

A reading from the prophecy of Hosea. (14.4-8)
> I will heal Israel's disloyalty;
>> I will love them freely,
>> for my anger has turned from them.
> I will be like the dew to Israel;
>> he shall blossom like the lily,
>> he shall strike root like the forests of Lebanon.
> His shoots shall spread out;
>> his beauty shall be like the olive tree,
>> and his fragrance like that of Lebanon.
> They shall again live beneath my shadow,
>> they shall flourish as a garden;
> they shall blossom like the vine,
>> their fragrance shall be like the wine of Lebanon.

> O Ephraim, what have I to do with idols?
>> It is I who answer and look after you.
> I am like an evergreen cypress;
>> your faithfulness comes from me.

Psalm 92.10-15

A reading from the First Letter of Peter. (2.4-10)
Come to him, a living stone, though rejected by mortals yet chosen
and precious in God's sight, and like living stones, let yourselves be
built into a spiritual house, to be a holy priesthood, to offer spiritual
sacrifices acceptable to God through Jesus Christ. For it stands in
scripture:
> 'See, I am laying in Zion a stone,
>> a cornerstone chosen and precious;
> and whoever believes in him will not be put to shame.'

To you then who believe, he is precious; but for those who do not
believe,
> 'The stone that the builders rejected
>> has become the very head of the corner,'

and
> 'A stone that makes them stumble,
>> and a rock that makes them fall.'

They stumble because they disobey the word, as they were destined to do.

But you are a chosen race, a royal priesthood, a holy nation, God's own people, in order that you may proclaim the mighty acts of him who called you out of darkness into his marvellous light.

Once you were not a people,
  but now you are God's people;
once you had not received mercy,
  but now you have received mercy.

Hear the Gospel of our Lord Jesus Christ according to John. (15.1-11) Jesus said to his disciples, 'I am the true vine, and my Father is the vinegrower. He removes every branch in me that bears no fruit. Every branch that bears fruit he prunes to make it bear more fruit. You have already been cleansed by the word that I have spoken to you. Abide in me as I abide in you. Just as the branch cannot bear fruit by itself unless it abides in the vine, neither can you unless you abide in me. I am the vine, you are the branches. Those who abide in me and I in them bear much fruit, because apart from me you can do nothing. Whoever does not abide in me is thrown away like a branch and withers; such branches are gathered, thrown into the fire, and burned. If you abide in me, and my words abide in you, ask for whatever you wish, and it will be done for you. My Father is glorified by this, that you bear much fruit and become my disciples. As the Father has loved me, so I have loved you; abide in my love. If you keep my commandments, you will abide in my love, just as I have kept my Father's commandments and abide in his love. I have said these things to you so that my joy may be in you, and that your joy may be complete.'

This is the Gospel of Christ.

Vigil, or Post-Baptismal Liturgy – Set I

A reading from the book Genesis. *(28.10-17)*

Jacob left Beer-sheba and went toward Haran. He came to a certain place and stayed there for the night, because the sun had set. Taking one of the stones of the place, he put it under his head and lay down in that place. And he dreamed that there was a ladder set up on the earth, the top of it reaching to heaven; and the angels of God were ascending and descending on it. And the Lord stood beside him and said, 'I am the Lord, the God of Abraham your father and the God of Isaac; the land on which you lie I will give to you and to your off-spring; and your offspring shall be like the dust of the earth, and you shall spread abroad to the west and to the east and to the north and to the south; and all the families of the earth shall be blessed in you and in your offspring. Know that I am with you and will keep you wherever you go, and will bring you back to this land; for I will not leave you until I have done what I have promised you.' Then Jacob woke from his sleep and said, 'Surely the Lord is in this place – and I did not know it!' And he was afraid, and said, 'How awesome is this place! This is none other than the house of God, and this is the gate of heaven.'

Psalm 121

A reading from the Letter to the Hebrews. *(10.12-23 or 19-23)*

[When Christ had offered for all time a single sacrifice for sins, 'he sat down at the right hand of God,' and since then has been waiting 'until his enemies would be made a footstool for his feet.' For by a single offering he has perfected for all time those who are sanctified. And the Holy Spirit also testifies to us, for after saying,

'This is the covenant that I will make with them
    after those days, says the Lord:
I will put my laws in their hearts,
    and I will write them on their minds,'
he also adds,
    'I will remember their sins and their lawless deeds no more.'
Where there is forgiveness of these, there is no longer any offering for sin.]

[19] Therefore, my friends, since we have confidence to enter the sanc-tuary by the blood of Jesus, by the new and living way that he opened for us through the curtain (that is, through his flesh), and since we have a great priest over the house of God, let us approach

with a true heart in full assurance of faith, with our hearts sprinkled clean from an evil conscience and our bodies washed with pure water. Let us hold fast to the confession of our hope without wavering, for he who has promised is faithful.

Hear the Gospel of our Lord Jesus Christ according to Mark.

(10.[13-16],17-27)

[People were bringing little children to Jesus in order that he might touch them; and the disciples spoke sternly to them. But when Jesus saw this, he was indignant and said to them, 'Let the little children come to me; do not stop them; for it is to such as these that the kingdom of God belongs. Truly I tell you, whoever does not receive the kingdom of God as a little child will never enter it.' And he took them up in his arms, laid his hands on them, and blessed them.]

As Jesus was setting out on a journey, a man ran up and knelt before him, and asked him, 'Good Teacher, what must I do to inherit eternal life?' Jesus said to him, 'Why do you call me good? No one is good but God alone. You know the commandments: "You shall not murder; You shall not commit adultery; You shall not steal; You shall not bear false witness; You shall not defraud; Honour your father and mother."' He said to him, 'Teacher, I have kept all these since my youth.' Jesus, looking at him, loved him and said, 'You lack one thing; go, sell what you own, and give the money to the poor, and you will have treasure in heaven; then come, follow me.' When he heard this, he was shocked and went away grieving, for he had many possessions.

Then Jesus looked around and said to his disciples, 'How hard it will be for those who have wealth to enter the kingdom of God!' And the disciples were perplexed at these words. But Jesus said to them again, 'Children, how hard it is to enter the kingdom of God! It is easier for a camel to go through the eye of a needle than for someone who is rich to enter the kingdom of God.' They were greatly astounded and said to one another, 'Then who can be saved?' Jesus looked at them and said, 'For mortals it is impossible, but not for God; for God all things are possible.'

This is the Gospel of Christ.

Vigil, or Post-Baptismal Liturgy – Set II

A reading from the Book of the Exodus. (3.1-15 or 7-15)

[Moses was keeping the flock of his father-in-law Jethro, the priest of Midian; he led his flock beyond the wilderness, and came to Horeb, the mountain of God. There the angel of the Lord appeared to him in a flame of fire out of a bush; he looked, and the bush was blazing, yet it was not consumed. Then Moses said, 'I must turn aside and look at this great sight, and see why the bush is not burned up.' When the Lord saw that he had turned aside to see, God called to him out of the bush, 'Moses, Moses!' And he said, 'Here I am.' Then he said, 'Come no closer! Remove the sandals from your feet, for the place on which you are standing is holy ground.' He said further, 'I am the God of your father, the God of Abraham, the God of Isaac, and the God of Jacob.' And Moses hid his face, for he was afraid to look at God.

⁷ Then] the Lord said, 'I have observed the misery of my people who are in Egypt; I have heard their cry on account of their taskmasters. Indeed, I know their sufferings, and I have come down to deliver them from the Egyptians, and to bring them up out of that land to a good and broad land, a land flowing with milk and honey, to the country of the Canaanites, the Hittites, the Amorites, the Perizzites, the Hivites, and the Jebusites. The cry of the Israelites has now come to me; I have also seen how the Egyptians oppress them. So come, I will send you to Pharaoh to bring my people, the Israelites, out of Egypt.' But Moses said to God, 'Who am I that I should go to Pharaoh, and bring the Israelites out of Egypt?' He said, 'I will be with you; and this shall be the sign for you that it is I who sent you: when you have brought the people out of Egypt, you shall worship God on this mountain.'

But Moses said to God, 'If I come to the Israelites and say to them, "The God of your ancestors has sent me to you," and they ask me, "What is his name?" what shall I say to them?' God said to Moses, 'I Am Who I Am.' He said further, 'Thus you shall say to the Israelites, "I Am has sent me to you."' God also said to Moses, 'Thus you shall say to the Israelites, "The Lord, the God of your ancestors, the God of Abraham, the God of Isaac, and the God of Jacob, has sent me to you":

This is my name for ever,
and this my title for all generations.'

Psalm 114

Baptism – Vigil, or Post-Baptismal Liturgy

A reading from the Letter to the Hebrews. (11.24-29)

By faith Moses, when he was grown up, refused to be called a son of Pharaoh's daughter, choosing rather to share ill-treatment with the people of God than to enjoy the fleeting pleasures of sin. He considered abuse suffered for the Christ to be greater wealth than the treasures of Egypt, for he was looking ahead to the reward. By faith he left Egypt, unafraid of the king's anger; for he persevered as though he saw him who is invisible. By faith he kept the Passover and the sprinkling of blood, so that the destroyer of the firstborn would not touch the firstborn of Israel.

By faith the people passed through the Red Sea as if it were dry land, but when the Egyptians attempted to do so they were drowned.

Hear the Gospel of our Lord Jesus Christ according to Luke.

(9.51-end or 57-end)

[When the days drew near for Jesus to be taken up, he set his face to go to Jerusalem. And he sent messengers ahead of him. On their way they entered a village of the Samaritans to make ready for him; but they did not receive him, because his face was set toward Jerusalem. When his disciples James and John saw it, they said, 'Lord, do you want us to command fire to come down from heaven and consume them?' But he turned and rebuked them. Then they went on to another village.]

[57] As they were going along the road, someone said to him, 'I will follow you wherever you go.' And Jesus said to him, 'Foxes have holes, and birds of the air have nests; but the Son of Man has nowhere to lay his head.' To another he said, 'Follow me.' But he said, 'Lord, first let me go and bury my father.' But Jesus said to him, 'Let the dead bury their own dead; but as for you, go and proclaim the kingdom of God.' Another said, 'I will follow you, Lord; but let me first say farewell to those at my home.' Jesus said to him, 'No one who puts a hand to the plough and looks back is fit for the kingdom of God.'

This is the Gospel of Christ.

Confirmation
& Affirmation or Reception

For Collect and Post-Communion Prayer, see page 20.

Two sets of readings are provided under each heading for use:
A at Confirmation
B when Affirmation or Reception take place, for which they are particularly suitable.

General – Set A1

A reading from the prophecy of Ezekiel. (36.24-28)
I will take you from the nations, and gather you from all the countries, and bring you into your own land. I will sprinkle clean water upon you, and you shall be clean from all your uncleannesses, and from all your idols I will cleanse you. A new heart I will give you, and a new spirit I will put within you; and I will remove from your body the heart of stone and give you a heart of flesh. I will put my spirit within you, and make you follow my statutes and be careful to observe my ordinances. Then you shall live in the land that I gave to your ancestors; and you shall be my people, and I will be your God.

Psalm 51.6-13

A reading from the Letter of Paul to the Titus. (3.3-7)
We ourselves were once foolish, disobedient, led astray, slaves to various passions and pleasures, passing our days in malice and envy, despicable, hating one another. But when the goodness and loving kindness of God our Saviour appeared, he saved us, not because of any works of righteousness that we had done, but according to his mercy, through the water of rebirth and renewal by the Holy Spirit. This Spirit he poured out on us richly through Jesus Christ our Saviour, so that, having been justified by his grace, we might become heirs according to the hope of eternal life.

Hear the Gospel of our Lord Jesus Christ according to John. (3.1-8)
There was a Pharisee named Nicodemus, a leader of the Jews. He came to Jesus by night and said to him, 'Rabbi, we know that you are a teacher who has come from God; for no one can do these signs that you do apart from the presence of God.' Jesus answered him, 'Very truly, I tell you, no one can see the kingdom of God without being

born from above.' Nicodemus said to him, 'How can anyone be born after having grown old? Can one enter a second time into the mother's womb and be born?' Jesus answered, 'Very truly, I tell you, no one can enter the kingdom of God without being born of water and Spirit. What is born of the flesh is flesh, and what is born of the Spirit is spirit. Do not be astonished that I said to you, "You must be born from above." The wind blows where it chooses, and you hear the sound of it, but you do not know where it comes from or where it goes. So it is with everyone who is born of the Spirit.'

This is the Gospel of Christ.

General – Set A2

A reading from the prophecy of Ezekiel. (47.1-10,12)
The man of God brought me back to the entrance of the temple; there, water was flowing from below the threshold of the temple toward the east (for the temple faced east); and the water was flowing down from below the south end of the threshold of the temple, south of the altar. Then he brought me out by way of the north gate, and led me around on the outside to the outer gate that faces toward the east; and the water was coming out on the south side.

Going on eastward with a cord in his hand, the man measured one thousand cubits, and then led me through the water; and it was ankle-deep. Again he measured one thousand, and led me through the water; and it was knee-deep. Again he measured one thousand, and led me through the water; and it was up to the waist. Again he measured one thousand, and it was a river that I could not cross, for the water had risen; it was deep enough to swim in, a river that could not be crossed. He said to me, 'Mortal, have you seen this?'

Then he led me back along the bank of the river. As I came back, I saw on the bank of the river a great many trees on the one side and on the other. He said to me, 'This water flows toward the eastern region and goes down into the Arabah; and when it enters the sea, the sea of stagnant waters, the water will become fresh. Wherever the river goes, every living creature that swarms will live, and there will be very many fish, once these waters reach there. It will become fresh; and everything will live where the river goes. People will stand fishing beside the sea from En-gedi to En-eglaim; it will be a place for the spreading of nets; its fish will be of a great many kinds, like the fish of the Great Sea.
¹² On the banks, on both sides of the river, there will grow all kinds of trees for food. Their leaves will not wither nor their fruit fail, but they will bear fresh fruit every month, because the water for them flows from the sanctuary. Their fruit will be for food, and their leaves for healing.'

Psalm 84.1-7

A reading from the First Letter of Paul to the Corinthians. (12.4-13)
There are varieties of gifts, but the same Spirit; and there are varieties of services, but the same Lord; and there are varieties of activities, but it is the same God who activates all of them in everyone. To each is given the manifestation of the Spirit for the common good. To one is

given through the Spirit the utterance of wisdom, and to another the utterance of knowledge according to the same Spirit, to another faith by the same Spirit, to another gifts of healing by the one Spirit, to another the working of miracles, to another prophecy, to another the discernment of spirits, to another various kinds of tongues, to another the interpretation of tongues. All these are activated by one and the same Spirit, who allots to each one individually just as the Spirit chooses.

For just as the body is one and has many members, and all the members of the body, though many, are one body, so it is with Christ. For in the one Spirit we were all baptized into one body – Jews or Greeks, slaves or free – and we were all made to drink of one Spirit.

Hear the Gospel of our Lord Jesus Christ according to John. (7.37-39) On the last day of the festival, the great day, while Jesus was standing there, he cried out, 'Let anyone who is thirsty come to me, and let the one who believes in me drink. As the scripture has said, "Out of the believer's heart shall flow rivers of living water."' Now he said this about the Spirit, which believers in him were to receive; for as yet there was no Spirit, because Jesus was not yet glorified.

This is the Gospel of Christ.

General – Set B1

A reading from the prophecy of Isaiah. (44.1-5)

Now hear, O Jacob my servant,
  Israel whom I have chosen!
Thus says the Lord who made you,
  who formed you in the womb and will help you:
Do not fear, O Jacob my servant,
  Jeshurun whom I have chosen.
For I will pour water on the thirsty land,
  and streams on the dry ground;
I will pour my spirit upon your descendants,
  and my blessing on your offspring.
They shall spring up like a green tamarisk,
  like willows by flowing streams.
This one will say, 'I am the Lord's,'
  another will be called by the name of Jacob,
yet another will write on the hand, 'The Lord's,'
  and adopt the name of Israel.

Psalm 18.30-37

A reading from the Letter of Paul to the Ephesians. (6.10-20)

Be strong in the Lord and in the strength of his power. Put on the whole armour of God, so that you may be able to stand against the wiles of the devil. For our struggle is not against enemies of blood and flesh, but against the rulers, against the authorities, against the cosmic powers of this present darkness, against the spiritual forces of evil in the heavenly places. Therefore take up the whole armour of God, so that you may be able to withstand on that evil day, and having done everything, to stand firm. Stand therefore, and fasten the belt of truth around your waist, and put on the breastplate of righteousness. As shoes for your feet put on whatever will make you ready to proclaim the gospel of peace. With all of these, take the shield of faith, with which you will be able to quench all the flaming arrows of the evil one. Take the helmet of salvation, and the sword of the Spirit, which is the word of God.

Pray in the Spirit at all times in every prayer and supplication. To that end keep alert and always persevere in supplication for all the saints. Pray also for me, so that when I speak, a message may be given to me to make known with boldness the mystery of the gospel, for which I am an ambassador in chains. Pray that I may declare it boldly, as I must speak.

Hear the Gospel of our Lord Jesus Christ according to Luke.

(24.44-49)

Then Jesus said to his disciples, 'These are my words that I spoke to you while I was still with you – that everything written about me in the law of Moses, the prophets, and the psalms must be fulfilled.' Then he opened their minds to understand the scriptures, and he said to them, 'Thus it is written, that the Messiah is to suffer and to rise from the dead on the third day, and that repentance and forgiveness of sins is to be proclaimed in his name to all nations, beginning from Jerusalem. You are witnesses of these things. And see, I am sending upon you what my Father promised; so stay here in the city until you have been clothed with power from on high.'

This is the Gospel of Christ.

General – Set B2

A reading from the prophecy of Isaiah. (62.1-7)
For Zion's sake I will not keep silent,
    and for Jerusalem's sake I will not rest,
until her vindication shines out like the dawn,
    and her salvation like a burning torch.
The nations shall see your vindication,
    and all the kings your glory;
and you shall be called by a new name
    that the mouth of the Lord will give.
You shall be a crown of beauty in the hand of the Lord,
    and a royal diadem in the hand of your God.
You shall no more be termed Forsaken,
    and your land shall no more be termed Desolate;
but you shall be called My Delight Is in Her,
    and your land Married;
for the Lord delights in you,
    and your land shall be married.
For as a young man marries a young woman,
    so shall your builder marry you,
and as the bridegroom rejoices over the bride,
    so shall your God rejoice over you.
Upon your walls, O Jerusalem,
    I have posted sentinels;
all day and all night
    they shall never be silent.
You who remind the Lord,
    take no rest,
and give him no rest
    until he establishes Jerusalem
    and makes it renowned throughout the earth.

Psalm 107.1-9

A reading from the Acts of the Apostles. (10.34-43)
Peter began to speak to Cornelius and his companions: 'I truly understand that God shows no partiality, but in every nation anyone who fears him and does what is right is acceptable to him. You know the message he sent to the people of Israel, preaching peace by Jesus Christ – he is Lord of all. That message spread throughout Judea, beginning in Galilee after the baptism that John announced: how God anointed Jesus of Nazareth with the Holy Spirit and with power; how

he went about doing good and healing all who were oppressed by the devil, for God was with him. We are witnesses to all that he did both in Judea and in Jerusalem. They put him to death by hanging him on a tree; but God raised him on the third day and allowed him to appear, not to all the people but to us who were chosen by God as witnesses, and who ate and drank with him after he rose from the dead. He commanded us to preach to the people and to testify that he is the one ordained by God as judge of the living and the dead. All the prophets testify about him that everyone who believes in him receives forgiveness of sins through his name.'

Hear the Gospel of our Lord Jesus Christ according to Luke. (4.14-19)
Jesus, filled with the power of the Spirit, returned to Galilee, and a report about him spread through all the surrounding country. He began to teach in their synagogues and was praised by everyone.

When he came to Nazareth, where he had been brought up, he went to the synagogue on the sabbath day, as was his custom. He stood up to read, and the scroll of the prophet Isaiah was given to him. He unrolled the scroll and found the place where it was written:
'The Spirit of the Lord is upon me,
  because he has anointed me
  to bring good news to the poor.
He has sent me to proclaim release to the captives
  and recovery of sight to the blind,
  to let the oppressed go free,
  to proclaim the year of the Lord's favour.'

This is the Gospel of Christ.

Epiphany / Baptism of Christ / Trinity – Set A

For Collects and Post-Communion Prayers, see pages 11 & 20.

A reading from the prophecy of Isaiah. (63.7-10,14 & 64.1-4)
> I will recount the gracious deeds of the Lord,
>> the praiseworthy acts of the Lord,
> because of all that the Lord has done for us,
>> and the great favour to the house of Israel
> that he has shown them according to his mercy,
>> according to the abundance of his steadfast love.
> For he said, 'Surely they are my people,
>> children who will not deal falsely';
> and he became their saviour
>> in all their distress.
> It was no messenger or angel
>> but his presence that saved them;
> in his love and in his pity he redeemed them;
>> he lifted them up and carried them all the days of old.
>
> But they rebelled
>> and grieved his holy spirit;
> therefore he became their enemy;
>> he himself fought against them.

[14] Like cattle that go down into the valley,
>> the spirit of the Lord gave them rest.
> Thus you led your people,
>> to make for yourself a glorious name.

[64.1] O that you would tear open the heavens and come down,
>> so that the mountains would quake at your presence –
> as when fire kindles brushwood
>> and the fire causes water to boil –
> to make your name known to your adversaries,
>> so that the nations might tremble at your presence!
> When you did awesome deeds that we did not expect,
>> you came down, the mountains quaked at your presence.
> From ages past no one has heard,
>> no ear has perceived,
> no eye has seen any God besides you,
>> who works for those who wait for him.

Psalm 27.1-8

A reading from the First Letter of Paul to the Corinthians. (2.7-12)
We speak God's wisdom, secret and hidden, which God decreed
before the ages for our glory. None of the rulers of this age under-
stood this; for if they had, they would not have crucified the Lord of
glory. But, as it is written,
　　'What no eye has seen, nor ear heard,
　　　nor the human heart conceived,
　　　what God has prepared for those who love him' –
these things God has revealed to us through the Spirit; for the Spirit
searches everything, even the depths of God. For what human being
knows what is truly human except the human spirit that is within?
So also no one comprehends what is truly God's except the Spirit of
God. Now we have received not the spirit of the world, but the Spirit that is from God, so that we may understand the gifts bestowed on
us by God.

Hear the Gospel of our Lord Jesus Christ according to Mark.
(1.1-13 or 4-11)
[The beginning of the good news of Jesus Christ, the Son of God.
　　As it is written in the prophet Isaiah,
　　'See, I am sending my messenger ahead of you,
　　　who will prepare your way;
　　the voice of one crying out in the wilderness:
　　　"Prepare the way of the Lord,
　　　make his paths straight,"']
⁴ John the baptizer appeared in the wilderness, proclaiming a baptism of repentance for the forgiveness of sins. And people from the
whole Judean countryside and all the people of Jerusalem were going
out to him, and were baptized by him in the river Jordan, confessing
their sins. Now John was clothed with camel's hair, with a leather
belt around his waist, and he ate locusts and wild honey. He proclaimed, 'The one who is more powerful than I is coming after me; I
am not worthy to stoop down and untie the thong of his sandals. I
have baptized you with water; but he will baptize you with the Holy
Spirit.'
　In those days Jesus came from Nazareth of Galilee and was baptized
by John in the Jordan. And just as he was coming up out of the water,
he saw the heavens torn apart and the Spirit descending like a dove
on him. And a voice came from heaven, 'You are my Son, the
Belovèd; with you I am well pleased.'
[¹² And the Spirit immediately drove him out into the wilderness. He
was in the wilderness forty days, tempted by Satan; and he was with
the wild beasts; and the angels waited on him.]

This is the Gospel of Christ.

Epiphany / Baptism of Christ / Trinity – Set B

For Collects and Post-Communion Prayers, see pages 11 & 20.

A reading from the Book of the Exodus. (33.12-20)

Moses said to the Lord, 'See, you have said to me, "Bring up this peo-ple"; but you have not let me know whom you will send with me. Yet you have said, "I know you by name, and you have also found favour in my sight." Now if I have found favour in your sight, show me your ways, so that I may know you and find favour in your sight. Consider too that this nation is your people.' The Lord said, 'My presence will go with you, and I will give you rest.' And Moses said to him, 'If your presence will not go, do not carry us up from here. For how shall it be known that I have found favour in your sight, I and your people, unless you go with us? In this way, we shall be dis-tinct, I and your people, from every people on the face of the earth.'

The Lord said to Moses, 'I will do the very thing that you have asked; for you have found favour in my sight, and I know you by name.' Moses said, 'Show me your glory, I pray.' And he said, 'I will make all my goodness pass before you, and will proclaim before you the name, "The Lord"; and I will be gracious to whom I will be gra-cious, and will show mercy on whom I will show mercy. But,' he said, 'you cannot see my face; for no one shall see me and live.'

Psalm 36.5-9

A reading from the Second Letter of Paul to the Corinthians.

(3.12 – 4.6)

Since we have such a hope, we act with great boldness, not like Moses, who put a veil over his face to keep the people of Israel from gazing at the end of the glory that was being set aside. But their minds were hardened. Indeed, to this very day, when they hear the reading of the old covenant, that same veil is still there, since only in Christ is it set aside. Indeed, to this very day whenever Moses is read, a veil lies over their minds; but when one turns to the Lord, the veil is removed. Now the Lord is the Spirit, and where the Spirit of the Lord is, there is freedom. And all of us, with unveiled faces, see-ing the glory of the Lord as though reflected in a mirror, are being transformed into the same image from one degree of glory to anoth-er; for this comes from the Lord, the Spirit.

Therefore, since it is by God's mercy that we are engaged in this ministry, we do not lose heart. We have renounced the shameful things that one hides; we refuse to practise cunning or to falsify God's word; but by the open statement of the truth we commend ourselves to the conscience of everyone in the sight of God. And even if our gospel is veiled, it is veiled to those who are perishing. In their case the god of this world has blinded the minds of the unbelievers, to keep them from seeing the light of the gospel of the glory of Christ, who is the image of God. For we do not proclaim ourselves; we proclaim Jesus Christ as Lord and ourselves as your slaves for Jesus' sake. For it is the God who said, 'Let light shine out of darkness,' who has shone in our hearts to give the light of the knowledge of the glory of God in the face of Jesus Christ.

Hear the Gospel of our Lord Jesus Christ according to John. (1.14-18) The Word became flesh and lived among us, and we have seen his glory, the glory as of a father's only son, full of grace and truth. (John testified to him and cried out, 'This was he of whom I said, "He who comes after me ranks ahead of me because he was before me."') From his fullness we have all received, grace upon grace. The law indeed was given through Moses; grace and truth came through Jesus Christ. No one has ever seen God. It is God the only Son, who is close to the Father's heart, who has made him known.

This is the Gospel of Christ.

Easter / Pentecost – Set A

For Collects and Post-Communion Prayers, see pages 11 & 27.

A reading from the prophecy of Ezekiel. (37.1-14)

The hand of the Lord came upon me, and he brought me out by the spirit of the Lord and set me down in the middle of a valley; it was full of bones. He led me all around them; there were very many lying in the valley, and they were very dry. He said to me, 'Mortal, can these bones live?' I answered, 'O Lord God, you know.' Then he said to me, 'Prophesy to these bones, and say to them: O dry bones, hear the word of the Lord. Thus says the Lord God to these bones: I will cause breath to enter you, and you shall live. I will lay sinews on you, and will cause flesh to come upon you, and cover you with skin, and put breath in you, and you shall live; and you shall know that I am the Lord.'

So I prophesied as I had been commanded; and as I prophesied, suddenly there was a noise, a rattling, and the bones came together, bone to its bone. I looked, and there were sinews on them, and flesh had come upon them, and skin had covered them; but there was no breath in them. Then he said to me, 'Prophesy to the breath, prophesy, mortal, and say to the breath: Thus says the Lord God: Come from the four winds, O breath, and breathe upon these slain, that they may live.' I prophesied as he commanded me, and the breath came into them, and they lived, and stood on their feet, a vast multitude.

Then he said to me, 'Mortal, these bones are the whole house of Israel. They say, "Our bones are dried up, and our hope is lost; we are cut off completely." Therefore prophesy, and say to them, Thus says the Lord God: I am going to open your graves, and bring you up from your graves, O my people; and I will bring you back to the land of Israel. And you shall know that I am the Lord, when I open your graves, and bring you up from your graves, O my people. I will put my spirit within you, and you shall live, and I will place you on your own soil; then you shall know that I, the Lord, have spoken and will act, says the Lord.'

Psalm 118.19-24 or Isaiah 12.2-6

A reading from the Letter of Paul to the Romans. (8.[1-4],5-11)

[There is now no condemnation for those who are in Christ Jesus. For the law of the Spirit of life in Christ Jesus has set you free from the law of sin and of death. For God has done what the law, weakened by the flesh, could not do: by sending his own Son in the likeness of sinful flesh, and to deal with sin, he condemned sin in the flesh, so that the just requirement of the law might be fulfilled in us, who walk not according to the flesh but according to the Spirit.] [5] For those who live according to the flesh set their minds on the things of the flesh, but those who live according to the Spirit set their minds on the things of the Spirit. To set the mind on the flesh is death, but to set the mind on the Spirit is life and peace. For this reason the mind that is set on the flesh is hostile to God; it does not submit to God's law – indeed it cannot, and those who are in the flesh cannot please God.

But you are not in the flesh; you are in the Spirit, since the Spirit of God dwells in you. Anyone who does not have the Spirit of Christ does not belong to him. But if Christ is in you, though the body is dead because of sin, the Spirit is life because of righteousness. If the Spirit of him who raised Jesus from the dead dwells in you, he who raised Christ from the dead will give life to your mortal bodies also through his Spirit that dwells in you.

Hear the Gospel of our Lord Jesus Christ according to John.

(20.19-23)

When it was evening on that day, the first day of the week, and the doors of the house where the disciples had met were locked for fear of the Jews, Jesus came and stood among them and said, 'Peace be with you.' After he said this, he showed them his hands and his side. Then the disciples rejoiced when they saw the Lord. Jesus said to them again, 'Peace be with you. As the Father has sent me, so I send you.' When he had said this, he breathed on them and said to them, 'Receive the Holy Spirit. If you forgive the sins of any, they are forgiven them; if you retain the sins of any, they are retained.'

This is the Gospel of Christ.

Easter / Pentecost – Set B

For Collects and Post-Communion Prayers, see pages 11 & 27.

A reading from the prophecy of Jeremiah. (31.31-34)
The days are surely coming, says the Lord, when I will make a new covenant with the house of Israel and the house of Judah. It will not be like the covenant that I made with their ancestors when I took them by the hand to bring them out of the land of Egypt – a covenant that they broke, though I was their husband, says the Lord. But this is the covenant that I will make with the house of Israel after those days, says the Lord: I will put my law within them, and I will write it on their hearts; and I will be their God, and they shall be my people. No longer shall they teach one another, or say to each other, 'Know the Lord,' for they shall all know me, from the least of them to the greatest, says the Lord; for I will forgive their iniquity, and remember their sin no more.

Psalm 119.105-112 or Psalm 104.27-30

A reading from the Letter of Paul to the Galatians. (5.22 – 6.2)
The fruit of the Spirit is love, joy, peace, patience, kindness, generosity, faithfulness, gentleness, and self-control. There is no law against such things. And those who belong to Christ Jesus have crucified the flesh with its passions and desires. If we live by the Spirit, let us also be guided by the Spirit. Let us not become conceited, competing against one another, envying one another.

My friends, if anyone is detected in a transgression, you who have received the Spirit should restore such a one in a spirit of gentleness. Take care that you yourselves are not tempted. Bear one another's burdens, and in this way you will fulfil the law of Christ.

Or:

A reading from the Acts of the Apostles. (2.1-18)
When the day of Pentecost had come, the apostles were all together in one place. And suddenly from heaven there came a sound like the rush of a violent wind, and it filled the entire house where they were sitting. Divided tongues, as of fire, appeared among them, and a tongue rested on each of them. All of them were filled with the Holy Spirit and began to speak in other languages, as the Spirit gave them ability.

Now there were devout Jews from every nation under heaven living in Jerusalem. And at this sound the crowd gathered and was bewildered, because each one heard them speaking in the native language of each. Amazed and astonished, they asked, 'Are not all these who are speaking Galileans? And how is it that we hear, each of us, in our own native language? Parthians, Medes, Elamites, and residents of Mesopotamia, Judea and Cappadocia, Pontus and Asia, Phrygia and Pamphylia, Egypt and the parts of Libya belonging to Cyrene, and visitors from Rome, both Jews and proselytes, Cretans and Arabs – in our own languages we hear them speaking about God's deeds of power.' All were amazed and perplexed, saying to one another, 'What does this mean?' But others sneered and said, 'They are filled with new wine.'

But Peter, standing with the eleven, raised his voice and addressed them, 'Men of Judea and all who live in Jerusalem, let this be known to you, and listen to what I say. Indeed, these are not drunk, as you suppose, for it is only nine o'clock in the morning. No, this is what was spoken through the prophet Joel:

"In the last days it will be, God declares,
    that I will pour out my Spirit upon all flesh,
and your sons and your daughters shall prophesy,
    and your young men shall see visions,
    and your old men shall dream dreams.
Even upon my slaves, both men and women,
    in those days I will pour out my Spirit;
    and they shall prophesy."'

Hear the Gospel of our Lord Jesus Christ according to John, *(14.15-18)*

Jesus said to his disciples, 'If you love me, you will keep my commandments. And I will ask the Father, and he will give you another Advocate, to be with you for ever. This is the Spirit of truth, whom the world cannot receive, because it neither sees him nor knows him. You know him, because he abides with you, and he will be in you.

'I will not leave you orphaned; I am coming to you.'

This is the Gospel of Christ.

Or:

Hear the Gospel of our Lord Jesus Christ according to John. *(4.23-26)*

Jesus said, 'The hour is coming, and is now here, when the true worshippers will worship the Father in spirit and truth, for the Father seeks such as these to worship him. God is spirit, and those who worship him must worship in spirit and truth.' The woman said to him, 'I know that Messiah is coming' (who is called Christ). 'When he comes, he will proclaim all things to us.' Jesus said to her, 'I am he, the one who is speaking to you.'

This is the Gospel of Christ.

All Saints – Set A

For Collects and Post-Communion Prayers, see pages 11 & 32.

A reading from the prophecy of Isaiah. (11.1-10)

A shoot shall come out from the stump of Jesse,
  and a branch shall grow out of his roots.
The spirit of the Lord shall rest on him,
  the spirit of wisdom and understanding,
the spirit of counsel and might,
  the spirit of knowledge and the fear of the Lord.
His delight shall be in the fear of the Lord.

He shall not judge by what his eyes see,
  or decide by what his ears hear;
but with righteousness he shall judge the poor,
  and decide with equity for the meek of the earth;
he shall strike the earth with the rod of his mouth,
  and with the breath of his lips he shall kill the wicked.
Righteousness shall be the belt around his waist,
  and faithfulness the belt around his loins.

The wolf shall live with the lamb,
  the leopard shall lie down with the kid,
the calf and the lion and the fatling together,
  and a little child shall lead them.
The cow and the bear shall graze,
  their young shall lie down together;
  and the lion shall eat straw like the ox.
The nursing child shall play over the hole of the asp,
  and the weaned child shall put its hand on the adder's den.
They will not hurt or destroy
  on all my holy mountain;
for the earth will be full of the knowledge of the Lord
  as the waters cover the sea.

On that day the root of Jesse shall stand as a signal to the peoples;
the nations shall inquire of him, and his dwelling shall be glorious.

Psalm 20.6-9

A reading from the Revelation to John. (5.6-10)
I saw between the throne and the four living creatures and among the elders a Lamb standing as if it had been slaughtered, having seven horns and seven eyes, which are the seven spirits of God sent out into all the earth. He went and took the scroll from the right hand of the one who was seated on the throne. When he had taken the scroll, the four living creatures and the twenty-four elders fell before the Lamb, each holding a harp and golden bowls full of incense, which are the prayers of the saints. They sing a new song:

'You are worthy to take the scroll
  and to open its seals,
for you were slaughtered and by your blood
    you ransomed for God
saints from every tribe and language and people and nation;
you have made them to be a kingdom
    and priests serving our God,
  and they will reign on earth.'

Hear the Gospel of our Lord Jesus Christ according to Matthew.

(28.16-end)

The eleven disciples went to Galilee, to the mountain to which Jesus had directed them. When they saw him, they worshipped him; but some doubted. And Jesus came and said to them, 'All authority in heaven and on earth has been given to me. Go therefore and make disciples of all nations, baptizing them in the name of the Father and of the Son and of the Holy Spirit, and teaching them to obey everything that I have commanded you. And remember, I am with you always, to the end of the age.'

This is the Gospel of Christ.

All Saints – Set B

For Collects and Post-Communion Prayers, see pages 11 & 32.

A reading from the Book of the Exodus. (19.3-8)

Moses went up to God; the Lord called to him from the mountain, saying, 'Thus you shall say to the house of Jacob, and tell the Israelites: You have seen what I did to the Egyptians, and how I bore you on eagles' wings and brought you to myself. Now therefore, if you obey my voice and keep my covenant, you shall be my treasured possession out of all the peoples. Indeed, the whole earth is mine, but you shall be for me a priestly kingdom and a holy nation. These are the words that you shall speak to the Israelites.'

So Moses came, summoned the elders of the people, and set before them all these words that the Lord had commanded him. The people all answered as one: 'Everything that the Lord has spoken we will do.' Moses reported the words of the people to the Lord.

Psalm 96.1-10

A reading from the First Letter of Peter. (2.4-10)

Come to Christ, a living stone, though rejected by mortals yet chosen and precious in God's sight and, like living stones, let yourselves be built into a spiritual house, to be a holy priesthood, to offer spiritual sacrifices acceptable to God through Jesus Christ. For it stands in scripture:
'See, I am laying in Zion a stone,
   a cornerstone chosen and precious;
and whoever believes in him will not be put to shame.'
To you then who believe, he is precious; but for those who do not believe,
'The stone that the builders rejected
   has become the very head of the corner,'
and
'A stone that makes them stumble,
   and a rock that makes them fall.'
They stumble because they disobey the word, as they were destined to do.

But you are a chosen race, a royal priesthood, a holy nation, God's own people, in order that you may proclaim the mighty acts of him who called you out of darkness into his marvellous light.
Once you were not a people,
   but now you are God's people;

once you had not received mercy,
　　but now you have received mercy.

Hear the Gospel of our Lord Jesus Christ according to Mark. *(1.14-20)*
After John was arrested, Jesus came to Galilee, proclaiming the good news of God, and saying, 'The time is fulfilled, and the kingdom of God has come near; repent, and believe in the good news.'

As Jesus passed along the Sea of Galilee, he saw Simon and his brother Andrew casting a net into the sea – for they were fishermen. And Jesus said to them, 'Follow me and I will make you fish for people.' And immediately they left their nets and followed him. As he went a little farther, he saw James son of Zebedee and his brother John, who were in their boat mending the nets. Immediately he called them; and they left their father Zebedee in the boat with the hired men, and followed him.

This is the Gospel of Christ.

Blank page 62

Marriage

Marriage

Collect
God our Father,
from the beginning
you have blessed creation with abundant life:
pour out your blessings upon N and N,
that they may be joined in mutual love and companionship
in holiness and commitment to each other;
we ask this through our Lord Jesus Christ your Son,
who is alive and reigns with you
in the unity of the Holy Spirit,
one God, now and for ever.

Post Communion
Gracious God,
may N and N,
who have been bound together in these holy mysteries,
become one in body and soul;
may they live in faithfulness and peace
and obtain those eternal joys
prepared for all who love you;
through your Son Jesus Christ our Lord.

The following readings are also appropriate at services celebrating an Engagement for Marriage and at services of Thanksgiving for Marriage and for the Renewal of Marriage Vows.

A reading from the book Genesis. *(1.26-28)*

God said, 'Let us make humankind in our image, according to our likeness; and let them have dominion over the fish of the sea, and over the birds of the air, and over the cattle, and over all the wild animals of the earth, and over every creeping thing that creeps upon the earth.'
   So God created humankind in his image,
     in the image of God he created them;
     male and female he created them.
God blessed them, and God said to them, 'Be fruitful and multiply, and fill the earth and subdue it; and have dominion over the fish of the sea and over the birds of the air and over every living thing that moves upon the earth.'

A reading from the Song of Solomon. *(2.10-13; 8.6-7)*

    My belovèd speaks and says to me:
    'Arise, my love, my fair one,
      and come away;
    for now the winter is past,
      the rain is over and gone.
    The flowers appear on the earth;
      the time of singing has come,
    and the voice of the turtledove
      is heard in our land.
    The fig tree puts forth its figs,
      and the vines are in blossom;
      they give forth fragrance.
    Arise, my love, my fair one,
      and come away.

8.6 Set me as a seal upon your heart,
      as a seal upon your arm;
    for love is strong as death,
      passion fierce as the grave.
    Its flashes are flashes of fire,
      a raging flame.
    Many waters cannot quench love,
      neither can floods drown it.
    If one offered for love
      all the wealth of one's house,
      it would be utterly scorned.

A reading from the prophecy of Jeremiah. *(31.31-34)*

The days are surely coming, says the Lord, when I will make a new covenant with the house of Israel and the house of Judah. It will not be like the covenant that I made with their ancestors when I took them by the hand to bring them out of the land of Egypt – a covenant that they broke, though I was their husband, says the Lord. But this is the covenant that I will make with the house of Israel after those days, says the Lord: I will put my law within them, and I will write it on their hearts; and I will be their God, and they shall be my people. No longer shall they teach one another, or say to each other, 'Know the Lord,' for they shall all know me, from the least of them to the greatest, says the Lord; for I will forgive their iniquity, and remember their sin no more.

A reading from the book Tobit. *(8.4-8)*

When the parents had gone out and shut the door of the room, Tobias got out of bed and said to Sarah, 'Sister, get up, and let us pray and implore our Lord that he grant us mercy and safety.' So she got up, and they began to pray and implore that they might be kept safe. Tobias began by saying,

'Blessèd are you, O God of our ancestors,
    and blessèd is your name in all generations for ever.
Let the heavens and the whole creation bless you for ever.
You made Adam, and for him you made his wife Eve
    as a helper and support.
    From the two of them the human race has sprung.
You said, "It is not good that the man should be alone;
    let us make a helper for him like himself."
I now am taking this kinswoman of mine,
    not because of lust,
    but with sincerity.
Grant that she and I may find mercy
    and that we may grow old together.'

And they both said, 'Amen, Amen.'

Psalm 67; Psalm 121; Psalm 127; Psalm 128

A reading from the Letter of Paul to the Romans. *(7.1-2,9-18)*

Do you not know, brothers and sisters – for I am speaking to those who know the law – that the law is binding on a person only during that person's lifetime? Thus a married woman is bound by the law to her husband as long as he lives; but if her husband dies, she is discharged from the law concerning the husband.

9 I was once alive apart from the law, but when the commandment came, sin revived and I died, and the very commandment that promised life proved to be death to me. For sin, seizing an opportunity in the commandment, deceived me and through it killed me. So the law is holy, and the commandment is holy and just and good.

Did what is good, then, bring death to me? By no means! It was sin, working death in me through what is good, in order that sin might be shown to be sin, and through the commandment might become sinful beyond measure.

For we know that the law is spiritual; but I am of the flesh, sold into slavery under sin. I do not understand my own actions. For I do not do what I want, but I do the very thing I hate. Now if I do what I do not want, I agree that the law is good. But in fact it is no longer I that do it, but sin that dwells within me. For I know that nothing good dwells within me, that is, in my flesh. I can will what is right, but I cannot do it.

A reading from the Letter of Paul to the Romans. (8.31-35,37-end)
What are we to say about these things? If God is for us, who is against us? He who did not withhold his own Son, but gave him up for all of us, will he not with him also give us everything else? Who will bring any charge against God's elect? It is God who justifies. Who is to condemn? It is Christ Jesus, who died, yes, who was raised, who is at the right hand of God, who indeed intercedes for us. Who will separate us from the love of Christ? Will hardship, or distress, or persecution, or famine, or nakedness, or peril, or sword? [37] No, in all these things we are more than conquerors through him who loved us. For I am convinced that neither death, nor life, nor angels, nor rulers, nor things present, nor things to come, nor powers, nor height, nor depth, nor anything else in all creation, will be able to separate us from the love of God in Christ Jesus our Lord.

A reading from the Letter of Paul to the Romans. (12.1-2,9-13)
I appeal to you therefore, brothers and sisters, by the mercies of God, to present your bodies as a living sacrifice, holy and acceptable to God, which is your spiritual worship. Do not be conformed to this world, but be transformed by the renewing of your minds, so that you may discern what is the will of God – what is good and acceptable and perfect.
[9] Let love be genuine; hate what is evil, hold fast to what is good; love one another with mutual affection; outdo one another in showing honour. Do not lag in zeal, be ardent in spirit, serve the Lord. Rejoice in hope, be patient in suffering, persevere in prayer. Contribute to the needs of the saints; extend hospitality to strangers.

A reading from the Letter of Paul to the Romans. (15.1-3,5-7,13)
We who are strong ought to put up with the failings of the weak, and not to please ourselves. Each of us must please our neighbour for the good purpose of building up the neighbour. For Christ did not please himself; but, as it is written, 'The insults of those who insult you have fallen on me.'
  May the God of steadfastness and encouragement grant you to live in harmony with one another, in accordance with Christ Jesus, so that together you may with one voice glorify the God and Father of our Lord Jesus Christ.

Welcome one another, therefore, just as Christ has welcomed you, for the glory of God.

May the God of hope fill you with all joy and peace in believing, so that you may abound in hope by the power of the Holy Spirit.

A reading from the First Letter of Paul to the Corinthians. (Chapter 13)
If I speak in the tongues of mortals and of angels, but do not have love, I am a noisy gong or a clanging cymbal. And if I have prophetic powers, and understand all mysteries and all knowledge, and if I have all faith, so as to remove mountains, but do not have love, I am nothing. If I give away all my possessions, and if I hand over my body so that I may boast, but do not have love, I gain nothing.

Love is patient; love is kind; love is not envious or boastful or arrogant or rude. It does not insist on its own way; it is not irritable or resentful; it does not rejoice in wrongdoing, but rejoices in the truth. It bears all things, believes all things, hopes all things, endures all things.

Love never ends. But as for prophecies, they will come to an end; as for tongues, they will cease; as for knowledge, it will come to an end. For we know only in part, and we prophesy only in part; but when the complete comes, the partial will come to an end. When I was a child, I spoke like a child, I thought like a child, I reasoned like a child; when I became an adult, I put an end to childish ways. For now we see in a mirror, dimly, but then we will see face to face. Now I know only in part; then I will know fully, even as I have been fully known. And now faith, hope, and love abide, these three; and the greatest of these is love.

A reading from the Letter of Paul to the Ephesians. (3.14-end)
I bow my knees before the Father, from whom every family in heaven and on earth takes its name. I pray that, according to the riches of his glory, he may grant that you may be strengthened in your inner being with power through his Spirit, and that Christ may dwell in your hearts through faith, as you are being rooted and grounded in love. I pray that you may have the power to comprehend, with all the saints, what is the breadth and length and height and depth, and to know the love of Christ that surpasses knowledge, so that you may be filled with all the fullness of God.

Now to him who by the power at work within us is able to accomplish abundantly far more than all we can ask or imagine, to him be glory in the church and in Christ Jesus to all generations, for ever and ever. Amen.

A reading from the Letter of Paul to the Ephesians. (4.1-6)
I, the prisoner in the Lord, beg you to lead a life worthy of the calling
to which you have been called, with all humility and gentleness, with
patience, bearing with one another in love, making every effort to
maintain the unity of the Spirit in the bond of peace. There is one
body and one Spirit, just as you were called to the one hope of your
calling, one Lord, one faith, one baptism, one God and Father of all,
who is above all and through all and in all.

A reading from the Letter of Paul to the Ephesians. (5.21-end)
Be subject to one another out of reverence for Christ.

Wives, be subject to your husbands as you are to the Lord. For the
husband is the head of the wife just as Christ is the head of the
church, the body of which he is the Saviour. Just as the church is
subject to Christ, so also wives ought to be, in everything, to their
husbands.

Husbands, love your wives, just as Christ loved the church and gave
himself up for her, in order to make her holy by cleansing her with
the washing of water by the word, so as to present the church to
himself in splendour, without a spot or wrinkle or anything of the
kind – yes, so that she may be holy and without blemish. In the same
way, husbands should love their wives as they do their own bodies.
He who loves his wife loves himself. For no one ever hates his own
body, but he nourishes and tenderly cares for it, just as Christ does
for the church, because we are members of his body. 'For this reason
a man will leave his father and mother and be joined to his wife, and
the two will become one flesh.' This is a great mystery, and I am
applying it to Christ and the church. Each of you, however, should
love his wife as himself, and a wife should respect her husband.

A reading from the Letter of Paul to the Philippians. (4.4-9)
Rejoice in the Lord always; again I will say, Rejoice. Let your gentleness be known to everyone. The Lord is near. Do not worry about
anything, but in everything by prayer and supplication with thanksgiving let your requests be made known to God. And the peace of
God, which surpasses all understanding, will guard your hearts and
your minds in Christ Jesus.

Finally, belovèd, whatever is true, whatever is honourable, whatever is just, whatever is pure, whatever is pleasing, whatever is
commendable, if there is any excellence and if there is anything
worthy of praise, think about these things. Keep on doing the things
that you have learned and received and heard and seen in me, and
the God of peace will be with you.

A reading from the Letter of Paul to the Colossians. (3.12-17)
As God's chosen ones, holy and belovèd, clothe yourselves with compassion, kindness, humility, meekness, and patience. Bear with one another and, if anyone has a complaint against another, forgive each other; just as the Lord has forgiven you, so you also must forgive. Above all, clothe yourselves with love, which binds everything together in perfect harmony. And let the peace of Christ rule in your hearts, to which indeed you were called in the one body. And be thankful. Let the word of Christ dwell in you richly; teach and admonish one another in all wisdom; and with gratitude in your hearts sing psalms, hymns, and spiritual songs to God. And whatever you do, in word or deed, do everything in the name of the Lord Jesus, giving thanks to God the Father through him.

A reading from the First Letter of John. (3.18-end)
Little children, let us love, not in word or speech, but in truth and action. And by this we will know that we are from the truth and will reassure our hearts before him whenever our hearts condemn us; for God is greater than our hearts, and he knows everything. Belovèd, if our hearts do not condemn us, we have boldness before God; and we receive from him whatever we ask, because we obey his commandments and do what pleases him.

And this is his commandment, that we should believe in the name of his Son Jesus Christ and love one another, just as he has commanded us. All who obey his commandments abide in him, and he abides in them. And by this we know that he abides in us, by the Spirit that he has given us.

A reading from the First Letter of John. (4.7-12)
Belovèd, let us love one another, because love is from God; everyone who loves is born of God and knows God. Whoever does not love does not know God, for God is love. God's love was revealed among us in this way: God sent his only Son into the world so that we might live through him. In this is love, not that we loved God but that he loved us and sent his Son to be the atoning sacrifice for our sins. Belovèd, since God loved us so much, we also ought to love one another. No one has ever seen God; if we love one another, God lives in us, and his love is perfected in us.

A reading from the Gospel according to Matthew. (5.1-10)
When Jesus saw the crowds, he went up the mountain; and after he sat down, his disciples came to him. Then he began to speak, and taught them, saying:
> 'Blessèd are the poor in spirit, for theirs is the kingdom of heaven.
> 'Blessèd are those who mourn, for they will be comforted.
> 'Blessèd are the meek, for they will inherit the earth.
> 'Blessèd are those who hunger and thirst for righteousness,
>   for they will be filled.
> 'Blessèd are the merciful, for they will receive mercy.
> 'Blessèd are the pure in heart, for they will see God.
> 'Blessèd are the peacemakers, for they will be called
>   children of God.
> 'Blessèd are those who are persecuted for righteousness' sake,
>   for theirs is the kingdom of heaven.'

A reading from the Gospel according to Matthew. (7.21,24-end)
Jesus said, 'Not everyone who says to me, "Lord, Lord," will enter the kingdom of heaven, but only the one who does the will of my Father in heaven.
²⁴ 'Everyone then who hears these words of mine and acts on them will be like a wise man who built his house on rock. The rain fell, the floods came, and the winds blew and beat on that house, but it did not fall, because it had been founded on rock. And everyone who hears these words of mine and does not act on them will be like a foolish man who built his house on sand. The rain fell, and the floods came, and the winds blew and beat against that house, and it fell – and great was its fall!'
   Now when Jesus had finished saying these things, the crowds were astounded at his teaching, for he taught them as one having authority, and not as their scribes.

A reading from the Gospel according to Mark. (10.6-9,13-16)
Jesus said to the Pharisees, 'From the beginning of creation, "God made them male and female." "For this reason a man shall leave his father and mother and be joined to his wife, and the two shall become one flesh." So they are no longer two, but one flesh. Therefore what God has joined together, let no one separate.'
¹³ People were bringing little children to him in order that he might touch them; and the disciples spoke sternly to them. But when Jesus saw this, he was indignant and said to them, 'Let the little children come to me; do not stop them; for it is to such as these that the

kingdom of God belongs. Truly I tell you, whoever does not receive the kingdom of God as a little child will never enter it.' And he took them up in his arms, laid his hands on them, and blessed them.

A reading from the Gospel according to John. (2.1-11)
On the third day there was a wedding in Cana of Galilee, and the mother of Jesus was there. Jesus and his disciples had also been invited to the wedding. When the wine gave out, the mother of Jesus said to him, 'They have no wine.' And Jesus said to her, 'Woman, what concern is that to you and to me? My hour has not yet come.' His mother said to the servants, 'Do whatever he tells you.' Now standing there were six stone water jars for the Jewish rites of purification, each holding twenty or thirty gallons. Jesus said to them, 'Fill the jars with water.' And they filled them up to the brim. He said to them, 'Now draw some out, and take it to the chief steward.' So they took it. When the steward tasted the water that had become wine, and did not know where it came from (though the servants who had drawn the water knew), the steward called the bridegroom and said to him, 'Everyone serves the good wine first, and then the inferior wine after the guests have become drunk. But you have kept the good wine until now.' Jesus did this, the first of his signs, in Cana of Galilee, and revealed his glory; and his disciples believed in him.

A reading from the Gospel according to John. (15.1-8)
Jesus said to his disciples, 'I am the true vine, and my Father is the vinegrower. He removes every branch in me that bears no fruit. Every branch that bears fruit he prunes to make it bear more fruit. You have already been cleansed by the word that I have spoken to you. Abide in me as I abide in you. Just as the branch cannot bear fruit by itself unless it abides in the vine, neither can you unless you abide in me. I am the vine, you are the branches. Those who abide in me and I in them bear much fruit, because apart from me you can do nothing. Whoever does not abide in me is thrown away like a branch and withers; such branches are gathered, thrown into the fire, and burned. If you abide in me, and my words abide in you, ask for whatever you wish, and it will be done for you. My Father is glorified by this, that you bear much fruit and become my disciples.'

A reading from the Gospel according to John. (15.9-17)
Jesus said to his disciples, 'As the Father has loved me, so I have loved you; abide in my love. If you keep my commandments, you will abide in my love, just as I have kept my Father's commandments

and abide in his love. I have said these things to you so that my joy may be in you, and that your joy may be complete.

'This is my commandment, that you love one another as I have loved you. No one has greater love than this, to lay down one's life for one's friends. You are my friends if you do what I command you. I do not call you servants any longer, because the servant does not know what the master is doing; but I have called you friends, because I have made known to you everything that I have heard from my Father. You did not choose me but I chose you. And I appointed you to go and bear fruit, fruit that will last, so that the Father will give you whatever you ask him in my name. I am giving you these commands so that you may love one another.'

Ministry

Ministry

Ordination

At the time of going to press, the Ordination Services for **Common Worship** *are yet to be authorized. Therefore, the text of the readings printed here are as authorized both by* The Ordinal *attached to* The Book of Common Prayer *and by* The Alternative Service Book 1980, *the Ordinal of which has had its authority extended to the year 2005.*

A rubric of The Alternative Service Book 1980 *Ordinal states that 'the presiding bishop may choose alternative Old Testament and New Testament readings suitable to the occasion.' There is no such rubric in* The Ordinal *attached to* The Book of Common Prayer, *neither is the situation affected by Canon.*

The text of the Collects and Post-Communion Prayers are from The Alternative Service Book 1980, *with authorized changes made by the House of Bishops.*

Ordination of Deacons

Collect (also used at the Ordination of Deacons and Priests)
God our Father, Lord of all the world,
we thank you that, through your Son,
you have called us into the fellowship of your universal Church:
hear our prayer for all your faithful people,
that in their vocation and ministry
they may be an instrument of your love;
and give your *servants*, now to be ordained
the needful gifts of grace;
through your Son our Lord and Saviour Jesus Christ,
who is alive and reigns with you
in the unity of the Holy Spirit,
one God, now and for ever.

Post Communion
Father,
you have taught the ministers of your Church
to be the willing servants of others:
give to *these* your *deacons*
skill and gentleness in the practice of *their* ministry
and perseverance always in prayer;
through Jesus Christ our Lord.

or, if deacons and priests are being ordained at the same service:
Father,
you have appointed your Son
to be our high priest for ever:
fulfil now your purpose in choosing these your servants
to be ministers and stewards
  of your word and sacraments;
and grant that they may be found faithful
in the ministry they have received;
through Jesus Christ our Lord.

BCP: 1 Timothy 3.8-13; Acts 6.2-7; Luke 12.35-38
or, if deacons and priests are being ordained at the same service:
Ephesians 4.7-13; Matthew 9.36-end *or* Luke 12.35-38 *(see page 82 ff)*

ASB: Isaiah 6.1-8; Psalm 119.33-38; Romans 12.1-12; Mark 10.35-45

A reading from the prophecy of Isaiah. (6.1-8)

In the year that King Uzziah died, I saw the Lord sitting on a throne, high and lofty; and the hem of his robe filled the temple. Seraphs were in attendance above him; each had six wings: with two they covered their faces, and with two they covered their feet, and with two they flew. And one called to another and said:

'Holy, holy, holy is the Lord of hosts;
    the whole earth is full of his glory.'

The pivots on the thresholds shook at the voices of those who called, and the house filled with smoke. And I said: 'Woe is me! I am lost, for I am a man of unclean lips, and I live among a people of unclean lips; yet my eyes have seen the King, the Lord of hosts!'

Then one of the seraphs flew to me, holding a live coal that had been taken from the altar with a pair of tongs. The seraph touched my mouth with it and said: 'Now that this has touched your lips, your guilt has departed and your sin is blotted out.' Then I heard the voice of the Lord saying, 'Whom shall I send, and who will go for us?' And I said, 'Here am I; send me!'

This is the word of the Lord.

Psalm 119.33-38

A reading from the Acts of the Apostles. (6.2-7)

The twelve called together the whole community of the disciples and said, 'It is not right that we should neglect the word of God in order to wait on tables. Therefore, friends, select from among yourselves seven men of good standing, full of the Spirit and of wisdom, whom we may appoint to this task, while we, for our part, will devote ourselves to prayer and to serving the word.' What they said pleased the whole community, and they chose Stephen, a man full of faith and the Holy Spirit, together with Philip, Prochorus, Nicanor, Timon, Parmenas, and Nicolaus, a proselyte of Antioch. They had these men stand before the apostles, who prayed and laid their hands on them.

The word of God continued to spread; the number of the disciples increased greatly in Jerusalem, and a great many of the priests became obedient to the faith.

This is the word of the Lord.

A reading from the Letter of Paul to the Romans. (12.1-12)
I appeal to you, brothers and sisters, by the mercies of God, to present your bodies as a living sacrifice, holy and acceptable to God, which is your spiritual worship. Do not be conformed to this world, but be transformed by the renewing of your minds, so that you may discern what is the will of God – what is good and acceptable and perfect.

For by the grace given to me I say to everyone among you not to think of yourself more highly than you ought to think, but to think with sober judgment, each according to the measure of faith that God has assigned. For as in one body we have many members, and not all the members have the same function, so we, who are many, are one body in Christ, and individually we are members one of another. We have gifts that differ according to the grace given to us: prophecy, in proportion to faith; ministry, in ministering; the teacher, in teaching; the exhorter, in exhortation; the giver, in generosity; the leader, in diligence; the compassionate, in cheerfulness.

Let love be genuine; hate what is evil, hold fast to what is good; love one another with mutual affection; outdo one another in showing honour. Do not lag in zeal, be ardent in spirit, serve the Lord. Rejoice in hope, be patient in suffering, persevere in prayer.

This is the word of the Lord.

A reading from the First Letter of Paul to Timothy. (3.8-13)
Deacons must be serious, not double-tongued, not indulging in much wine, not greedy for money; they must hold fast to the mystery of the faith with a clear conscience. And let them first be tested; then, if they prove themselves blameless, let them serve as deacons. Women likewise must be serious, not slanderers, but temperate, faithful in all things. Let deacons be married only once, and let them manage their children and their households well; for those who serve well as deacons gain a good standing for themselves and great boldness in the faith that is in Christ Jesus.

This is the word of the Lord.

Hear the Gospel of our Lord Jesus Christ according to Mark.

(10.35-45)

James and John, the sons of Zebedee, came forward to Jesus and said to him, 'Teacher, we want you to do for us whatever we ask of you.' And he said to them, 'What is it you want me to do for you?' And they said to him, 'Grant us to sit, one at your right hand and one at your left, in your glory.' But Jesus said to them, 'You do not know what you are asking. Are you able to drink the cup that I drink, or be baptized with the baptism that I am baptized with?' They replied, 'We are able.' Then Jesus said to them, 'The cup that I drink you will drink; and with the baptism with which I am baptized, you will be baptized; but to sit at my right hand or at my left is not mine to grant, but it is for those for whom it has been prepared.'

When the ten heard this, they began to be angry with James and John. So Jesus called them and said to them, 'You know that among the Gentiles those whom they recognize as their rulers lord it over them, and their great ones are tyrants over them. But it is not so among you; but whoever wishes to become great among you must be your servant, and whoever wishes to be first among you must be slave of all. For the Son of Man came not to be served but to serve, and to give his life a ransom for many.'

This is the Gospel of the Lord.

Hear the Gospel of our Lord Jesus Christ according to Luke.

(12.35-38)

Jesus said to his disciples, 'Be dressed for action and have your lamps lit; be like those who are waiting for their master to return from the wedding banquet, so that they may open the door for him as soon as he comes and knocks. Blessèd are those slaves whom the master finds alert when he comes; truly I tell you, he will fasten his belt and have them sit down to eat, and he will come and serve them. If he comes during the middle of the night, or near dawn, and finds them so, blessèd are those slaves.'

This is the Gospel of the Lord.

Ordination of Priests

Collect
God our Father, Lord of all the world,
we thank you that, through your Son,
you have called us into the fellowship of your universal Church:
hear our prayer for all your faithful people,
that in their vocation and ministry
they may be an instrument of your love;
and give your *servants*, now to be ordained priest
the needful gifts of grace;
through your Son our Lord and Saviour Jesus Christ,
who is alive and reigns with you
in the unity of the Holy Spirit,
one God, now and for ever.

Post Communion
Father,
you have appointed your Son
to be our high priest for ever:
fulfil now your purpose in choosing *these* your *servants*
to be *ministers* and *stewards*
  of your word and sacraments;
and grant that *they* may be found faithful
in the ministry *they have* received;
through Jesus Christ our Lord.

BCP: Ephesians 4.7-13; Matthew 9.36-end *or* John 10.1-16
ASB: Isaiah 61.1-3*a or* Malachi 2.5-7; Psalm 145.1-7,22;
2 Corinthians 5.14-19; John 20.19-23 *& see note on page 77.*

A reading from the prophecy of Isaiah. *(61.1-3a)*
    The spirit of the Lord God is upon me,
        because the Lord has anointed me;
    he has sent me to bring good news to the oppressed,
        to bind up the broken-hearted,
    to proclaim liberty to the captives,
        and release to the prisoners;
    to proclaim the year of the Lord's favour,
        and the day of vengeance of our God;
        to comfort all who mourn;
    to provide for those who mourn in Zion –

to give them a garland instead of ashes,
the oil of gladness instead of mourning,
the mantle of praise instead of a faint spirit.

This is the word of the Lord.

A reading from the prophecy of Malachi. (2.5-7)
My covenant with him was a covenant of life and well-being, which
I gave him; this called for reverence, and he revered me and stood in
awe of my name. True instruction was in his mouth, and no wrong
was found on his lips. He walked with me in integrity and upright-
ness, and he turned many from iniquity. For the lips of a priest
should guard knowledge, and people should seek instruction from
his mouth, for he is the messenger of the Lord of hosts.

This is the word of the Lord.

Psalm 145.1-7,22

A reading from the Second Letter of Paul to the Corinthians. (5.14-19)
The love of Christ urges us on, because we are convinced that one has
died for all; therefore all have died. And he died for all, so that those
who live might live no longer for themselves, but for him who died
and was raised for them.

From now on, therefore, we regard no one from a human point of
view; even though we once knew Christ from a human point of view,
we know him no longer in that way. So if anyone is in Christ, there
is a new creation: everything old has passed away; see, everything
has become new! All this is from God, who reconciled us to himself
through Christ, and has given us the ministry of reconciliation; that
is, in Christ God was reconciling the world to himself, not counting
their trespasses against them, and entrusting the message of
reconciliation to us.

This is the word of the Lord.

A reading from the Letter of Paul to the Ephesians. (4.7-13)
Each of us was given grace according to the measure of Christ's gift.
Therefore it is said,
'When he ascended on high he made captivity itself a captive;
he gave gifts to his people.'
(When it says, 'He ascended,' what does it mean but that he had also
descended into the lower parts of the earth? He who descended is
the same one who ascended far above all the heavens, so that he

might fill all things.)   The gifts he gave were that some would be apostles, some prophets, some evangelists, some pastors and teachers, to equip the saints for the work of ministry, for building up the body of Christ, until all of us come to the unity of the faith and of the knowledge of the Son of God, to maturity, to the measure of the full stature of Christ.

This is the word of the Lord.

Hear the Gospel of our Lord Jesus Christ according to Matthew.
(9.36-end)
When Jesus saw the crowds, he had compassion for them, because they were harassed and helpless, like sheep without a shepherd. Then he said to his disciples, 'The harvest is plentiful, but the labourers are few; therefore ask the Lord of the harvest to send out labourers into his harvest.'

This is the Gospel of the Lord.

Hear the Gospel of our Lord Jesus Christ according to John.
(10.1-16)
Jesus said to the Pharisees, 'Very truly, I tell you, anyone who does not enter the sheepfold by the gate but climbs in by another way is a thief and a bandit. The one who enters by the gate is the shepherd of the sheep. The gatekeeper opens the gate for him, and the sheep hear his voice. He calls his own sheep by name and leads them out. When he has brought out all his own, he goes ahead of them, and the sheep follow him because they know his voice. They will not follow a stranger, but they will run from him because they do not know the voice of strangers.' Jesus used this figure of speech with them, but they did not understand what he was saying to them.

So again Jesus said to them, 'Very truly, I tell you, I am the gate for the sheep. All who came before me are thieves and bandits; but the sheep did not listen to them. I am the gate. Whoever enters by me will be saved, and will come in and go out and find pasture. The thief comes only to steal and kill and destroy. I came that they may have life, and have it abundantly.

'I am the good shepherd. The good shepherd lays down his life for the sheep. The hired hand, who is not the shepherd and does not own the sheep, sees the wolf coming and leaves the sheep and runs away – and the wolf snatches them and scatters them. The hired hand runs away because a hired hand does not care for the sheep. I am the good shepherd. I know my own and my own know me, just as the Father knows me and I know the Father. And I lay down my life for the sheep. I have other sheep that do not belong to this fold. I must bring them also, and they will listen to my voice. So there will be one flock, one shepherd.'

This is the Gospel of the Lord.

Hear the Gospel of our Lord Jesus Christ according to John.
(20.19-23)

When it was evening on that day, the first day of the week, and the doors of the house where the disciples had met were locked for fear of the Jews, Jesus came and stood among them and said, 'Peace be with you.' After he said this, he showed them his hands and his side. Then the disciples rejoiced when they saw the Lord. Jesus said to them again, 'Peace be with you. As the Father has sent me, so I send you.' When he had said this, he breathed on them and said to them, 'Receive the Holy Spirit. If you forgive the sins of any, they are forgiven them; if you retain the sins of any, they are retained.'

This is the Gospel of the Lord.

Ordination of Bishops

Collect
God our Father, Lord of all the world,
we thank you that, through your Son,
you have called us into the fellowship
of your universal Church:
hear our prayer for all your faithful people,
that in their vocation and ministry
they may be an instrument of your love,
and give your *servants*, now to be ordained bishop
the needful gifts of grace;
through your Son our Lord and Saviour Jesus Christ,
who is alive and reigns with you
in the unity of the Holy Spirit,
one God, now and for ever.

Post Communion
God our Father,
shepherd and guide of all your faithful people:
look with favour on *N & N* your *servants*
whom you have chosen to be *pastors* over your Church;
and grant that by word and example
they may lead the people committed to *their* charge
and with them come to your eternal kingdom;
through Jesus Christ our Lord.

BCP: *The title of the service indicates that the ordination 'is always to be performed upon some Sunday or holy-day', though no provision is made for the use of readings proper to those days, either in rubric or in Canon. The given readings are:* 1 Timothy 3.1-7; Acts 20.17-35;
Matthew 28.18-end *or* John 20.19-23 *or* John 21.15-17
ASB: Numbers 27.15-20,22-end; Psalm 119.165-174;
2 Corinthians 4.1-10; John 21.15-17 *& see note on page 77.*

A reading from the book Numbers. *(27.15-20,22-end)*
Moses spoke to the Lord, saying, 'Let the Lord, the God of the spirits of all flesh, appoint someone over the congregation who shall go out before them and come in before them, who shall lead them out and bring them in, so that the congregation of the Lord may not be like sheep without a shepherd.' So the Lord said to Moses, 'Take Joshua son of Nun, a man in whom is the spirit, and lay your hand

upon him; have him stand before Eleazar the priest and all the congregation, and commission him in their sight. You shall give him some of your authority, so that all the congregation of the Israelites may obey.

22 So Moses did as the Lord commanded him. He took Joshua and had him stand before Eleazar the priest and the whole congregation; he laid his hands on him and commissioned him – as the Lord had directed through Moses.

This is the word of the Lord.

Psalm 119.165-174

A reading from the Acts of the Apostles. (20.17-35)
From Miletus Paul sent a message to Ephesus, asking the elders of the church to meet him. When they came to him, he said to them:

'You yourselves know how I lived among you the entire time from the first day that I set foot in Asia, serving the Lord with all humility and with tears, enduring the trials that came to me through the plots of the Jews. I did not shrink from doing anything helpful, proclaiming the message to you and teaching you publicly and from house to house, as I testified to both Jews and Greeks about repentance toward God and faith toward our Lord Jesus. And now, as a captive to the Spirit, I am on my way to Jerusalem, not knowing what will happen to me there, except that the Holy Spirit testifies to me in every city that imprisonment and persecutions are waiting for me. But I do not count my life of any value to myself, if only I may finish my course and the ministry that I received from the Lord Jesus, to testify to the good news of God's grace.

'And now I know that none of you, among whom I have gone about proclaiming the kingdom, will ever see my face again. Therefore I declare to you this day that I am not responsible for the blood of any of you, for I did not shrink from declaring to you the whole purpose of God. Keep watch over yourselves and over all the flock, of which the Holy Spirit has made you overseers, to shepherd the church of God that he obtained with the blood of his own Son. I know that after I have gone, savage wolves will come in among you, not sparing the flock. Some even from your own group will come distorting the truth in order to entice the disciples to follow them. Therefore be alert, remembering that for three years I did not cease night or day to warn everyone with tears. And now I commend you to God and to the message of his grace, a message that is able to build you up and to give you the inheritance among all who are sanctified.

I coveted no one's silver or gold or clothing. You know for yourselves that I worked with my own hands to support myself and my companions. In all this I have given you an example that by such work we must support the weak, remembering the words of the Lord Jesus, for he himself said, "It is more blessèd to give than to receive."'

This is the word of the Lord.

A reading from the Second Letter of Paul to the Corinthians. (4.1-10)
Since it is by God's mercy that we are engaged in this ministry, we do not lose heart. We have renounced the shameful things that one hides; we refuse to practise cunning or to falsify God's word; but by the open statement of the truth we commend ourselves to the conscience of everyone in the sight of God. And even if our gospel is veiled, it is veiled to those who are perishing. In their case the god of this world has blinded the minds of the unbelievers, to keep them from seeing the light of the gospel of the glory of Christ, who is the image of God. For we do not proclaim ourselves; we proclaim Jesus Christ as Lord and ourselves as your slaves for Jesus' sake. 6 For it is the God who said, 'Let light shine out of darkness,' who has shone in our hearts to give the light of the knowledge of the glory of God in the face of Jesus Christ.

But we have this treasure in clay jars, so that it may be made clear that this extraordinary power belongs to God and does not come from us. We are afflicted in every way, but not crushed; perplexed, but not driven to despair; persecuted, but not forsaken; struck down, but not destroyed; always carrying in the body the death of Jesus, so that the life of Jesus may also be made visible in our bodies.

This is the word of the Lord.

A reading from the First Letter of Paul to Timothy. (3.1-7)
The saying is sure: whoever aspires to the office of bishop desires a noble task. Now a bishop must be above reproach, married only once, temperate, sensible, respectable, hospitable, an apt teacher, not a drunkard, not violent but gentle, not quarrelsome, and not a lover of money. He must manage his own household well, keeping his children submissive and respectful in every way – for if someone does not know how to manage his own household, how can he take care of God's church? He must not be a recent convert, or he may be puffed up with conceit and fall into the condemnation of the devil. Moreover, he must be well thought of by outsiders, so that he may not fall into disgrace and the snare of the devil.

This is the word of the Lord.

Ministry – Ordination of Bishops

Hear the Gospel of our Lord Jesus Christ according to Matthew.
(28.18-end)

Jesus came and said to his disciples, 'All authority in heaven and on earth has been given to me. Go therefore and make disciples of all nations, baptizing them in the name of the Father and of the Son and of the Holy Spirit, and teaching them to obey everything that I have commanded you. And remember, I am with you always, to the end of the age.'

This is the Gospel of the Lord.

Hear the Gospel of our Lord Jesus Christ according to John.
(20.19-23)

When it was evening on that day, the first day of the week, and the doors of the house where the disciples had met were locked for fear of the Jews, Jesus came and stood among them and said, 'Peace be with you.' After he said this, he showed them his hands and his side. Then the disciples rejoiced when they saw the Lord. Jesus said to them again, 'Peace be with you. As the Father has sent me, so I send you.' When he had said this, he breathed on them and said to them, 'Receive the Holy Spirit. If you forgive the sins of any, they are forgiven them; if you retain the sins of any, they are retained.'

This is the Gospel of the Lord.

Hear the Gospel of our Lord Jesus Christ according to John.
(21.15-17)

When they had finished breakfast, Jesus said to Simon Peter, 'Simon son of John, do you love me more than these?' He said to him, 'Yes, Lord; you know that I love you.' Jesus said to him, 'Feed my lambs.' A second time he said to him, 'Simon son of John, do you love me?' He said to him, 'Yes, Lord; you know that I love you.' Jesus said to him, 'Tend my sheep.' He said to him the third time, 'Simon son of John, do you love me?' Peter felt hurt because he said to him the third time, 'Do you love me?' And he said to him, 'Lord, you know everything; you know that I love you.' Jesus said to him, 'Feed my sheep.'

This is the Gospel of the Lord.

Ministry – General

Ember Days

Collect (for the ministry of all Christian people)
Almighty and everlasting God,
by whose Spirit the whole body of the Church
  is governed and sanctified:
hear our prayer which we offer for all your faithful people,
that in their vocation and ministry
they may serve you in holiness and truth
to the glory of your name;
through our Lord and Saviour Jesus Christ,
who is alive and reigns with you
in the unity of the Holy Spirit,
one God, now and for ever.

Collect (for those to be ordained)
Almighty God, the giver of all good gifts,
by your Holy Spirit
you have appointed various orders of ministry in the Church:
look with mercy and favour on your servants
  now called to be deacons and priests;
maintain them in truth and renew them in holiness,
that by word and good example they may faithfully serve you
to the glory of your name and the benefit of your Church;
through the merits of our Saviour Jesus Christ,
who is alive and reigns with you
in the unity of the Holy Spirit,
one God, now and for ever.

Collect (for vocations)
Almighty God,
you have entrusted to your Church
a share in the ministry of your Son, our great High Priest:
inspire by your Holy Spirit the hearts of many
to offer themselves for the ministry of your Church
that strengthened by his power,
they may work for the increase of your kingdom
and set forward the eternal praise of your name;
through Jesus Christ your Son our Lord,
who is alive and reigns with you
in the unity of the Holy Spirit,
one God, now and for ever.

Post Communion
Heavenly Father,
whose ascended Son gave gifts of leadership and service
  to the Church:
strengthen us who have received this holy food
to be good stewards of your manifold grace;
through him who came not to be served but to serve
  and give his life as a ransom for many,
Jesus Christ our Lord.

Or:

Lord of the harvest,
you have fed your people in this sacrament
with the fruits of creation made holy by your Spirit:
by your grace
raise up among us faithful labourers
to sow your word and reap the harvest of souls;
through Jesus Christ our Lord.

A reading from the book Numbers. (11.16-17,24-29)
The Lord said to Moses, 'Gather for me seventy of the elders of Israel,
whom you know to be the elders of the people and officers over
them; bring them to the tent of meeting, and have them take their
place there with you. I will come down and talk with you there; and
I will take some of the spirit that is on you and put it on them; and
they shall bear the burden of the people along with you so that you
will not bear it all by yourself.'
²⁴ So Moses went out and told the people the words of the Lord; and
he gathered seventy elders of the people, and placed them all around
the tent. Then the Lord came down in the cloud and spoke to him,
and took some of the spirit that was on him and put it on the seventy
elders; and when the spirit rested upon them, they prophesied. But
they did not do so again.
   Two men remained in the camp, one named Eldad, and the other
named Medad, and the spirit rested on them; they were among
those registered, but they had not gone out to the tent, and so they
prophesied in the camp. And a young man ran and told Moses,
'Eldad and Medad are prophesying in the camp.' And Joshua son of
Nun, the assistant of Moses, one of his chosen men, said, 'My lord
Moses, stop them!' But Moses said to him, 'Are you jealous for my
sake? Would that all the Lord's people were prophets, and that the
Lord would put his spirit on them!'

A reading from the book Numbers. (27.15-end)

Moses spoke to the Lord, saying, 'Let the Lord, the God of the spirits of all flesh, appoint someone over the congregation who shall go out before them and come in before them, who shall lead them out and bring them in, so that the congregation of the Lord may not be like sheep without a shepherd.' So the Lord said to Moses, 'Take Joshua son of Nun, a man in whom is the spirit, and lay your hand upon him; have him stand before Eleazar the priest and all the congregation, and commission him in their sight. You shall give him some of your authority, so that all the congregation of the Israelites may obey. But he shall stand before Eleazar the priest, who shall inquire for him by the decision of the Urim before the Lord; at his word they shall go out, and at his word they shall come in, both he and all the Israelites with him, the whole congregation.' So Moses did as the Lord commanded him. He took Joshua and had him stand before Eleazar the priest and the whole congregation; he laid his hands on him and commissioned him – as the Lord had directed through Moses.

A reading from the First Book of Samuel. (16.1-13a)

The Lord said to Samuel, 'How long will you grieve over Saul? I have rejected him from being king over Israel. Fill your horn with oil and set out; I will send you to Jesse the Bethlehemite, for I have provided for myself a king among his sons.' Samuel said, How can I go? If Saul hears of it, he will kill me.' And the Lord said, 'Take a heifer with you, and say, "I have come to sacrifice to the Lord." Invite Jesse to the sacrifice, and I will show you what you shall do; and you shall anoint for me the one whom I name to you.' Samuel did what the Lord commanded, and came to Bethlehem. The elders of the city came to meet him trembling, and said, 'Do you come peaceably?' He said, 'Peaceably; I have come to sacrifice to the Lord; sanctify yourselves and come with me to the sacrifice.' And he sanctified Jesse and his sons and invited them to the sacrifice.

When they came, he looked on Eliab and thought, 'Surely the Lord's anointed is now before the Lord.' But the Lord said to Samuel, 'Do not look on his appearance or on the height of his stature, because I have rejected him; for the Lord does not see as mortals see; they look on the outward appearance, but the Lord looks on the heart.' Then Jesse called Abinadab, and made him pass before Samuel. He said, 'Neither has the Lord chosen this one.' Then Jesse made Shammah pass by. And he said, 'Neither has the Lord chosen this one.' Jesse made seven of his sons pass before Samuel, and Samuel said to Jesse,

'The Lord has not chosen any of these.' Samuel said to Jesse, 'Are all your sons here?' And he said, 'There remains yet the youngest, but he is keeping the sheep.' And Samuel said to Jesse, 'Send and bring him; for we will not sit down until he comes here.' He sent and brought him in. Now he was ruddy, and had beautiful eyes, and was handsome. The Lord said, 'Rise and anoint him; for this is the one.' Then Samuel took the horn of oil, and anointed him in the presence of his brothers; and the spirit of the Lord came mightily upon David from that day forward.

A reading from the prophecy of Isaiah. (6.1-8)
In the year that King Uzziah died, I saw the Lord sitting on a throne, high and lofty; and the hem of his robe filled the temple. Seraphs were in attendance above him; each had six wings: with two they covered their faces, and with two they covered their feet, and with two they flew. And one called to another and said:
   'Holy, holy, holy is the Lord of hosts;
     the whole earth is full of his glory.'
The pivots on the thresholds shook at the voices of those who called, and the house filled with smoke. And I said: 'Woe is me! I am lost, for I am a man of unclean lips, and I live among a people of unclean lips; yet my eyes have seen the King, the Lord of hosts!'
  Then one of the seraphs flew to me, holding a live coal that had been taken from the altar with a pair of tongs. The seraph touched my mouth with it and said: 'Now that this has touched your lips, your guilt has departed and your sin is blotted out.' Then I heard the voice of the Lord saying, 'Whom shall I send, and who will go for us?' And I said, 'Here am I; send me!'

A reading from the prophecy of Isaiah. (61.1-3)
   The spirit of the Lord God is upon me,
     because the Lord has anointed me;
   he has sent me to bring good news to the oppressed,
     to bind up the broken-hearted,
   to proclaim liberty to the captives,
     and release to the prisoners;
   to proclaim the year of the Lord's favour,
     and the day of vengeance of our God;
     to comfort all who mourn;
   to provide for those who mourn in Zion –
     to give them a garland instead of ashes,
   the oil of gladness instead of mourning,

the mantle of praise instead of a faint spirit.
They will be called oaks of righteousness,
  the planting of the Lord, to display his glory.

A reading from the prophecy of Jeremiah. (1.4-10)
The word of the Lord came to me saying,
  'Before I formed you in the womb I knew you,
    and before you were born I consecrated you;
    I appointed you a prophet to the nations.'
Then I said, 'Ah, Lord God! Truly I do not know how to speak, for I
am only a boy.' But the Lord said to me,
  'Do not say, "I am only a boy";
    for you shall go to all to whom I send you,
    and you shall speak whatever I command you.
  Do not be afraid of them,
    for I am with you to deliver you,
        says the Lord.'
Then the Lord put out his hand and touched my mouth; and the Lord
said to me,
  'Now I have put my words in your mouth.
  See, today I appoint you over nations and over kingdoms,
    to pluck up and to pull down,
    to destroy and to overthrow,
    to build and to plant.'

Psalm 40.8-13; Psalm 84.8-12; Psalm 89.19-25; Psalm 101.1-5,7;
Psalm 122

A reading from the Acts of the Apostles. (20.28-35)
Paul said to the elders of the Church at Ephesus: 'Keep watch over
yourselves and over all the flock, of which the Holy Spirit has made
you overseers, to shepherd the church of God that he obtained with
the blood of his own Son. I know that after I have gone, savage
wolves will come in among you, not sparing the flock. Some even
from your own group will come distorting the truth in order to entice
the disciples to follow them. Therefore be alert, remembering that for
three years I did not cease night or day to warn everyone with tears.
And now I commend you to God and to the message of his grace, a
message that is able to build you up and to give you the inheritance
among all who are sanctified. I coveted no one's silver or gold or
clothing. You know for yourselves that I worked with my own hands
to support myself and my companions. In all this I have given

you an example that by such work we must support the weak, remembering the words of the Lord Jesus, for he himself said, "It is more blessèd to give than to receive."'

A reading from the First Letter of Paul to the Corinthians. (3.3-11)
As long as there is jealousy and quarrelling among you, are you not of the flesh, and behaving according to human inclinations? For when one says, 'I belong to Paul,' and another, 'I belong to Apollos,' are you not merely human?

What then is Apollos? What is Paul? Servants through whom you came to believe, as the Lord assigned to each. I planted, Apollos watered, but God gave the growth. So neither the one who plants nor the one who waters is anything, but only God who gives the growth. The one who plants and the one who waters have a common purpose, and each will receive wages according to the labour of each. For we are God's servants, working together; you are God's field, God's building.

According to the grace of God given to me, like a skilled master builder I laid a foundation, and someone else is building on it. Each builder must choose with care how to build on it. For no one can lay any foundation other than the one that has been laid; that foundation is Jesus Christ.

A reading from the Letter of Paul to the Ephesians. (4.4-16)
There is one body and one Spirit, just as you were called to the one hope of your calling, one Lord, one faith, one baptism, one God and Father of all, who is above all and through all and in all.

But each of us was given grace according to the measure of Christ's gift. Therefore it is said,
    'When he ascended on high he made captivity itself a captive;
        he gave gifts to his people.'
(When it says, 'He ascended,' what does it mean but that he had also descended into the lower parts of the earth? He who descended is the same one who ascended far above all the heavens, so that he might fill all things.) The gifts he gave were that some would be apostles, some prophets, some evangelists, some pastors and teachers, to equip the saints for the work of ministry, for building up the body of Christ, until all of us come to the unity of the faith and of the knowledge of the Son of God, to maturity, to the measure of the full stature of Christ. We must no longer be children, tossed to and fro and blown about by every wind of doctrine, by people's trickery, by their craftiness in deceitful scheming. But speaking the truth in

love, we must grow up in every way into him who is the head, into Christ, from whom the whole body, joined and knit together by every ligament with which it is equipped, as each part is working properly, promotes the body's growth in building itself up in love.

A reading from the Letter of Paul to the Philippians. (3.7-14)
Whatever gains I had, these I have come to regard as loss because of Christ. More than that, I regard everything as loss because of the surpassing value of knowing Christ Jesus my Lord. For his sake I have suffered the loss of all things, and I regard them as rubbish, in order that I may gain Christ and be found in him, not having a righteousness of my own that comes from the law, but one that comes through faith in Christ, the righteousness from God based on faith. I want to know Christ and the power of his resurrection and the sharing of his sufferings by becoming like him in his death, if somehow I may attain the resurrection from the dead.

Not that I have already obtained this or have already reached the goal; but I press on to make it my own, because Christ Jesus has made me his own. Belovèd, I do not consider that I have made it my own; but this one thing I do: forgetting what lies behind and straining forward to what lies ahead, I press on toward the goal for the prize of the heavenly call of God in Christ Jesus.

A reading from the Gospel according to Luke. (4.16-21)
When Jesus came to Nazareth, where he had been brought up, he went to the synagogue on the sabbath day, as was his custom. He stood up to read, and the scroll of the prophet Isaiah was given to him. He unrolled the scroll and found the place where it was written:
'The Spirit of the Lord is upon me,
because he has anointed me
to bring good news to the poor.
He has sent me to proclaim release to the captives
and recovery of sight to the blind,
to let the oppressed go free,
to proclaim the year of the Lord's favour.'
And he rolled up the scroll, gave it back to the attendant, and sat down. The eyes of all in the synagogue were fixed on him. Then he began to say to them, 'Today this scripture has been fulfilled in your hearing.'

A reading from the Gospel according to Luke. (12.35-43)
Jesus said to his disciples, 'Be dressed for action and have your lamps lit; be like those who are waiting for their master to return from the wedding banquet, so that they may open the door for him as soon as he comes and knocks. Blessèd are those slaves whom the master finds alert when he comes; truly I tell you, he will fasten his belt and have them sit down to eat, and he will come and serve them. If he comes during the middle of the night, or near dawn, and finds them so, blessèd are those slaves.

'But know this: if the owner of the house had known at what hour the thief was coming, he would not have let his house be broken into. You also must be ready, for the Son of Man is coming at an unexpected hour.'

Peter said, 'Lord, are you telling this parable for us or for everyone?' And the Lord said, 'Who then is the faithful and prudent manager whom his master will put in charge of his slaves, to give them their allowance of food at the proper time? Blessèd is that slave whom his master will find at work when he arrives.'

A reading from the Gospel according to Luke. (22.24-27)
A dispute arose among the apostles as to which one of them was to be regarded as the greatest. But Jesus said to them, 'The kings of the Gentiles lord it over them; and those in authority over them are called benefactors. But not so with you; rather the greatest among you must become like the youngest, and the leader like one who serves. For who is greater, the one who is at the table or the one who serves? Is it not the one at the table? But I am among you as one who serves.'

A reading from the Gospel according to John. (4.31-38)
The disciples were urging Jesus, 'Rabbi, eat something.' But he said to them, 'I have food to eat that you do not know about.' So the disciples said to one another, 'Surely no one has brought him something to eat?' Jesus said to them, 'My food is to do the will of him who sent me and to complete his work. Do you not say, "Four months more, then comes the harvest"? But I tell you, look around you, and see how the fields are ripe for harvesting. The reaper is already receiving wages and is gathering fruit for eternal life, so that sower and reaper may rejoice together. For here the saying holds true, "One sows and another reaps." I sent you to reap that for which you did not labour. Others have laboured, and you have entered into their labour.'

A reading from the Gospel according to John. (15.5-17)
Jesus said to his disciples, 'I am the vine, you are the branches. Those who abide in me and I in them bear much fruit, because apart from me you can do nothing. Whoever does not abide in me is thrown away like a branch and withers; such branches are gathered, thrown into the fire, and burned. If you abide in me, and my words abide in you, ask for whatever you wish, and it will be done for you. My Father is glorified by this, that you bear much fruit and become my disciples. As the Father has loved me, so I have loved you; abide in my love. If you keep my commandments, you will abide in my love, just as I have kept my Father's commandments and abide in his love. I have said these things to you so that my joy may be in you, and that your joy may be complete.

'This is my commandment, that you love one another as I have loved you. No one has greater love than this, to lay down one's life for one's friends. You are my friends if you do what I command you. I do not call you servants any longer, because the servant does not know what the master is doing; but I have called you friends, because I have made known to you everything that I have heard from my Father. You did not choose me but I chose you. And I appointed you to go and bear fruit, fruit that will last, so that the Father will give you whatever you ask him in my name. I am giving you these commands so that you may love one another.'

For the Appointment of a Bishop or Incumbent

Collect
Almighty God,
the giver of all good gifts:
guide with your heavenly wisdom
those who are to choose a faithful pastor
  for this *diocese / parish*:
that we may receive one who will speak your word
  and serve your people
according to your will;
through Jesus Christ your Son our Lord,
who is alive and reigns with you
in the unity of the Holy Spirit,
one God, now and for ever.

Post Communion
Heavenly Father,
whose ascended Son gave gifts of leadership and service
  to the Church:
strengthen us who have received this holy food
to be good stewards of your manifold grace,
through him who came not to be served but to serve
  and give his life as a ransom for many,
Jesus Christ our Lord.

A reading from the book Numbers. (11.16-17,24-29)
The Lord said to Moses, 'Gather for me seventy of the elders of Israel,
whom you know to be the elders of the people and officers over
them; bring them to the tent of meeting, and have them take their
place there with you. I will come down and talk with you there; and
I will take some of the spirit that is on you and put it on them; and
they shall bear the burden of the people along with you so that you
will not bear it all by yourself.'
24 So Moses went out and told the people the words of the Lord; and
he gathered seventy elders of the people, and placed them all around
the tent. Then the Lord came down in the cloud and spoke to him,
and took some of the spirit that was on him and put it on the seventy
elders; and when the spirit rested upon them, they prophesied. But
they did not do so again.
  Two men remained in the camp, one named Eldad, and the other
named Medad, and the spirit rested on them; they were among those

registered, but they had not gone out to the tent, and so they prophesied in the camp. And a young man ran and told Moses, 'Eldad and Medad are prophesying in the camp.' And Joshua son of Nun, the assistant of Moses, one of his chosen men, said, 'My lord Moses, stop them!' But Moses said to him, 'Are you jealous for my sake? Would that all the Lord's people were prophets, and that the Lord would put his spirit on them!'

A reading from the First Book of Samuel. (16.1-13a)
The Lord said to Samuel, 'How long will you grieve over Saul? I have rejected him from being king over Israel. Fill your horn with oil and set out; I will send you to Jesse the Bethlehemite, for I have provided for myself a king among his sons.' Samuel said, How can I go? If Saul hears of it, he will kill me.' And the Lord said, 'Take a heifer with you, and say, "I have come to sacrifice to the Lord." Invite Jesse to the sacrifice, and I will show you what you shall do; and you shall anoint for me the one whom I name to you.' Samuel did what the Lord commanded, and came to Bethlehem. The elders of the city came to meet him trembling, and said, 'Do you come peaceably?' He said, 'Peaceably; I have come to sacrifice to the Lord; sanctify yourselves and come with me to the sacrifice.' And he sanctified Jesse and his sons and invited them to the sacrifice.

When they came, he looked on Eliab and thought, 'Surely the Lord's anointed is now before the Lord.' But the Lord said to Samuel, 'Do not look on his appearance or on the height of his stature, because I have rejected him; for the Lord does not see as mortals see; they look on the outward appearance, but the Lord looks on the heart.' Then Jesse called Abinadab, and made him pass before Samuel. He said, 'Neither has the Lord chosen this one.' Then Jesse made Shammah pass by. And he said, 'Neither has the Lord chosen this one.' Jesse made seven of his sons pass before Samuel, and Samuel said to Jesse, 'The Lord has not chosen any of these.' Samuel said to Jesse, 'Are all your sons here?' And he said, 'There remains yet the youngest, but he is keeping the sheep.' And Samuel said to Jesse, 'Send and bring him; for we will not sit down until he comes here.' He sent and brought him in. Now he was ruddy, and had beautiful eyes, and was handsome. The Lord said, 'Rise and anoint him; for this is the one.' Then Samuel took the horn of oil, and anointed him in the presence of his brothers; and the spirit of the Lord came mightily upon David from that day forward.

Psalm 15; Psalm 25.1-5

For the Appointment of a Bishop or Incumbent

A reading from the Acts of the Apostles. (1.15-17,20-end)
Peter stood up among the believers (together, the crowd numbered about one hundred twenty persons) and said, 'Friends, the scripture had to be fulfilled, which the Holy Spirit through David foretold concerning Judas, who became a guide for those who arrested Jesus – for he was numbered among us and was allotted his share in this ministry.
[20] 'For it is written in the book of Psalms,
"Let his homestead become desolate,
and let there be no one to live in it";
and
"Let another take his position of overseer."
'So one of the men who have accompanied us during all the time that the Lord Jesus went in and out among us, beginning from the baptism of John until the day when he was taken up from us – one of these must become a witness with us to his resurrection.'

So they proposed two, Joseph called Barsabbas, who was also known as Justus, and Matthias. Then they prayed and said, 'Lord, you know everyone's heart. Show us which one of these two you have chosen to take the place in this ministry and apostleship from which Judas turned aside to go to his own place.' And they cast lots for them, and the lot fell on Matthias; and he was added to the eleven apostles.

A reading from the Letter of Paul to the Ephesians. (4.7-16)
Each of us was given grace according to the measure of Christ's gift. Therefore it is said,
'When he ascended on high he made captivity itself a captive;
he gave gifts to his people.'
(When it says, 'He ascended,' what does it mean but that he had also descended into the lower parts of the earth? He who descended is the same one who ascended far above all the heavens, so that he might fill all things.) The gifts he gave were that some would be apostles, some prophets, some evangelists, some pastors and teachers, to equip the saints for the work of ministry, for building up the body of Christ, until all of us come to the unity of the faith and of the knowledge of the Son of God, to maturity, to the measure of the full stature of Christ. We must no longer be children, tossed to and fro and blown about by every wind of doctrine, by people's trickery, by their craftiness in deceitful scheming. But speaking the truth in love, we must grow up in every way into him who is the head, into Christ, from whom the whole body, joined and knit together by

every ligament with which it is equipped, as each part is working properly, promotes the body's growth in building itself up in love.

A reading from the Gospel according to John. (4.34-38)
Jesus said to his disciples, 'My food is to do the will of him who sent me and to complete his work. Do you not say, "Four months more, then comes the harvest"? But I tell you, look around you, and see how the fields are ripe for harvesting. The reaper is already receiving wages and is gathering fruit for eternal life, so that sower and reaper may rejoice together. For here the saying holds true, "One sows and another reaps." I sent you to reap that for which you did not labour. Others have laboured, and you have entered into their labour.'

A reading from the Gospel according to John. (15.9-17)
Jesus said to his disciples, 'As the Father has loved me, so I have loved you; abide in my love. If you keep my commandments, you will abide in my love, just as I have kept my Father's commandments and abide in his love. I have said these things to you so that my joy may be in you, and that your joy may be complete.

'This is my commandment, that you love one another as I have loved you. No one has greater love than this, to lay down one's life for one's friends. You are my friends if you do what I command you. I do not call you servants any longer, because the servant does not know what the master is doing; but I have called you friends, because I have made known to you everything that I have heard from my Father. You did not choose me but I chose you. And I appointed you to go and bear fruit, fruit that will last, so that the Father will give you whatever you ask him in my name. I am giving you these commands so that you may love one another.'

For an Enthronement or an Installation or an Induction

Collect
God our Father, Lord of all the world,
through your Son you have called us into the fellowship
  of your universal Church:
hear our prayer for all your faithful people,
that in their vocation and ministry
they may be an instrument of your love;
and give your *servant N*, now to be . . . *(enthroned, installed, inducted)*
the needful gifts of grace;
through your Son our Lord and Saviour Jesus Christ,
who is alive and reigns with you
in the unity of the Holy Spirit,
one God, now and for ever.

Post Communion
Heavenly Father,
whose ascended Son gave gifts of leadership and service
  to the Church:
strengthen us who have received this holy food
to be good stewards of your manifold grace,
through him who came not to be served but to serve
  and to give his life as a ransom for many,
Jesus Christ our Lord.

A reading from the book Numbers. *(3.5-9)*
The Lord spoke to Moses, saying: Bring the tribe of Levi near, and
set them before Aaron the priest, so that they may assist him. They
shall perform duties for him and for the whole congregation in front
of the tent of meeting, doing service at the tabernacle; they shall be in
charge of all the furnishings of the tent of meeting, and attend to the
duties for the Israelites as they do service at the tabernacle. You shall
give the Levites to Aaron and his descendants; they are unreservedly
given to him from among the Israelites.

A reading from the prophecy of Isaiah. (61.1-3)

The spirit of the Lord God is upon me,
    because the Lord has anointed me;
he has sent me to bring good news to the oppressed,
    to bind up the brokenhearted,
to proclaim liberty to the captives,
    and release to the prisoners;
to proclaim the year of the Lord's favour,
    and the day of vengeance of our God;
    to comfort all who mourn;
to provide for those who mourn in Zion –
    to give them a garland instead of ashes,
the oil of gladness instead of mourning,
    the mantle of praise instead of a faint spirit.
They will be called oaks of righteousness,
    the planting of the Lord, to display his glory.

Psalm 95.1-7; Psalm 101

A reading from the Letter of Paul to the Ephesians. (4.1-7)

I, the prisoner in the Lord, beg you to lead a life worthy of the calling to which you have been called, with all humility and gentleness, with patience, bearing with one another in love, making every effort to maintain the unity of the Spirit in the bond of peace. There is one body and one Spirit, just as you were called to the one hope of your calling, one Lord, one faith, one baptism, one God and Father of all, who is above all and through all and in all.

But each of us was given grace according to the measure of Christ's gift.

A reading from the First Letter of Peter. (5.1-11)

As an elder myself and a witness of the sufferings of Christ, as well as one who shares in the glory to be revealed, I exhort the elders among you to tend the flock of God that is in your charge, exercising the oversight, not under compulsion but willingly, as God would have you do it – not for sordid gain but eagerly. Do not lord it over those in your charge, but be examples to the flock. And when the chief shepherd appears, you will win the crown of glory that never fades away.

In the same way, you who are younger must accept the authority of the elders. And all of you must clothe yourselves with humility in your dealings with one another, for

'God opposes the proud,
but gives grace to the humble.'
Humble yourselves therefore under the mighty hand of God, so that
he may exalt you in due time. Cast all your anxiety on him, because
he cares for you.

  Discipline yourselves, keep alert. Like a roaring lion your adversary
the devil prowls around, looking for someone to devour. Resist him,
steadfast in your faith, for you know that your brothers and sisters in
all the world are undergoing the same kinds of suffering. And after
you have suffered for a little while, the God of all grace, who has
called you to his eternal glory in Christ, will himself restore, support,
strengthen, and establish you. To him be the power for ever and
ever. Amen.

A reading from the Gospel according to Luke. (10.1-9)
The Lord appointed seventy others and sent them on ahead of him in
pairs to every town and place where he himself intended to go. He
said to them, 'The harvest is plentiful, but the labourers are few;
therefore ask the Lord of the harvest to send out labourers into his
harvest. Go on your way. See, I am sending you out like lambs into
the midst of wolves. Carry no purse, no bag, no sandals; and greet
no one on the road. Whatever house you enter, first say, "Peace to
this house!" And if anyone is there who shares in peace, your peace
will rest on that person; but if not, it will return to you. Remain in
the same house, eating and drinking whatever they provide, for the
labourer deserves to be paid. Do not move about from house to
house. Whenever you enter a town and its people welcome you, eat
what is set before you; cure the sick who are there, and say to them,
"The kingdom of God has come near to you."'

A reading from the Gospel according to John. (10.11-16)
Jesus said, 'I am the good shepherd. The good shepherd lays down
his life for the sheep. The hired hand, who is not the shepherd and
does not own the sheep, sees the wolf coming and leaves the sheep
and runs away – and the wolf snatches them and scatters them. The
hired hand runs away because a hired hand does not care for the
sheep. I am the good shepherd. I know my own and my own know
me, just as the Father knows me and I know the Father. And I lay
down my life for the sheep. I have other sheep that do not belong to
this fold. I must bring them also, and they will listen to my voice. So
there will be one flock, one shepherd.'

The Religious Life

For Vocations to the Religious Life

Collect
Almighty and everlasting God,
by whose spirit the whole body of the Church
  is governed and sanctified:
hear our prayer which we offer for all your faithful people,
that in their vocation and ministry
they may serve you in holiness and truth
to the glory of your name;
through our Lord and Saviour Jesus Christ,
who is alive and reigns with you
in the unity of the Holy Spirit,
one God, now and for ever.

Post Communion
Heavenly Father,
you have fed your people in this sacrament
with the fruits of creation made holy by your Spirit:
by your grace
raise up among us faithful men and women
to work for the increase of your kingdom
and set forward the eternal praise of your name;
through him who came not to be served but to serve
  and to give his life as a ransom for many,
Jesus Christ our Lord.

A reading from the prophecy of Jeremiah. (1.4-9)
The word of the Lord came to me saying,
    'Before I formed you in the womb I knew you,
        and before you were born I consecrated you;
        I appointed you a prophet to the nations.'
Then I said, 'Ah, Lord God! Truly I do not know how to speak,
for I am only a boy.' But the Lord said to me,
    'Do not say, "I am only a boy";
        for you shall go to all to whom I send you,
        and you shall speak whatever I command you.
    Do not be afraid of them,
        for I am with you to deliver you,
                says the Lord.'

Then the Lord put out his hand and touched my mouth; and the Lord said to me,

'Now I have put my words in your mouth.'

Psalm 63.1-9

A reading from the Letter of Paul to the Philippians. (3.7-14)
Whatever gains I had, these I have come to regard as loss because of Christ. More than that, I regard everything as loss because of the surpassing value of knowing Christ Jesus my Lord. For his sake I have suffered the loss of all things, and I regard them as rubbish, in order that I may gain Christ and be found in him, not having a righteousness of my own that comes from the law, but one that comes through faith in Christ, the righteousness from God based on faith. I want to know Christ and the power of his resurrection and the sharing of his sufferings by becoming like him in his death, if somehow I may attain the resurrection from the dead.

Not that I have already obtained this or have already reached the goal; but I press on to make it my own, because Christ Jesus has made me his own. Belovèd, I do not consider that I have made it my own; but this one thing I do: forgetting what lies behind and straining forward to what lies ahead, I press on toward the goal for the prize of the heavenly call of God in Christ Jesus.

A reading from the Gospel according to Matthew. (6.24-end)
Jesus said, 'No one can serve two masters; for a slave will either hate the one and love the other, or be devoted to the one and despise the other. You cannot serve God and wealth.

'Therefore I tell you, do not worry about your life, what you will eat or what you will drink, or about your body, what you will wear. Is not life more than food, and the body more than clothing? Look at the birds of the air; they neither sow nor reap nor gather into barns, and yet your heavenly Father feeds them. Are you not of more value than they? And can any of you by worrying add a single hour to your span of life? And why do you worry about clothing? Consider the lilies of the field, how they grow; they neither toil nor spin, yet I tell you, even Solomon in all his glory was not clothed like one of these. But if God so clothes the grass of the field, which is alive today and tomorrow is thrown into the oven, will he not much more clothe you – you of little faith? Therefore do not worry, saying, "What will we eat?" or "What will we drink?" or "What will we wear?" For it is the Gentiles who strive for all these things; and indeed your heavenly Father knows that you need all these things. But strive first for the kingdom of God and his righteousness, and all these things will be given to you as well.

'So do not worry about tomorrow, for tomorrow will bring worries of its own. Today's trouble is enough for today.'

For those taking Vows

Collect
Almighty God,
by whose grace alone we are accepted
  and called to your service:
strengthen us by your Holy Spirit
and make us worthy of our calling;
through Jesus Christ your Son our Lord,
who is alive and reigns with you
in the unity of the Holy Spirit,
one God, now and for ever.

Or:

Merciful God,
through the grace of baptism
and the call of your Holy Spirit,
you draw men and women to your service
for the building up of your kingdom:
grant that your *servants N & N*
may always strive to follow your Son
and, in seeking the perfection of the gospel
may increase the holiness of your Church
and so fulfil its mission;
through Jesus Christ your Son our Lord,
who is alive and reigns with you
in the unity of the Holy Spirit,
one God, now and for ever.

Post Communion
Heavenly Father,
you have fed your people in this sacrament
with the fruits of creation made holy by your Spirit:
by your grace
raise up among us faithful men and women
to work for the increase of your kingdom
and set forward the eternal praise of your name;
through him who came not to be served but to serve
  and to give his life as a ransom for many,
Jesus Christ our Lord.

A reading from the First Book of Samuel. (1.19b-end)

Elkanah knew his wife Hannah, and the Lord remembered her. In due time Hannah conceived and bore a son. She named him Samuel, for she said, 'I have asked him of the Lord.'

The man Elkanah and all his household went up to offer to the Lord the yearly sacrifice, and to pay his vow. But Hannah did not go up, for she said to her husband, 'As soon as the child is weaned, I will bring him, that he may appear in the presence of the Lord, and remain there for ever; I will offer him as a nazirite for all time.' Her husband Elkanah said to her, 'Do what seems best to you, wait until you have weaned him; only – may the Lord establish his word.' So the woman remained and nursed her son, until she weaned him. When she had weaned him, she took him up with her, along with a three-year-old bull, an ephah of flour, and a skin of wine. She brought him to the house of the Lord at Shiloh; and the child was young. Then they slaughtered the bull, and they brought the child to Eli. And she said, 'Oh, my lord! As you live, my lord, I am the woman who was standing here in your presence, praying to the Lord. For this child I prayed; and the Lord has granted me the petition that I made to him. Therefore I have lent him to the Lord; as long as he lives, he is given to the Lord.'

She left him there for the Lord.

Psalm 99; Psalm 101

A reading from the Letter of Paul to the Ephesians. (1.3-14)

Blessèd be the God and Father of our Lord Jesus Christ, who has blessed us in Christ with every spiritual blessing in the heavenly places, just as he chose us in Christ before the foundation of the world to be holy and blameless before him in love. He destined us for adoption as his children through Jesus Christ, according to the good pleasure of his will, to the praise of his glorious grace that he freely bestowed on us in the Belovèd. In him we have redemption through his blood, the forgiveness of our trespasses, according to the riches of his grace that he lavished on us. With all wisdom and insight he has made known to us the mystery of his will, according to his good pleasure that he set forth in Christ, as a plan for the fullness of time, to gather up all things in him, things in heaven and things on earth.

In Christ we have also obtained an inheritance, having been destined according to the purpose of him who accomplishes all things according to his counsel and will, so that we, who were the first to set our hope on Christ, might live for the praise of his glory. In him you also, when you had heard the word of truth, the gospel of your salvation, and had believed in him, were marked with the seal of the promised Holy Spirit; this is the pledge of our inheritance toward redemption as God's own people, to the praise of his glory.

A reading from the Letter of Paul to the Philippians. (3.7-14)
Whatever gains I had, these I have come to regard as loss because of Christ. More than that, I regard everything as loss because of the surpassing value of knowing Christ Jesus my Lord. For his sake I have suffered the loss of all things, and I regard them as rubbish, in order that I may gain Christ and be found in him, not having a righteousness of my own that comes from the law, but one that comes through faith in Christ, the righteousness from God based on faith. I want to know Christ and the power of his resurrection and the sharing of his sufferings by becoming like him in his death, if somehow I may attain the resurrection from the dead.

Not that I have already obtained this or have already reached the goal; but I press on to make it my own, because Christ Jesus has made me his own. Belovèd, I do not consider that I have made it my own; but this one thing I do: forgetting what lies behind and straining forward to what lies ahead, I press on toward the goal for the prize of the heavenly call of God in Christ Jesus.

A reading from the Gospel according to Luke. (10.38-end)
Jesus entered a certain village, where a woman named Martha welcomed him into her home. She had a sister named Mary, who sat at the Lord's feet and listened to what he was saying. But Martha was distracted by her many tasks; so she came to him and asked, 'Lord, do you not care that my sister has left me to do all the work by myself? Tell her then to help me.' But the Lord answered her, 'Martha, Martha, you are worried and distracted by many things; there is need of only one thing. Mary has chosen the better part, which will not be taken away from her.'

A reading from the Gospel according to John. (12.24-26)
Jesus said, 'Very truly, I tell you, unless a grain of wheat falls into the earth and dies, it remains just a single grain; but if it dies, it bears much fruit. Those who love their life lose it, and those who hate their life in this world will keep it for eternal life. Whoever serves me must follow me, and where I am, there will my servant be also. Whoever serves me, the Father will honour.'

The Installation & Blessing
of a Religious Superior

Collect
God our Father, Lord of all the world,
through your Son you have called us into the fellowship
  of your universal Church:
hear our prayer for all your faithful people,
that in their vocation and ministry
they may be an instrument of your love;
and give your *servant N*, now to be . . . *(installed, blessed, etc.)*
the needful gifts of grace;
through your Son our Lord and Saviour Jesus Christ,
who is alive and reigns with you
in the unity of the Holy Spirit,
one God, now and for ever.

Post Communion
Heavenly Father,
whose ascended Son gave gifts of leadership and service
  to the Church:
strengthen us who have received this holy food
to be good stewards of your manifold grace;
through him who came not to be served but to serve
  and to give his life as a ransom for many,
Jesus Christ our Lord.

A reading from the book Proverbs. *(2.1-9)*
> My child, if you accept my words
>   and treasure up my commandments within you,
> making your ear attentive to wisdom
>   and inclining your heart to understanding;
> if you indeed cry out for insight,
>   and raise your voice for understanding;
> if you seek it like silver,
>   and search for it as for hidden treasures –
> then you will understand the fear of the Lord
>   and find the knowledge of God.
> For the Lord gives wisdom;
>   from his mouth come knowledge and understanding;
> he stores up sound wisdom for the upright;
>   he is a shield to those who walk blamelessly,

guarding the paths of justice
   and preserving the way of his faithful ones.
Then you will understand righteousness and justice
   and equity, every good path.

A reading from the book Proverbs. (4.7-13)
   The beginning of wisdom is this: Get wisdom,
      and whatever else you get, get insight.
   Prize her highly, and she will exalt you;
      she will honour you if you embrace her.
   She will place on your head a fair garland;
      she will bestow on you a beautiful crown.'

   Hear, my child, and accept my words,
      that the years of your life may be many.
   I have taught you the way of wisdom;
      I have led you in the paths of uprightness.
   When you walk, your step will not be hampered;
      and if you run, you will not stumble.
   Keep hold of instruction; do not let go;
      guard her, for she is your life.

Psalm 133

A reading from the Letter of Paul to the Ephesians. (4.1-7)
I, the prisoner in the Lord, beg you to lead a life worthy of the calling
to which you have been called, with all humility and gentleness, with
patience, bearing with one another in love, making every effort to
maintain the unity of the Spirit in the bond of peace. There is one
body and one Spirit, just as you were called to the one hope of your
calling, one Lord, one faith, one baptism, one God and Father of all,
who is above all and through all and in all.
   But each of us was given grace according to the measure of Christ's
gift.

A reading from the Letter of Paul to the Colossians. (3.12-17)
As God's chosen ones, holy and belovèd, clothe yourselves with
compassion, kindness, humility, meekness, and patience. Bear with
one another and, if anyone has a complaint against another, forgive
each other; just as the Lord has forgiven you, so you also must
forgive. Above all, clothe yourselves with love, which binds everything together in perfect harmony. And let the peace of Christ rule
in your hearts, to which indeed you were called in the one body.

And be thankful. Let the word of Christ dwell in you richly; teach and admonish one another in all wisdom; and with gratitude in your hearts sing psalms, hymns, and spiritual songs to God. And whatever you do, in word or deed, do everything in the name of the Lord Jesus, giving thanks to God the Father through him.

A reading from the Gospel according to Luke. (12.35-38)
Jesus said to his disciples, 'Be dressed for action and have your lamps lit; be like those who are waiting for their master to return from the wedding banquet, so that they may open the door for him as soon as he comes and knocks. Blessèd are those slaves whom the master finds alert when he comes; truly I tell you, he will fasten his belt and have them sit down to eat, and he will come and serve them. If he comes during the middle of the night, or near dawn, and finds them so, blessèd are those slaves.'

A reading from the Gospel according to Luke. (22.25-27)
Jesus said to his disciples, 'The kings of the Gentiles lord it over them; and those in authority over them are called benefactors. But not so with you; rather the greatest among you must become like the youngest, and the leader like one who serves. For who is greater, the one who is at the table or the one who serves? Is it not the one at the table? But I am among you as one who serves.'

Wholeness and Healing

Wholeness and Healing

Collect
Heavenly Father,
you anointed your Son Jesus Christ
with the Holy Spirit and with power
to bring to us the blessings of your kingdom:
anoint your Church with the same Holy Spirit,
that we who share in his suffering and victory
may bear witness to the gospel of salvation;
through Jesus Christ your Son our Lord,
who is alive and reigns with you
in the unity of the Holy Spirit,
one God, now and for ever.

Post Communion
God of all compassion,
by the dying and rising of your Christ
you restore us to yourself and enfold us in your love:
may we who have been refreshed
with the bread of life and cup of salvation
be renewed by your healing Spirit
and made ready for the coming of your kingdom;
through Jesus Christ our Lord.

Advent
Birth pangs of a new age

A reading from the prophecy of Isaiah. (26.16-19)
> O Lord, in distress the nation sought you,
>> they poured out a prayer
>> when your chastening was on them.
> Like a woman with child,
>> who writhes and cries out in her pangs
>> when she is near her time,
> so were we because of you, O Lord;
>> we were with child, we writhed,
>> but we gave birth only to wind.
> We have won no victories on earth,
>> and no one is born to inhabit the world.
> Your dead shall live, their corpses shall rise.
>> O dwellers in the dust, awake and sing for joy!
> For your dew is a radiant dew,
>> and the earth will give birth to those long dead.

Psalm 46.1-7

A reading from the Letter of Paul to the Romans. (8.18-23)
I consider that the sufferings of this present time are not worth comparing with the glory about to be revealed to us. For the creation waits with eager longing for the revealing of the children of God; for the creation was subjected to futility, not of its own will but by the will of the one who subjected it, in hope that the creation itself will be set free from its bondage to decay and will obtain the freedom of the glory of the children of God. We know that the whole creation has been groaning in labour pains until now; and not only the creation, but we ourselves, who have the first fruits of the Spirit, groan inwardly while we wait for adoption, the redemption of our bodies.

Hear the Gospel of our Lord Jesus Christ according to Matthew.
(24.3-13)
When Jesus was sitting on the Mount of Olives, the disciples came to him privately, saying, 'Tell us, when will this be, and what will be the sign of your coming and of the end of the age?' Jesus answered them, 'Beware that no one leads you astray. For many will come in my name, saying, "I am the Messiah!" and they will lead many astray. And you will hear of wars and rumours of wars; see that you are not

alarmed; for this must take place, but the end is not yet. For nation will rise against nation, and kingdom against kingdom, and there will be famines and earthquakes in various places: all this is but the beginning of the birth pangs.

'Then they will hand you over to be tortured and will put you to death, and you will be hated by all nations because of my name. Then many will fall away, and they will betray one another and hate one another. And many false prophets will arise and lead many astray. And because of the increase of lawlessness, the love of many will grow cold. But the one who endures to the end will be saved.'

This is the Gospel of the Lord.

Dismissal Gospel
Hear the words of the Gospel according to Matthew. *(5.14-16)*
Jesus said to his disciples, 'You are the light of the world. A city built on a hill cannot be hid. No one after lighting a lamp puts it under the bushel basket, but on the lampstand, and it gives light to all in the house. In the same way, let your light shine before others, so that they may see your good works and give glory to your Father in heaven.'

This is the Gospel of the Lord.

Christmas
Bread of life

A reading from the prophecy of Isaiah. (55.1-3,10-11)
>Ho, everyone who thirsts,
>>come to the waters;
>and you that have no money,
>>come, buy and eat!
>Come, buy wine and milk
>>without money and without price.
>Why do you spend your money for that which is not bread,
>>and your labour for that which does not satisfy?
>Listen carefully to me, and eat what is good,
>>and delight yourselves in rich food.
>Incline your ear, and come to me;
>>listen, so that you may live.
>I will make with you an everlasting covenant,
>>my steadfast, sure love for David.

10 For as the rain and the snow come down from heaven,
>>and do not return there until they have watered the earth,
>making it bring forth and sprout,
>>giving seed to the sower and bread to the eater,
>so shall my word be that goes out from my mouth;
>>it shall not return to me empty,
>but it shall accomplish that which I purpose,
>>and succeed in the thing for which I sent it.

Psalm 145.14-end

A reading from the Letter of Paul to the Colossians. (3.14-17)
Clothe yourselves with love, which binds everything together in perfect harmony. And let the peace of Christ rule in your hearts, to which indeed you were called in the one body. And be thankful. Let the word of Christ dwell in you richly; teach and admonish one another in all wisdom; and with gratitude in your hearts sing psalms, hymns, and spiritual songs to God. And whatever you do, in word or deed, do everything in the name of the Lord Jesus, giving thanks to God the Father through him.

Hear the Gospel of our Lord Jesus Christ according to John. *(6.47-51)*
Jesus said to the Jews, 'Very truly, I tell you, whoever believes has eternal life. I am the bread of life. Your ancestors ate the manna in the wilderness, and they died. This is the bread that comes down from heaven, so that one may eat of it and not die. I am the living bread that came down from heaven. Whoever eats of this bread will live for ever; and the bread that I will give for the life of the world is my flesh.'

This is the Gospel of the Lord.

Dismissal Gospel
Hear the words of the Gospel according to John. *(6.63-64,66-69)*
Jesus said to his disciples, 'It is the spirit that gives life; the flesh is useless. The words that I have spoken to you are spirit and life. But among you there are some who do not believe.' For Jesus knew from the first who were the ones that did not believe, and who was the one that would betray him.
⁶⁶ Because of this many of his disciples turned back and no longer went about with him. So Jesus asked the twelve, 'Do you also wish to go away?' Simon Peter answered him, 'Lord, to whom can we go? You have the words of eternal life. We have come to believe and know that you are the Holy One of God.'

This is the Gospel of the Lord.

Epiphany
The opening of eyes

A reading from the prophecy of Isaiah. (42.1-7)
> Here is my servant, whom I uphold,
> > my chosen, in whom my soul delights;
> I have put my spirit upon him;
> > he will bring forth justice to the nations.
> He will not cry or lift up his voice,
> > or make it heard in the street;
> a bruised reed he will not break,
> > and a dimly burning wick he will not quench;
> > he will faithfully bring forth justice.
> He will not grow faint or be crushed
> > until he has established justice in the earth;
> > and the coastlands wait for his teaching.
>
> Thus says God, the Lord,
> > who created the heavens and stretched them out,
> > who spread out the earth and what comes from it,
> who gives breath to the people upon it
> > and spirit to those who walk in it:
> I am the Lord, I have called you in righteousness,
> > I have taken you by the hand and kept you;
> I have given you as a covenant to the people,
> > a light to the nations,
> > to open the eyes that are blind,
> to bring out the prisoners from the dungeon,
> > from the prison those who sit in darkness.

Psalm 27.1-6 *or* **Psalm 27.1-10**

A reading from the Acts of the Apostles. (9.10-19a)
There was a disciple in Damascus named Ananias. The Lord said to him in a vision, 'Ananias.' He answered, 'Here I am, Lord.' The Lord said to him, 'Get up and go to the street called Straight, and at the house of Judas look for a man of Tarsus named Saul. At this moment he is praying, and he has seen in a vision a man named Ananias come in and lay his hands on him so that he might regain his sight.' But Ananias answered, 'Lord, I have heard from many about this man, how much evil he has done to your saints in Jerusalem; and here he has authority from the chief priests to bind all who invoke your

name.' But the Lord said to him, 'Go, for he is an instrument whom I have chosen to bring my name before Gentiles and kings and before the people of Israel; I myself will show him how much he must suffer for the sake of my name.'

So Ananias went and entered the house. He laid his hands on Saul and said, 'Brother Saul, the Lord Jesus, who appeared to you on your way here, has sent me so that you may regain your sight and be filled with the Holy Spirit.' And immediately something like scales fell from his eyes, and his sight was restored. Then he got up and was baptized, and after taking some food, he regained his strength.

Hear the Gospel of our Lord Jesus Christ according to John. (9.1-7)
As Jesus walked along, he saw a man blind from birth. His disciples asked him, 'Rabbi, who sinned, this man or his parents, that he was born blind?' Jesus answered, 'Neither this man nor his parents sinned; he was born blind so that God's works might be revealed in him. We must work the works of him who sent me while it is day; night is coming when no one can work. As long as I am in the world, I am the light of the world.' When he had said this, he spat on the ground and made mud with the saliva and spread the mud on the man's eyes, saying to him, 'Go, wash in the pool of Siloam' (which means Sent). Then he went and washed and came back able to see.

This is the Gospel of the Lord.

Dismissal Gospel
Hear the words of the Gospel according to John. (9.35-38)
Jesus heard that the Pharisees had driven out of the synagogue the man Jesus had cured of his blindness, and when Jesus found him, he said, 'Do you believe in the Son of Man?' He answered, 'And who is he, sir? Tell me, so that I may believe in him.' Jesus said to him, 'You have seen him, and the one speaking with you is he.' He said, 'Lord, I believe.' And he worshipped him.

This is the Gospel of the Lord.

Lent – Set I
Sin and Forgiveness

A reading from the prophecy of Isaiah. (53.3-6)
> He was despised and rejected by others;
>> a man of suffering and acquainted with infirmity;
> and as one from whom others hide their faces
>> he was despised, and we held him of no account.

> Surely he has borne our infirmities
>> and carried our diseases;
> yet we accounted him stricken,
>> struck down by God, and afflicted.
> But he was wounded for our transgressions,
>> crushed for our iniquities;
> upon him was the punishment that made us whole,
>> and by his bruises we are healed.
> All we like sheep have gone astray;
>> we have all turned to our own way,
> and the Lord has laid on him
>> the iniquity of us all.

Psalm 103.1-5,8-14

A reading from the Letter of Paul to the Romans. (5.6-11)
While we were still weak, at the right time Christ died for the ungodly. Indeed, rarely will anyone die for a righteous person – though perhaps for a good person someone might actually dare to die. But God proves his love for us in that while we still were sinners Christ died for us. Much more surely then, now that we have been justified by his blood, will we be saved through him from the wrath of God. For if while we were enemies, we were reconciled to God through the death of his Son, much more surely, having been reconciled, will we be saved by his life. But more than that, we even boast in God through our Lord Jesus Christ, through whom we have now received reconciliation.

Hear the Gospel of our Lord Jesus Christ according to Mark. (2.1-12)
When Jesus returned to Capernaum after some days, it was reported
that he was at home. So many gathered around that there was no
longer room for them, not even in front of the door; and he was
speaking the word to them. Then some people came, bringing to him
a paralysed man, carried by four of them. And when they could not
bring him to Jesus because of the crowd, they removed the roof above
him; and after having dug through it, they let down the mat on which
the paralytic lay. When Jesus saw their faith, he said to the paralytic,
'Son, your sins are forgiven.' Now some of the scribes were sitting
there, questioning in their hearts, 'Why does this fellow speak in this
way? It is blasphemy! Who can forgive sins but God alone?' At once
Jesus perceived in his spirit that they were discussing these questions
among themselves; and he said to them, 'Why do you raise such
questions in your hearts? Which is easier, to say to the paralytic,
"Your sins are forgiven," or to say, "Stand up and take your mat and
walk"? But so that you may know that the Son of Man has authority
on earth to forgive sins' – he said to the paralytic – 'I say to you,
stand up, take your mat and go to your home.' And he stood up, and
immediately took the mat and went out before all of them; so that
they were all amazed and glorified God, saying, 'We have never seen
anything like this!'

This is the Gospel of the Lord.

Dismissal Gospel
Hear the words of the Gospel according to Mark. *(5.18-20)*
As Jesus was getting into the boat, the man who had been possessed
by demons begged him that he might be with him. But Jesus refused,
and said to him, 'Go home to your friends, and tell them how much
the Lord has done for you, and what mercy he has shown you.' And
he went away and began to proclaim in the Decapolis how much
Jesus had done for him; and everyone was amazed.

This is the Gospel of the Lord.

Lent – Set II
Powerlessness and Grace

A reading from the Lamentations of Jeremiah. (3.17-24)
>My soul is bereft of peace;
>>I have forgotten what happiness is;
>so I say, 'Gone is my glory,
>>and all that I had hoped for from the Lord.'

>The thought of my affliction and my homelessness
>>is wormwood and gall!
>My soul continually thinks of it
>>and is bowed down within me.
>But this I call to mind,
>>and therefore I have hope:

>The steadfast love of the Lord never ceases,
>>his mercies never come to an end;
>they are new every morning;
>>great is your faithfulness.
>'The Lord is my portion,' says my soul,
>>'therefore I will hope in him.'

Psalm 38.9-15

A reading from the Second Letter of Paul to the Corinthians. (12.7b-10)
To keep me from being too elated, a thorn was given me in the flesh, a messenger of Satan to torment me, to keep me from being too elated. Three times I appealed to the Lord about this, that it would leave me, but he said to me, 'My grace is sufficient for you, for power is made perfect in weakness.' So, I will boast all the more gladly of my weaknesses, so that the power of Christ may dwell in me. Therefore I am content with weaknesses, insults, hardships, persecutions, and calamities for the sake of Christ; for whenever I am weak, then I am strong.

Hear the Gospel of our Lord Jesus Christ according to Mark.

(14.32-38)

Jesus and his disciples went to a place called Gethsemane; and he said to his disciples, 'Sit here while I pray.' He took with him Peter and James and John, and began to be distressed and agitated. And he said to them, 'I am deeply grieved, even to death; remain here, and keep awake.' And going a little farther, he threw himself on the ground and prayed that, if it were possible, the hour might pass from him. He said, 'Abba, Father, for you all things are possible; remove this cup from me; yet, not what I want, but what you want.' He came and found them sleeping; and he said to Peter, 'Simon, are you asleep? Could you not keep awake one hour? Keep awake and pray that you may not come into the time of trial; the spirit indeed is willing, but the flesh is weak.'

This is the Gospel of the Lord.

Dismissal Gospel
Hear the words of the Gospel according to Mark. *(13.3-5a,34-36)*
When Jesus was sitting on the Mount of Olives opposite the temple, Peter, James, John, and Andrew asked him privately, 'Tell us, when will this be, and what will be the sign that all these things are about to be accomplished? Then Jesus began to say to them,
[34] 'It is like a man going on a journey, when he leaves home and puts his slaves in charge, each with his work, and commands the door-keeper to be on the watch. Therefore, keep awake – for you do not know when the master of the house will come, in the evening, or at midnight, or at cockcrow, or at dawn, or else he may find you asleep when he comes suddenly.

This is the Gospel of the Lord.

Lent – Set III
Anointing

A reading from the Second Book of the Chronicles. (28.15)
Those who were mentioned by name got up and took the captives, and with the booty they clothed all that were naked among them; they clothed them, gave them sandals, provided them with food and drink, and anointed them; and carrying all the feeble among them on donkeys, they brought them to their kindred at Jericho, the city of palm trees. Then they returned to Samaria.

Or:

A reading from the prophecy of Jeremiah. (17.5-10,14)
Thus says the Lord:
>   Cursed are those who trust in mere mortals
>   and make mere flesh their strength,
>   whose hearts turn away from the Lord.
>   They shall be like a shrub in the desert,
>   and shall not see when relief comes.
>   They shall live in the parched places of the wilderness,
>   in an uninhabited salt land.
>
>   Blessèd are those who trust in the Lord,
>   whose trust is the Lord.
>   They shall be like a tree planted by water,
>   sending out its roots by the stream.
>   It shall not fear when heat comes,
>   and its leaves shall stay green;
>   in the year of drought it is not anxious,
>   and it does not cease to bear fruit.
>
>   The heart is devious above all else;
>   it is perverse –
>   who can understand it?
>   I the Lord test the mind
>   and search the heart,
>   to give to all according to their ways,
>   according to the fruit of their doings.

14   Heal me, O Lord, and I shall be healed;
>   save me, and I shall be saved;
>   for you are my praise.

Psalm 23

A reading from the Letter of James. (5.14-16)
Are any among you sick? They should call for the elders of the
church and have them pray over them, anointing them with oil in the
name of the Lord. The prayer of faith will save the sick, and the Lord
will raise them up; and anyone who has committed sins will be
forgiven. Therefore confess your sins to one another, and pray for
one another, so that you may be healed. The prayer of the righteous
is powerful and effective.

Hear the Gospel of our Lord Jesus Christ according to Mark. *(6.7-13)*
Jesus called the twelve and began to send them out two by two, and
gave them authority over the unclean spirits. He ordered them to
take nothing for their journey except a staff; no bread, no bag, no
money in their belts; but to wear sandals and not to put on two
tunics. He said to them, 'Wherever you enter a house, stay there until
you leave the place. If any place will not welcome you and they
refuse to hear you, as you leave, shake off the dust that is on your feet
as a testimony against them.' So they went out and proclaimed that
all should repent. They cast out many demons, and anointed with oil
many who were sick and cured them.

This is the Gospel of the Lord.

Dismissal Gospel
Hear the words of the Gospel according to Mark. *(6.54-end)*
When Jesus and his disciples got out of the boat, people at once
recognized him, and rushed about that whole region and began
to bring the sick on mats to wherever they heard he was. And
wherever he went, into villages or cities or farms, they laid the sick in
the market-places, and begged him that they might touch even the
fringe of his cloak; and all who touched it were healed.

This is the Gospel of the Lord.

Easter

Resurrection

A reading from the First Book of the Kings. *(17.17-end)*

The son of the widow of Zarephath, the mistress of the house, became ill; his illness was so severe that there was no breath left in him. She then said to Elijah, 'What have you against me, O man of God? You have come to me to bring my sin to remembrance, and to cause the death of my son!' But he said to her, 'Give me your son.' He took him from her bosom, carried him up into the upper chamber where he was lodging, and laid him on his own bed. He cried out to the Lord, 'O Lord my God, have you brought calamity even upon the widow with whom I am staying, by killing her son?' Then he stretched himself upon the child three times, and cried out to the Lord, 'O Lord my God, let this child's life come into him again.' The Lord listened to the voice of Elijah; the life of the child came into him again, and he revived. Elijah took the child, brought him down from the upper chamber into the house, and gave him to his mother; then Elijah said, 'See, your son is alive.' So the woman said to Elijah, 'Now I know that you are a man of God, and that the word of the Lord in your mouth is truth.'

Psalm 30.6-12

A reading from the Acts of the Apostles. *(20.7-12)*

On the first day of the week, when we met to break bread, Paul was holding a discussion with the disciples; since he intended to leave the next day, he continued speaking until midnight. There were many lamps in the room upstairs where we were meeting. A young man named Eutychus, who was sitting in the window, began to sink off into a deep sleep while Paul talked still longer. Overcome by sleep, he fell to the ground three floors below and was picked up dead. But Paul went down, and bending over him took him in his arms, and said, 'Do not be alarmed, for his life is in him.' Then Paul went upstairs, and after he had broken bread and eaten, he continued to converse with them until dawn; then he left. Meanwhile they had taken the boy away alive and were not a little comforted.

Hear the Gospel of our Lord Jesus Christ according to Mark.

(5.35-end)

Some people came from Jairus's house to say, 'Your daughter is dead. Why trouble the teacher any further?' But overhearing what they said, Jesus said to the leader of the synagogue, 'Do not fear, only believe.' He allowed no one to follow him except Peter, James, and John, the brother of James. When they came to the house of the leader of the synagogue, he saw a commotion, people weeping and wailing loudly. When he had entered, he said to them, 'Why do you make a commotion and weep? The child is not dead but sleeping.' And they laughed at him. Then he put them all outside, and took the child's father and mother and those who were with him, and went in where the child was. He took her by the hand and said to her, 'Talitha cum,' which means, 'Little girl, get up!' And immediately the girl got up and began to walk about (she was twelve years of age). At this they were overcome with amazement. He strictly ordered them that no one should know this, and told them to give her something to eat.

This is the Gospel of the Lord.

Dismissal Gospel
Hear the words of the Gospel according to Mark. *(6.7-13)*
Jesus called the twelve and began to send them out two by two, and gave them authority over the unclean spirits. He ordered them to take nothing for their journey except a staff; no bread, no bag, no money in their belts; but to wear sandals and not to put on two tunics. He said to them, 'Wherever you enter a house, stay there until you leave the place. If any place will not welcome you and they refuse to hear you, as you leave, shake off the dust that is on your feet as a testimony against them.' So they went out and proclaimed that all should repent. They cast out many demons, and anointed with oil many who were sick and cured them.

This is the Gospel of the Lord.

Pentecost
Power of the Spirit

A reading from the prophecy of Isaiah. (61.1-3)

The spirit of the Lord God is upon me,
   because the Lord has anointed me;
he has sent me to bring good news to the oppressed,
   to bind up the broken-hearted,
to proclaim liberty to the captives,
   and release to the prisoners;
to proclaim the year of the Lord's favour,
   and the day of vengeance of our God;
   to comfort all who mourn;
to provide for those who mourn in Zion –
   to give them a garland instead of ashes,
the oil of gladness instead of mourning,
   the mantle of praise instead of a faint spirit.
They will be called oaks of righteousness,
   the planting of the Lord, to display his glory.

Psalm 139.1-17 or 139.1-11

A reading from the Letter of Paul to the Romans. (8.12-17)

Brothers and sisters, we are debtors, not to the flesh, to live according to the flesh – for if you live according to the flesh, you will die; but if by the Spirit you put to death the deeds of the body, you will live. For all who are led by the Spirit of God are children of God. For you did not receive a spirit of slavery to fall back into fear, but you have received a spirit of adoption. When we cry, 'Abba! Father!' it is that very Spirit bearing witness with our spirit that we are children of God, and if children, then heirs, heirs of God and joint heirs with Christ – if, in fact, we suffer with him so that we may also be glorified with him.

Hear the Gospel of our Lord Jesus Christ according to Luke. (4.16-21)
When Jesus came to Nazareth, where he had been brought up, he
went to the synagogue on the sabbath day, as was his custom.
He stood up to read, and the scroll of the prophet Isaiah was given
to him. He unrolled the scroll and found the place where it was
written:

'The Spirit of the Lord is upon me,
because he has anointed me
to bring good news to the poor.
He has sent me to proclaim release to the captives
and recovery of sight to the blind,
to let the oppressed go free,
to proclaim the year of the Lord's favour.'

And he rolled up the scroll, gave it back to the attendant, and sat
down. The eyes of all in the synagogue were fixed on him. Then he
began to say to them, 'Today this scripture has been fulfilled in your
hearing.'

This is the Gospel of the Lord.

Dismissal Gospel
Hear the words of the Gospel according to Luke. (4.33-37)
In the synagogue, there was a man who had the spirit of an unclean
demon, and he cried out with a loud voice, 'Let us alone! What have
you to do with us, Jesus of Nazareth? Have you come to destroy us?
I know who you are, the Holy One of God.' But Jesus rebuked him,
saying, 'Be silent, and come out of him!' When the demon had
thrown him down before them, he came out of him without having
done him any harm. They were all amazed and kept saying to one
another, 'What kind of utterance is this? For with authority and
power he commands the unclean spirits, and out they come!' And a
report about him began to reach every place in the region.

This is the Gospel of the Lord.

All Saints

Healing of the nations

A reading from the prophecy of Ezekiel. (47.1-12)

The man, whose appearance shone like bronze with a linen cord and measuring reed in his hand, brought me back to the entrance of the temple; there, water was flowing from below the threshold of the temple toward the east (for the temple faced east); and the water was flowing down from below the south end of the threshold of the temple, south of the altar. Then he brought me out by way of the north gate, and led me around on the outside to the outer gate that faces toward the east; and the water was coming out on the south side.

Going on eastward with a cord in his hand, the man measured one thousand cubits, and then led me through the water; and it was ankle-deep. Again he measured one thousand, and led me through the water; and it was knee-deep. Again he measured one thousand, and led me through the water; and it was up to the waist. Again he measured one thousand, and it was a river that I could not cross, for the water had risen; it was deep enough to swim in, a river that could not be crossed. He said to me, 'Mortal, have you seen this?'

Then he led me back along the bank of the river. As I came back, I saw on the bank of the river a great many trees on the one side and on the other. He said to me, 'This water flows toward the eastern region and goes down into the Arabah; and when it enters the sea, the sea of stagnant waters, the water will become fresh. Wherever the river goes, every living creature that swarms will live, and there will be very many fish, once these waters reach there. It will become fresh; and everything will live where the river goes. People will stand fishing beside the sea from En-gedi to En-eglaim; it will be a place for the spreading of nets; its fish will be of a great many kinds, like the fish of the Great Sea. But its swamps and marshes will not become fresh; they are to be left for salt. On the banks, on both sides of the river, there will grow all kinds of trees for food. Their leaves will not wither nor their fruit fail, but they will bear fresh fruit every month, because the water for them flows from the sanctuary. Their fruit will be for food, and their leaves for healing.'

Psalm 87

A reading from the Revelation to John. (21.22; 22.5)
I saw no temple in the city, for its temple is the Lord God the Almighty and the Lamb.
[22.5] And there will be no more night; they need no light of lamp or sun, for the Lord God will be their light, and they will reign for ever and ever.

Hear the Gospel of our Lord Jesus Christ according to Matthew.
(28.16-end)
The eleven disciples went to Galilee, to the mountain to which Jesus had directed them. When they saw him, they worshipped him; but some doubted. And Jesus came and said to them, 'All authority in heaven and on earth has been given to me. Go therefore and make disciples of all nations, baptizing them in the name of the Father and of the Son and of the Holy Spirit, and teaching them to obey everything that I have commanded you. And remember, I am with you always, to the end of the age.'

This is the Gospel of the Lord.

Dismissal Gospel
Hear the words of the Gospel according to Matthew. (28.9-10)
Jesus met the disciples and said, 'Greetings!' And they came to him, took hold of his feet, and worshipped him. Then Jesus said to them, 'Do not be afraid; go and tell my brothers to go to Galilee; there they will see me.'

This is the Gospel of the Lord.

Eucharist
Bread of life

A reading from the prophecy of Isaiah. (55.1-3,10-11)
> Ho, everyone who thirsts,
>> come to the waters;
> and you that have no money,
>> come, buy and eat!
> Come, buy wine and milk
>> without money and without price.
> Why do you spend your money for that which is not bread,
>> and your labour for that which does not satisfy?
> Listen carefully to me, and eat what is good,
>> and delight yourselves in rich food.
> Incline your ear, and come to me;
>> listen, so that you may live.
> I will make with you an everlasting covenant,
>> my steadfast, sure love for David.

10 For as the rain and the snow come down from heaven,
>> and do not return there until they have watered the earth,
> making it bring forth and sprout,
>> giving seed to the sower and bread to the eater,
> so shall my word be that goes out from my mouth;
>> it shall not return to me empty,
> but it shall accomplish that which I purpose,
>> and succeed in the thing for which I sent it.

Psalm 145.14-end

A reading from the Letter of Paul to the Colossians. (3.14-17)
Clothe yourselves with love, which binds everything together in perfect harmony. And let the peace of Christ rule in your hearts, to which indeed you were called in the one body. And be thankful. Let the word of Christ dwell in you richly; teach and admonish one another in all wisdom; and with gratitude in your hearts sing psalms, hymns, and spiritual songs to God. And whatever you do, in word or deed, do everything in the name of the Lord Jesus, giving thanks to God the Father through him.

Hear the Gospel of our Lord Jesus Christ according to John. *(6.47-51)*
Jesus said to the Jews, 'Very truly, I tell you, whoever believes has
eternal life. I am the bread of life. Your ancestors ate the manna in
the wilderness, and they died. This is the bread that comes down
from heaven, so that one may eat of it and not die. I am the living
bread that came down from heaven. Whoever eats of this bread will
live for ever; and the bread that I will give for the life of the world is
my flesh.'

This is the Gospel of the Lord.

Dismissal Gospel
Hear the words of the Gospel according to John. *(6.63-64,66-69)*
Jesus said to his disciples, 'It is the spirit that gives life; the flesh is
useless. The words that I have spoken to you are spirit and life. But
among you there are some who do not believe.' For Jesus knew from
the first who were the ones that did not believe, and who was the one
that would betray him.
⁶⁶ Because of this many of his disciples turned back and no longer
went about with him. So Jesus asked the twelve, 'Do you also wish
to go away?' Simon Peter answered him, 'Lord, to whom can we go?
You have the words of eternal life. We have come to believe and
know that you are the Holy One of God.'

This is the Gospel of the Lord.

General – Set I
Cleansing & Response

A reading from the Second Book of the Kings. (5.9-14)

Naaman came with his horses and chariots, and halted at the entrance of Elisha's house. Elisha sent a messenger to him, saying, 'Go, wash in the Jordan seven times, and your flesh shall be restored and you shall be clean.' But Naaman became angry and went away, saying, 'I thought that for me he would surely come out, and stand and call on the name of the Lord his God, and would wave his hand over the spot, and cure the leprosy! Are not Abana and Pharpar, the rivers of Damascus, better than all the waters of Israel? Could I not wash in them, and be clean?' He turned and went away in a rage. But his servants approached and said to him, 'Father, if the prophet had commanded you to do something difficult, would you not have done it? How much more, when all he said to you was, "Wash, and be clean"?'

So he went down and immersed himself seven times in the Jordan, according to the word of the man of God; his flesh was restored like the flesh of a young boy, and he was clean.

Psalm 66.15-end

A reading from the Letter of Paul to the Romans. (10.5-11)

Moses writes concerning the righteousness that comes from the law, that 'the person who does these things will live by them.' But the righteousness that comes from faith says, 'Do not say in your heart, "Who will ascend into heaven?"' (that is, to bring Christ down) 'or "Who will descend into the abyss?"' (that is, to bring Christ up from the dead). But what does it say?

    'The word is near you,

      on your lips and in your heart'

(that is, the word of faith that we proclaim); because if you confess with your lips that Jesus is Lord and believe in your heart that God raised him from the dead, you will be saved. For one believes with the heart and so is justified, and one confesses with the mouth and so is saved. The scripture says, 'No one who believes in him will be put to shame.'

Hear the Gospel of our Lord Jesus Christ according to Luke.

(17.11-19)

On the way to Jerusalem, Jesus was going through the region between Samaria and Galilee. As he entered a village, ten lepers approached him. Keeping their distance, they called out, saying, 'Jesus, Master, have mercy on us!' When he saw them, he said to them, 'Go and show yourselves to the priests.' And as they went, they were made clean. Then one of them, when he saw that he was healed, turned back, praising God with a loud voice. He prostrated himself at Jesus' feet and thanked him. And he was a Samaritan. Then Jesus asked, 'Were not ten made clean? But the other nine, where are they? Was none of them found to return and give praise to God except this foreigner?' Then he said to him, 'Get up and go on your way; your faith has made you well.'

This is the Gospel of the Lord.

Dismissal Gospel
Hear the words of the Gospel according to Luke. *(17.20-21)*
Once, Jesus was asked by the Pharisees when the kingdom of God was coming, and he answered, 'The kingdom of God is not coming with things that can be observed; nor will they say, "Look, here it is!" or "There it is!" For, in fact, the kingdom of God is among you.'

This is the Gospel of the Lord.

General – Set II
Prayer

A reading from the Second Book of the Kings. (20.1-5)
Hezekiah became sick and was at the point of death. The prophet
Isaiah son of Amoz came to him, and said to him, 'Thus says
the Lord: Set your house in order, for you shall die; you shall not
recover.' Then Hezekiah turned his face to the wall and prayed to the
Lord: 'Remember now, O Lord, I implore you, how I have walked
before you in faithfulness with a whole heart, and have done what is
good in your sight.' Hezekiah wept bitterly. Before Isaiah had gone
out of the middle court, the word of the Lord came to him: 'Turn
back, and say to Hezekiah prince of my people, Thus says the Lord,
the God of your ancestor David: I have heard your prayer, I have
seen your tears; indeed, I will heal you; on the third day you shall go
up to the house of the Lord.'

Psalm 130

A reading from the Letter of James. (5.13-16)
Are any among you suffering? They should pray. Are any cheerful?
They should sing songs of praise. Are any among you sick? They
should call for the elders of the church and have them pray over
them, anointing them with oil in the name of the Lord. The prayer of
faith will save the sick, and the Lord will raise them up; and anyone
who has committed sins will be forgiven. Therefore confess your sins
to one another, and pray for one another, so that you may be healed.
The prayer of the righteous is powerful and effective.

Hear the Gospel of our Lord Jesus Christ according to Mark. (9.16-29)
Jesus asked the crowd, 'What are you arguing about with the
disciples?' Someone from the crowd answered him, 'Teacher, I
brought you my son; he has a spirit that makes him unable to speak;
and whenever it seizes him, it dashes him down; and he foams and
grinds his teeth and becomes rigid; and I asked your disciples to cast
it out, but they could not do so.' He answered them, 'You faithless
generation, how much longer must I be among you? How much
longer must I put up with you? Bring him to me.' And they brought
the boy to him. When the spirit saw him, immediately it convulsed
the boy, and he fell on the ground and rolled about, foaming at the
mouth. Jesus asked the father, 'How long has this been happening to
him?' And he said, 'From childhood. It has often cast him into the

fire and into the water, to destroy him; but if you are able to do anything, have pity on us and help us.' Jesus said to him, '"If you are able"! – All things can be done for the one who believes.' Immediately the father of the child cried out, 'I believe; help my unbelief!' When Jesus saw that a crowd came running together, he rebuked the unclean spirit, saying to it, 'You spirit that keeps this boy from speaking and hearing, I command you, come out of him, and never enter him again!' After crying out and convulsing him terribly, it came out, and the boy was like a corpse, so that most of them said, 'He is dead.' But Jesus took him by the hand and lifted him up, and he was able to stand. When he had entered the house, his disciples asked him privately, 'Why could we not cast it out?' He said to them, 'This kind can come out only through prayer.'

This is the Gospel of the Lord.

Dismissal Gospel
Hear the words of the Gospel according to Mark. *(9.38-40)*
John said to Jesus, 'Teacher, we saw someone casting out demons in your name, and we tried to stop him, because he was not following us.' But Jesus said, 'Do not stop him; for no one who does a deed of power in my name will be able soon afterward to speak evil of me. Whoever is not against us is for us.'

This is the Gospel of the Lord.

General – Set III
Deliverance

A reading from the First Book of Samuel. (16.14-end)

The spirit of the Lord departed from Saul, and an evil spirit from the Lord tormented him. And Saul's servants said to him, 'See now, an evil spirit from God is tormenting you. Let our lord now command the servants who attend you to look for someone who is skilful in playing the lyre; and when the evil spirit from God is upon you, he will play it, and you will feel better.' So Saul said to his servants, 'Provide for me someone who can play well, and bring him to me.' One of the young men answered, 'I have seen a son of Jesse the Bethlehemite who is skilful in playing, a man of valour, a warrior, prudent in speech, and a man of good presence; and the Lord is with him.' So Saul sent messengers to Jesse, and said, 'Send me your son David who is with the sheep.' Jesse took a donkey loaded with bread, a skin of wine, and a kid, and sent them by his son David to Saul. And David came to Saul, and entered his service. Saul loved him greatly, and he became his armour-bearer. Saul sent to Jesse, saying, 'Let David remain in my service, for he has found favour in my sight.' And whenever the evil spirit from God came upon Saul, David took the lyre and played it with his hand, and Saul would be relieved and feel better, and the evil spirit would depart from him.

Psalm 91.1-6,9-13

A reading from the Acts of the Apostles. (10.36-43)

You know the message God sent to the people of Israel, preaching peace by Jesus Christ – he is Lord of all. That message spread throughout Judea, beginning in Galilee after the baptism that John announced: how God anointed Jesus of Nazareth with the Holy Spirit and with power; how he went about doing good and healing all who were oppressed by the devil, for God was with him. We are witnesses to all that he did both in Judea and in Jerusalem. They put him to death by hanging him on a tree; but God raised him on the third day and allowed him to appear, not to all the people but to us who were chosen by God as witnesses, and who ate and drank with him after he rose from the dead. He commanded us to preach to the people and to testify that he is the one ordained by God as judge of the living and the dead. All the prophets testify about him that everyone who believes in him receives forgiveness of sins through his name.'

Hear the Gospel of our Lord Jesus Christ according to Mark. (1.21-28)
Jesus and his disciples went to Capernaum; and when the sabbath
came, he entered the synagogue and taught. They were astounded at
his teaching, for he taught them as one having authority, and not as
the scribes. Just then there was in their synagogue a man with an
unclean spirit, and he cried out, 'What have you to do with us, Jesus
of Nazareth? Have you come to destroy us? I know who you are, the
Holy One of God.' But Jesus rebuked him, saying, 'Be silent, and
come out of him!' And the unclean spirit, convulsing him and crying
with a loud voice, came out of him. They were all amazed, and they
kept on asking one another, 'What is this? A new teaching – with
authority! He commands even the unclean spirits, and they obey
him.' At once his fame began to spread throughout the surrounding
region of Galilee.

This is the Gospel of the Lord.

Or:

Hear the Gospel of our Lord Jesus Christ according to Mark. (5.1-20)
Jesus and his disciples came to the other side of the sea, to the
country of the Gerasenes. And when he had stepped out of the boat,
immediately a man out of the tombs with an unclean spirit met him.
He lived among the tombs; and no one could restrain him any more,
even with a chain; for he had often been restrained with shackles and
chains, but the chains he wrenched apart, and the shackles he broke
in pieces; and no one had the strength to subdue him. Night and day
among the tombs and on the mountains he was always howling and
bruising himself with stones. When he saw Jesus from a distance, he
ran and bowed down before him; and he shouted at the top of his
voice, 'What have you to do with me, Jesus, Son of the Most High
God? I adjure you by God, do not torment me.' For he had said to
him, 'Come out of the man, you unclean spirit!' Then Jesus asked
him, 'What is your name?' He replied, 'My name is Legion; for
we are many.' He begged him earnestly not to send them out of
the country. Now there on the hillside a great herd of swine was
feeding; and the unclean spirits begged him, 'Send us into the swine;
let us enter them.' So he gave them permission. And the unclean
spirits came out and entered the swine; and the herd, numbering
about two thousand, rushed down the steep bank into the sea, and
were drowned in the sea.

The swineherds ran off and told it in the city and in the country.
Then people came to see what it was that had happened. They came
to Jesus and saw the demoniac sitting there, clothed and in his right

mind, the very man who had had the legion; and they were afraid. Those who had seen what had happened to the demoniac and to the swine reported it. Then they began to beg Jesus to leave their neighbourhood. As he was getting into the boat, the man who had been possessed by demons begged him that he might be with him. But Jesus refused, and said to him, 'Go home to your friends, and tell them how much the Lord has done for you, and what mercy he has shown you.' And he went away and began to proclaim in the Decapolis how much Jesus had done for him; and everyone was amazed.

This is the Gospel of the Lord.

Dismissal Gospel
Hear the words of the Gospel according to Mark. *(5.25-34)*
There was a woman who had been suffering from haemorrhages for twelve years. She had endured much under many physicians, and had spent all that she had; and she was no better, but rather grew worse. She had heard about Jesus, and came up behind him in the crowd and touched his cloak, for she said, 'If I but touch his clothes, I will be made well.' Immediately her haemorrhage stopped; and she felt in her body that she was healed of her disease. Immediately aware that power had gone forth from him, Jesus turned about in the crowd and said, 'Who touched my clothes?' And his disciples said to him, 'You see the crowd pressing in on you; how can you say, "Who touched me?"' He looked all around to see who had done it. But the woman, knowing what had happened to her, came in fear and trembling, fell down before him, and told him the whole truth. He said to her, 'Daughter, your faith has made you well; go in peace, and be healed of your disease.'

This is the Gospel of the Lord.

Ministry
at the Time of Death

Collect
Eternal God,
grant to your servant
[and to us who surround *him/her* with our prayers]
your peace beyond understanding;
give us faith,
the comfort of your presence
and the words to say to one another
and to you
as we gather in the name of Jesus Christ our Lord.

Post Communion (adapted from the Commendation)
Holy Lord, almighty and eternal God,
hear our prayers as we entrust to you *N*,
as you summon *him/her* out of this world;
forgive *his/her* sins and failings
and grant *him/her* a haven of light and peace;
let *him/her* pass unharmed through the gates of death
to dwell with the blessèd in light,
as you promised to Abraham and his children for ever;
accept *N* into your safe keeping
and on the great day of judgement
raise *him/her* up with all the saints
to inherit your eternal kingdom;
we ask this through Christ our Lord.

A reading from the book Joshua. *(23.1-8)*
When the Lord had given rest to Israel from all their enemies
all around, and Joshua was old and well advanced in years, Joshua
summoned all Israel, their elders and heads, their judges and officers,
and said to them, "I am now old and well advanced in years; and you
have seen all that the Lord your God has done to all these nations for
your sake, for it is the Lord your God who has fought for you. I have
allotted to you as an inheritance for your tribes those nations that
remain, along with all the nations that I have already cut off, from
the Jordan to the Great Sea in the west. The Lord your God will
push them back before you, and drive them out of your sight; and
you shall possess their land, as the Lord your God promised you.

Therefore be very steadfast to observe and do all that is written in the book of the law of Moses, turning aside from it neither to the right nor to the left, so that you may not be mixed with these nations left here among you, or make mention of the names of their gods, or swear by them, or serve them, or bow yourselves down to them, but hold fast to the Lord your God, as you have done to this day.

A reading from the prophecy of Isaiah. *(53.3-5)*

He was despised and rejected by others;
   a man of suffering and acquainted with infirmity;
and as one from whom others hide their faces
   he was despised, and we held him of no account.

Surely he has borne our infirmities
   and carried our diseases;
yet we accounted him stricken,
   struck down by God, and afflicted.
But he was wounded for our transgressions,
   crushed for our iniquities;
upon him was the punishment that made us whole,
   and by his bruises we are healed.

Psalm 23; Psalm 139

A reading from the Letter of Paul to the Romans. *(8.35,37-end)*

Who will separate us from the love of Christ? Will hardship, or distress, or persecution, or famine, or nakedness, or peril, or sword? [37] No, in all these things we are more than conquerors through him who loved us. For I am convinced that neither death, nor life, nor angels, nor rulers, nor things present, nor things to come, nor powers, nor height, nor depth, nor anything else in all creation, will be able to separate us from the love of God in Christ Jesus our Lord.

A reading from the Letter of Paul to the Philippians. *(1.20-26)*

It is my eager expectation and hope that I will not be put to shame in any way, but that by my speaking with all boldness, Christ will be exalted now as always in my body, whether by life or by death. For to me, living is Christ and dying is gain. If I am to live in the flesh, that means fruitful labour for me; and I do not know which I prefer. I am hard pressed between the two: my desire is to depart and be with Christ, for that is far better; but to remain in the flesh is more necessary for you. Since I am convinced of this, I know that I will remain and continue with all of you for your progress and joy in

Ministry at the time of Death

faith, so that I may share abundantly in your boasting in Christ Jesus when I come to you again.

A reading from the Gospel according to Luke. *(23.39-46)*
One of the criminals who were hanged there kept deriding Jesus and saying, 'Are you not the Messiah? Save yourself and us!' But the other rebuked him, saying, 'Do you not fear God, since you are under the same sentence of condemnation? And we indeed have been condemned justly, for we are getting what we deserve for our deeds, but this man has done nothing wrong.' Then he said, 'Jesus, remember me when you come into your kingdom.' He replied, 'Truly I tell you, today you will be with me in Paradise.'

It was now about noon, and darkness came over the whole land until three in the afternoon, while the sun's light failed; and the curtain of the temple was torn in two. Then Jesus, crying with a loud voice, said, 'Father, into your hands I commend my spirit.' Having said this, he breathed his last.

A reading from the Gospel according to John. *(6.35-40,[53-58])*
Jesus said to the crowd, 'I am the bread of life. Whoever comes to me will never be hungry, and whoever believes in me will never be thirsty. But I said to you that you have seen me and yet do not believe. Everything that the Father gives me will come to me, and anyone who comes to me I will never drive away; for I have come down from heaven, not to do my own will, but the will of him who sent me. And this is the will of him who sent me, that I should lose nothing of all that he has given me, but raise it up on the last day. This is indeed the will of my Father, that all who see the Son and believe in him may have eternal life; and I will raise them up on the last day.'
[53 'Very truly, I tell you, unless you eat the flesh of the Son of Man and drink his blood, you have no life in you. Those who eat my flesh and drink my blood have eternal life, and I will raise them up on the last day; for my flesh is true food and my blood is true drink. Those who eat my flesh and drink my blood abide in me, and I in them. Just as the living Father sent me, and I live because of the Father, so whoever eats me will live because of me. This is the bread that came down from heaven, not like that which your ancestors ate, and they died. But the one who eats this bread will live for ever.']

A reading from the Gospel according to John. (14.1-3)
Jesus said to his disciples, 'Do not let your hearts be troubled. Believe in God, believe also in me. In my Father's house there are many dwelling places. If it were not so, would I have told you that I go to prepare a place for you? And if I go and prepare a place for you, I will come again and will take you to myself, so that where I am, there you may be also.'

Death

Death

At Home before the Funeral

A reading from the First Letter of Paul to the Thessalonians. *(4.13-15)*
We do not want you to be uninformed, brothers and sisters, about
those who have died, so that you may not grieve as others do who
have no hope. For since we believe that Jesus died and rose again,
even so, through Jesus, God will bring with him those who have
died. For this we declare to you by the word of the Lord, that we
who are alive, who are left until the coming of the Lord, will by no
means precede those who have died.

Psalm 121

A reading from the Gospel according to John. *(11.21-24)*
Martha said to Jesus, 'Lord, if you had been here, my brother
would not have died. But even now I know that God will give you
what-ever you ask of him.' Jesus said to her, 'Your brother will rise
again.' Martha said to him, 'I know that he will rise again in the
resurrection on the last day.'

Receiving the Coffin at Church before the Funeral

A reading from the Gospel according to John. *(14.1-6)*
Jesus said to his disciples, 'Do not let your hearts be troubled. Believe
in God, believe also in me. In my Father's house there are many
dwelling places. If it were not so, would I have told you that I go to
prepare a place for you? And if I go and prepare a place for you, I
will come again and will take you to myself, so that where I am, there
you may be also. And you know the way to the place where I am
going.' Thomas said to him, 'Lord, we do not know where you are
going. How can we know the way?' Jesus said to him, 'I am the way,
and the truth, and the life. No one comes to the Father except
through me.'

At a Funeral Vigil
Assurance & Comfort

A reading from the prophecy of Isaiah. (61.1-3)
> The spirit of the Lord God is upon me,
>   because the Lord has anointed me;
> he has sent me to bring good news to the oppressed,
>   to bind up the broken-hearted,
> to proclaim liberty to the captives,
>   and release to the prisoners;
> to proclaim the year of the Lord's favour,
>   and the day of vengeance of our God;
>   to comfort all who mourn;
> to provide for those who mourn in Zion –
>   to give them a garland instead of ashes,
> the oil of gladness instead of mourning,
>   the mantle of praise instead of a faint spirit.
> They will be called oaks of righteousness,
>   the planting of the Lord, to display his glory.

Psalm 139

A reading from the First Letter of Peter. (1.3-9)
Blessèd be the God and Father of our Lord Jesus Christ! By his great mercy he has given us a new birth into a living hope through the resurrection of Jesus Christ from the dead, and into an inheritance that is imperishable, undefiled, and unfading, kept in heaven for you, who are being protected by the power of God through faith for a salvation ready to be revealed in the last time. In this you rejoice, even if now for a little while you have had to suffer various trials, so that the genuineness of your faith – being more precious than gold that, though perishable, is tested by fire – may be found to result in praise and glory and honour when Jesus Christ is revealed. Although you have not seen him, you love him; and even though you do not see him now, you believe in him and rejoice with an indescribable and glorious joy, for you are receiving the outcome of your faith, the salvation of your souls.

A reading from the Gospel according to John. *(14.1-6)*
Jesus said to his disciples, 'Do not let your hearts be troubled. Believe in God, believe also in me. In my Father's house there are many dwelling places. If it were not so, would I have told you that I go to prepare a place for you? And if I go and prepare a place for you, I will come again and will take you to myself, so that where I am, there you may be also. And you know the way to the place where I am going.' Thomas said to him, 'Lord, we do not know where you are going. How can we know the way?' Jesus said to him, 'I am the way, and the truth, and the life. No one comes to the Father except through me.'

The Faithfulness of God

A reading from the prophecy of Isaiah. (53.1-10)

Who has believed what we have heard?
And to whom has the arm of the Lord been revealed?
For he grew up before him like a young plant,
and like a root out of dry ground;
he had no form or majesty that we should look at him,
nothing in his appearance that we should desire him.
He was despised and rejected by others;
a man of suffering and acquainted with infirmity;
and as one from whom others hide their faces
he was despised, and we held him of no account.

Surely he has borne our infirmities
and carried our diseases;
yet we accounted him stricken,
struck down by God, and afflicted.
But he was wounded for our transgressions,
crushed for our iniquities;
upon him was the punishment that made us whole,
and by his bruises we are healed.
All we like sheep have gone astray;
we have all turned to our own way,
and the Lord has laid on him
the iniquity of us all.

He was oppressed, and he was afflicted,
yet he did not open his mouth;
like a lamb that is led to the slaughter,
and like a sheep that before its shearers is silent,
so he did not open his mouth.
By a perversion of justice he was taken away.
Who could have imagined his future?
For he was cut off from the land of the living,
stricken for the transgression of my people.
They made his grave with the wicked
and his tomb with the rich,
although he had done no violence,
and there was no deceit in his mouth.
Yet it was the will of the Lord to crush him with pain.
When you make his life an offering for sin,
he shall see his offspring, and shall prolong his days;
through him the will of the Lord shall prosper.

Psalm 116.1-8,[9-17]

A reading from the Letter of Paul to the Romans. *(8.31-end)*
What are we to say about these things? If God is for us, who is
against us? He who did not withhold his own Son, but gave him up
for all of us, will he not with him also give us everything else? Who
will bring any charge against God's elect? It is God who justifies.
Who is to condemn? It is Christ Jesus, who died, yes, who was
raised, who is at the right hand of God, who indeed intercedes for us.
Who will separate us from the love of Christ? Will hardship, or
distress, or persecution, or famine, or nakedness, or peril, or sword?
As it is written,
  'For your sake we are being killed all day long;
    we are accounted as sheep to be slaughtered.'
No, in all these things we are more than conquerors through
him who loved us. For I am convinced that neither death, nor life,
nor angels, nor rulers, nor things present, nor things to come, nor
powers, nor height, nor depth, nor anything else in all creation, will
be able to separate us from the love of God in Christ Jesus our Lord.

A reading from the Revelation to John. *(21.1-7)*
I saw a new heaven and a new earth; for the first heaven and the first
earth had passed away, and the sea was no more. And I saw the
holy city, the new Jerusalem, coming down out of heaven from God,
prepared as a bride adorned for her husband. And I heard a loud
voice from the throne saying,
  See, the home of God is among mortals.
    He will dwell with them as their God;
  they will be his peoples,
    and God himself will be with them;
    he will wipe every tear from their eyes.
  Death will be no more;
    mourning and crying and pain will be no more,
    for the first things have passed away.'
And the one who was seated on the throne said, 'See, I am making
all things new.' Also he said, 'Write this, for these words are trustworthy and true.' Then he said to me, 'It is done! I am the Alpha
and the Omega, the beginning and the end. To the thirsty I will
give water as a gift from the spring of the water of life. Those who
conquer will inherit these things, and I will be their God and they
will be my children.'

A reading from the Gospel according to John. *(6.35-40,[53-58])*

Jesus said to the crowd, 'I am the bread of life. Whoever comes to me will never be hungry, and whoever believes in me will never be thirsty. But I said to you that you have seen me and yet do not believe. Everything that the Father gives me will come to me, and anyone who comes to me I will never drive away; for I have come down from heaven, not to do my own will, but the will of him who sent me. And this is the will of him who sent me, that I should lose nothing of all that he has given me, but raise it up on the last day. This is indeed the will of my Father, that all who see the Son and believe in him may have eternal life; and I will raise them up on the last day.'

[53 'Very truly, I tell you, unless you eat the flesh of the Son of Man and drink his blood, you have no life in you. Those who eat my flesh and drink my blood have eternal life, and I will raise them up on the last day; for my flesh is true food and my blood is true drink. Those who eat my flesh and drink my blood abide in me, and I in them. Just as the living Father sent me, and I live because of the Father, so whoever eats me will live because of me. This is the bread that came down from heaven, not like that which your ancestors ate, and they died. But the one who eats this bread will live for ever.']

The Hope of Heaven

A reading from the Wisdom of Solomon. (3.1-5,9)
   The souls of the righteous are in the hand of God,
   and no torment will ever touch them.
   In the eyes of the foolish they seemed to have died,
   and their departure was thought to be a disaster,
   and their going from us to be their destruction;
   but they are at peace.
   For though in the sight of others they were punished,
   their hope is full of immortality.
   Having been disciplined a little, they will receive great good,
   because God tested them and found them worthy of himself.
⁹   Those who trust in him will understand truth,
   and the faithful will abide with him in love,
   because grace and mercy are upon his holy ones,
   and he watches over his elect.

Psalm 25.1-9

A reading from the Letter of Paul to the Romans. (8.18-25,[26-30])
I consider that the sufferings of this present time are not worth
comparing with the glory about to be revealed to us. For the creation
waits with eager longing for the revealing of the children of God; for
the creation was subjected to futility, not of its own will but by the
will of the one who subjected it, in hope that the creation itself will be
set free from its bondage to decay and will obtain the freedom of the
glory of the children of God. We know that the whole creation has
been groaning in labour pains until now; and not only the creation,
but we ourselves, who have the first fruits of the Spirit, groan
inwardly while we wait for adoption, the redemption of our bodies.
For in hope we were saved. Now hope that is seen is not hope. For
who hopes for what is seen? But if we hope for what we do not see,
we wait for it with patience.
[²⁶ Likewise the Spirit helps us in our weakness; for we do not know
how to pray as we ought, but that very Spirit intercedes with sighs
too deep for words. And God, who searches the heart, knows what
is the mind of the Spirit, because the Spirit intercedes for the saints
according to the will of God.
   We know that all things work together for good for those who love
God, who are called according to his purpose. For those whom he
foreknew he also predestined to be conformed to the image of his

Son, in order that he might be the firstborn within a large family. And those whom he predestined he also called; and those whom he called he also justified; and those whom he justified he also glorified.]

A reading from the Gospel according to John. (14.1-6)
Jesus said to his disciples, 'Do not let your hearts be troubled. Believe in God, believe also in me. In my Father's house there are many dwelling places. If it were not so, would I have told you that I go to prepare a place for you? And if I go and prepare a place for you, I will come again and will take you to myself, so that where I am, there you may be also. And you know the way to the place where I am going.' Thomas said to him, 'Lord, we do not know where you are going. How can we know the way?' Jesus said to him, 'I am the way, and the truth, and the life. No one comes to the Father except through me.'

Advent

A reading from the Book of Daniel. (12.1-3,[5-9])
'At the time of the end Michael, the great prince, the protector of your people, shall arise. There shall be a time of anguish, such as has never occurred since nations first came into existence. But at that time your people shall be delivered, everyone who is found written in the book. Many of those who sleep in the dust of the earth shall awake, some to everlasting life, and some to shame and everlasting contempt. Those who are wise shall shine like the brightness of the sky, and those who lead many to righteousness, like the stars for ever and ever.'
[⁵ Then I, Daniel, looked, and two others appeared, one standing on this bank of the stream and one on the other. One of them said to the man clothed in linen, who was upstream, 'How long shall it be until the end of these wonders?' The man clothed in linen, who was upstream, raised his right hand and his left hand toward heaven. And I heard him swear by the one who lives for ever that it would be for a time, two times, and half a time, and that when the shattering of the power of the holy people comes to an end, all these things would be accomplished. I heard but could not understand; so I said, 'My lord, what shall be the outcome of these things?' He said, 'Go your way, Daniel, for the words are to remain secret and sealed until the time of the end.']

Psalm 27

A reading from the First Letter of Paul to the Thessalonians. (4.13-end)
We do not want you to be uninformed, brothers and sisters, about those who have died, so that you may not grieve as others do who have no hope. For since we believe that Jesus died and rose again, even so, through Jesus, God will bring with him those who have died. For this we declare to you by the word of the Lord, that we who are alive, who are left until the coming of the Lord, will by no means precede those who have died. For the Lord himself, with a cry of command, with the archangel's call and with the sound of God's trumpet, will descend from heaven, and the dead in Christ will rise first. Then we who are alive, who are left, will be caught up in the clouds together with them to meet the Lord in the air; and so we will be with the Lord for ever. Therefore encourage one another with these words.

A reading from the Gospel according to Matthew. (25.31-end)

Jesus said to his disciples, 'When the Son of Man comes in his glory, and all the angels with him, then he will sit on the throne of his glory. All the nations will be gathered before him, and he will separate people one from another as a shepherd separates the sheep from the goats, and he will put the sheep at his right hand and the goats at the left.

Then the king will say to those at his right hand, "Come, you that are blessed by my Father, inherit the kingdom prepared for you from the foundation of the world; for I was hungry and you gave me food, I was thirsty and you gave me something to drink, I was a stranger and you welcomed me, I was naked and you gave me clothing, I was sick and you took care of me, I was in prison and you visited me." Then the righteous will answer him, "Lord, when was it that we saw you hungry and gave you food, or thirsty and gave you something to drink? And when was it that we saw you a stranger and welcomed you, or naked and gave you clothing? And when was it that we saw you sick or in prison and visited you?" And the king will answer them, "Truly I tell you, just as you did it to one of the least of these who are members of my family, you did it to me."

Then he will say to those at his left hand, "You that are accursed, depart from me into the eternal fire prepared for the devil and his angels; for I was hungry and you gave me no food, I was thirsty and you gave me nothing to drink, I was a stranger and you did not welcome me, naked and you did not give me clothing, sick and in prison and you did not visit me." Then they also will answer, "Lord, when was it that we saw you hungry or thirsty or a stranger or naked or sick or in prison, and did not take care of you?" Then he will answer them, "Truly I tell you, just as you did not do it to one of the least of these, you did not do it to me." And these will go away into eternal punishment, but the righteous into eternal life.'

Easter

A reading from the Book of Job. *(19.23-27)*
Job said:
'O that my words were written down!
  O that they were inscribed in a book!
O that with an iron pen and with lead
  they were engraved on a rock for ever!
For I know that my Redeemer lives,
  and that at the last he will stand upon the earth;
and after my skin has been thus destroyed,
  then in my flesh I shall see God,
whom I shall see on my side,
  and my eyes shall behold, and not another.
My heart faints within me!'

Psalm 32

A reading from the Second Letter of Paul to Timothy. *(2.8-13)*
Remember Jesus Christ, raised from the dead, a descendant of David
– that is my gospel, for which I suffer hardship, even to the point of
being chained like a criminal. But the word of God is not chained.
Therefore I endure everything for the sake of the elect, so that they
may also obtain the salvation that is in Christ Jesus, with eternal
glory. The saying is sure:
  If we have died with him, we will also live with him;
  if we endure, we will also reign with him;
  if we deny him, he will also deny us;
  if we are faithless, he remains faithful –
  for he cannot deny himself.

A reading from the Gospel according to John. *(11.17-27)*
When Jesus arrived in Bethany, he found that Lazarus had already
been in the tomb four days. Now Bethany was near Jerusalem, some
two miles away, and many of the Jews had come to Martha and Mary
to console them about their brother. When Martha heard that Jesus
was coming, she went and met him, while Mary stayed at home.
Martha said to Jesus, 'Lord, if you had been here, my brother
would not have died. But even now I know that God will give you
whatever you ask of him.' Jesus said to her, 'Your brother will rise
again.' Martha said to him, 'I know that he will rise again in the
resurrection on the last day.' Jesus said to her, 'I am the resurrection

and the life. Those who believe in me, even though they die, will live, and everyone who lives and believes in me will never die. Do you believe this?' She said to him, 'Yes, Lord, I believe that you are the Messiah, the Son of God, the one coming into the world.'

An Unexpected Death

A reading from the Wisdom of Solomon. (4.8-11,13-15)
Old age is not honoured for length of time,
or measured by number of years;
but understanding is grey hair for anyone,
and a blameless life is ripe old age.

There were some who pleased God and were loved by him,
and while living among sinners were taken up.
They were caught up so that evil
might not change their understanding
or guile deceive their souls.

13 Being perfected in a short time, they fulfilled long years;
for their souls were pleasing to the Lord,
therefore he took them quickly from the midst of wickedness.
Yet the peoples saw and did not understand,
or take such a thing to heart,
that God's grace and mercy are with his elect,
and that he watches over his holy ones.

Psalm 6

A reading from the Second Letter of Paul to the Corinthians. (4.7-15)
We have this treasure in clay jars, so that it may be made clear that
this extraordinary power belongs to God and does not come from us.
We are afflicted in every way, but not crushed; perplexed, but not
driven to despair; persecuted, but not forsaken; struck down, but not
destroyed; always carrying in the body the death of Jesus, so that the
life of Jesus may also be made visible in our bodies. For while we
live, we are always being given up to death for Jesus' sake, so that the
life of Jesus may be made visible in our mortal flesh. So death is at
work in us, but life in you.
But just as we have the same spirit of faith that is in accordance with
scripture – 'I believed, and so I spoke' – we also believe, and so we
speak, because we know that the one who raised the Lord Jesus will
raise us also with Jesus, and will bring us with you into his presence.
Yes, everything is for your sake, so that grace, as it extends to more
and more people, may increase thanksgiving, to the glory of God.

A reading from the Gospel according to Luke. (12.35-40)
Jesus said to his disciples, 'Be dressed for action and have your lamps lit; be like those who are waiting for their master to return from the wedding banquet, so that they may open the door for him as soon as he comes and knocks. Blessèd are those slaves whom the master finds alert when he comes; truly I tell you, he will fasten his belt and have them sit down to eat, and he will come and serve them. If he comes during the middle of the night, or near dawn, and finds them so, blessèd are those slaves.

'But know this: if the owner of the house had known at what hour the thief was coming, he would not have let his house be broken into. You also must be ready, for the Son of Man is coming at an unexpected hour.'

A Child

A reading from the Second Book of Samuel. (12.16-23)
David pleaded with God for the child; David fasted, and went in and lay all night on the ground. The elders of his house stood beside him, urging him to rise from the ground; but he would not, nor did he eat food with them. On the seventh day the child died. And the servants of David were afraid to tell him that the child was dead; for they said, 'While the child was still alive, we spoke to him, and he did not listen to us; how then can we tell him the child is dead? He may do himself some harm.' But when David saw that his servants were whispering together, he perceived that the child was dead; and David said to his servants, 'Is the child dead?' They said, 'He is dead.'
  Then David rose from the ground, washed, anointed himself, and changed his clothes. He went into the house of the Lord, and worshipped; he then went to his own house; and when he asked, they set food before him and he ate. Then his servants said to him, 'What is this thing that you have done? You fasted and wept for the child while it was alive; but when the child died, you rose and ate food.' He said, 'While the child was still alive, I fasted and wept; for I said, "Who knows? The Lord may be gracious to me, and the child may live." But now he is dead; why should I fast? Can I bring him back again? I shall go to him, but he will not return to me.'

Psalm 38.9-end

A reading from the Wisdom of Solomon. (4.8-11,13-15)
>   Old age is not honoured for length of time,
>   or measured by number of years;
>   but understanding is grey hair for anyone,
>   and a blameless life is ripe old age.
>   There were some who pleased God and were loved by him,
>   and while living among sinners were taken up.
>   They were caught up so that evil
>   might not change their understanding
>   or guile deceive their souls.

13   Being perfected in a short time, they fulfilled long years;
>   for their souls were pleasing to the Lord,
>   therefore he took them quickly from the midst of wickedness.
>   Yet the peoples saw and did not understand,
>   or take such a thing to heart,
>   that God's grace and mercy are with his elect,
>   and that he watches over his holy ones.

A reading from the First Letter of John. (3.1-3)

See what love the Father has given us, that we should be called children of God; and that is what we are. The reason the world does not know us is that it did not know him. Belovèd, we are God's children now; what we will be has not yet been revealed. What we do know is this: when he is revealed, we will be like him, for we will see him as he is. And all who have this hope in him purify themselves, just as he is pure.

A reading from the Gospel according to Luke. (12.35-40)

Jesus said to his disciples, 'Be dressed for action and have your lamps lit; be like those who are waiting for their master to return from the wedding banquet, so that they may open the door for him as soon as he comes and knocks. Blessèd are those slaves whom the master finds alert when he comes; truly I tell you, he will fasten his belt and have them sit down to eat, and he will come and serve them. If he comes during the middle of the night, or near dawn, and finds them so, blessèd are those slaves.

'But know this: if the owner of the house had known at what hour the thief was coming, he would not have let his house be broken into. You also must be ready, for the Son of Man is coming at an unexpected hour.'

On the Morning of the Funeral

A reading from the Lamentations of Jeremiah. (3.22-26,31-33)

The steadfast love of the Lord never ceases,
   his mercies never come to an end;
they are new every morning;
   great is your faithfulness.
'The Lord is my portion,' says my soul,
'therefore I will hope in him.'

The Lord is good to those who wait for him,
   to the soul that seeks him.
It is good that one should wait quietly
   for the salvation of the Lord.

31   For the Lord will not
   reject for ever.
Although he causes grief, he will have compassion
   according to the abundance of his steadfast love;
for he does not willingly afflict
   or grieve anyone.

The Funeral Service
& for use at Memorial Services

Collect
Merciful Father,
hear our prayers and comfort us;
renew our trust in your Son,
whom you raised from the dead;
strengthen our faith
that all who have died in the love of Christ
will share in his resurrection;
who is alive and reigns with you
in the unity of the Holy Spirit,
one God, now and for ever.

Or:

Eternal God, our maker and redeemer,
grant us [*with N*] and all the faithful departed
the sure benefits of your Son's saving passion
  and glorious resurrection:
that, in the last day,
when you gather up all things in Christ,
we may with them enjoy the fullness of your promises;
through Jesus Christ your Son our Lord,
who is alive and reigns with you
in the unity of the Holy Spirit,
one God, now and for ever.

Post Communion
Gracious God,
we thank you that in your great love
you have fed us with the spiritual food and drink
  of the body and blood of your Son Jesus Christ
and have given us a foretaste of your heavenly banquet:
grant that this sacrament may be to us
a comfort in affliction
and a pledge of our inheritance
in that kingdom where there is no death,
neither sorrow nor crying,
but fullness of joy with all your saints;
through Jesus Christ our Saviour.

A reading from the book Genesis. *(42.29-end)*
When his sons came to their father Jacob in the land of Canaan, they told him all that had happened to them, saying, 'The man, the lord of the land, spoke harshly to us, and charged us with spying on the land. But we said to him, "We are honest men, we are not spies. We are twelve brothers, sons of our father; one is no more, and the youngest is now with our father in the land of Canaan." Then the man, the lord of the land, said to us, "By this I shall know that you are honest men: leave one of your brothers with me, take grain for the famine of your households, and go your way. Bring your youngest brother to me, and I shall know that you are not spies but honest men. Then I will release your brother to you, and you may trade in the land."'

As they were emptying their sacks, there in each one's sack was his bag of money. When they and their father saw their bundles of money, they were dismayed. And their father Jacob said to them, 'I am the one you have bereaved of children: Joseph is no more, and Simeon is no more, and now you would take Benjamin. All this has happened to me!' Then Reuben said to his father, 'You may kill my two sons if I do not bring him back to you. Put him in my hands, and I will bring him back to you.' But he said, 'My son shall not go down with you, for his brother is dead, and he alone is left. If harm should come to him on the journey that you are to make, you would bring down my grey hairs with sorrow to Sheol.'

A reading from the Second Book Samuel. *(1.17,23-end)*
David intoned this lamentation over Saul and his son Jonathan. (He ordered that The Song of the Bow be taught to the people of Judah; it is written in the Book of Jashar.) He said:
²³ Saul and Jonathan, belovèd and lovely!
    In life and in death they were not divided;
they were swifter than eagles,
    they were stronger than lions.

O daughters of Israel, weep over Saul,
    who clothed you with crimson, in luxury,
    who put ornaments of gold on your apparel.

How the mighty have fallen
    in the midst of the battle!
Jonathan lies slain upon your high places.
    I am distressed for you, my brother Jonathan;
greatly beloved were you to me;

your love to me was wonderful,
   passing the love of women.

How the mighty have fallen,
   and the weapons of war perished!

A reading from the Second Book of Samuel. (12.16-23)
David pleaded with God for the child; David fasted, and went in and
lay all night on the ground. The elders of his house stood beside him,
urging him to rise from the ground; but he would not, nor did he eat
food with them. On the seventh day the child died. And the servants
of David were afraid to tell him that the child was dead; for they said,
'While the child was still alive, we spoke to him, and he did not
listen to us; how then can we tell him the child is dead? He may do
himself some harm.' But when David saw that his servants were
whispering together, he perceived that the child was dead; and
David said to his servants, 'Is the child dead?' They said, 'He is dead.'

Then David rose from the ground, washed, anointed himself,
and changed his clothes. He went into the house of the Lord, and
worshipped; he then went to his own house; and when he asked,
they set food before him and he ate. Then his servants said to him,
'What is this thing that you have done? You fasted and wept for the
child while it was alive; but when the child died, you rose and ate
food.' He said, 'While the child was still alive, I fasted and wept; for
I said, "Who knows? The Lord may be gracious to me, and the child
may live." But now he is dead; why should I fast? Can I bring him
back again? I shall go to him, but he will not return to me.'

A reading from the Book of Job. (19.23-27)
Job said:
   'O that my words were written down!
      O that they were inscribed in a book!
   O that with an iron pen and with lead
      they were engraved on a rock for ever!
   For I know that my Redeemer lives,
      and that at the last he will stand upon the earth;
   and after my skin has been thus destroyed,
      then in my flesh I shall see God,
   whom I shall see on my side,
      and my eyes shall behold, and not another.
      My heart faints within me!'

A reading from the Song of Solomon. *(2.10-13)*
My belovèd speaks and says to me:
  'Arise, my love, my fair one,
    and come away;
  for now the winter is past,
    the rain is over and gone.
  The flowers appear on the earth;
    the time of singing has come,
  and the voice of the turtledove
    is heard in our land.
  The fig tree puts forth its figs,
    and the vines are in blossom;
    they give forth fragrance.
  Arise, my love, my fair one,
    and come away.'

A reading from the prophecy of Isaiah. *(49.15-16)*
  Can a woman forget her nursing child,
    or show no compassion for the child of her womb?
  Even these may forget,
    yet I will not forget you.
  See, I have inscribed you on the palms of my hands;
    your walls are continually before me.

A reading from the prophecy of Isaiah. *(53.1-10)*
  Who has believed what we have heard?
    And to whom has the arm of the Lord been revealed?
  For he grew up before him like a young plant,
    and like a root out of dry ground;
  he had no form or majesty that we should look at him,
    nothing in his appearance that we should desire him.
  He was despised and rejected by others;
    a man of suffering and acquainted with infirmity;
  and as one from whom others hide their faces
    he was despised, and we held him of no account.

  Surely he has borne our infirmities
    and carried our diseases;
  yet we accounted him stricken,
    struck down by God, and afflicted.
  But he was wounded for our transgressions,
    crushed for our iniquities;
  upon him was the punishment that made us whole,

and by his bruises we are healed.
All we like sheep have gone astray;
   we have all turned to our own way,
and the Lord has laid on him
   the iniquity of us all.

He was oppressed, and he was afflicted,
   yet he did not open his mouth;
like a lamb that is led to the slaughter,
   and like a sheep that before its shearers is silent,
   so he did not open his mouth.
By a perversion of justice he was taken away.
   Who could have imagined his future?
For he was cut off from the land of the living,
   stricken for the transgression of my people.
They made his grave with the wicked
   and his tomb with the rich,
although he had done no violence,
   and there was no deceit in his mouth.

Yet it was the will of the Lord to crush him with pain.
   When you make his life an offering for sin,
he shall see his offspring, and shall prolong his days;
   through him the will of the Lord shall prosper.

A reading from the prophecy of Isaiah. (61.1-3)
   The spirit of the Lord God is upon me,
      because the Lord has anointed me;
   he has sent me to bring good news to the oppressed,
      to bind up the broken-hearted,
   to proclaim liberty to the captives,
      and release to the prisoners;
   to proclaim the year of the Lord's favour,
      and the day of vengeance of our God;
      to comfort all who mourn;
   to provide for those who mourn in Zion –
      to give them a garland instead of ashes,
   the oil of gladness instead of mourning,
      the mantle of praise instead of a faint spirit.
   They will be called oaks of righteousness,
      the planting of the Lord, to display his glory.

A reading from the prophecy of Jeremiah. (1.4-8)
 The word of the Lord came to me saying,
 'Before I formed you in the womb I knew you,
 and before you were born I consecrated you;
 I appointed you a prophet to the nations.'
Then I said, 'Ah, Lord God! Truly I do not know how to speak, for
I am only a boy.' But the Lord said to me,
 'Do not say, "I am only a boy";
 for you shall go to all to whom I send you,
 and you shall speak whatever I command you.
 Do not be afraid of them,
 for I am with you to deliver you,' says the Lord.

A reading from the prophecy of Jeremiah. (31.15-17)
Thus says the Lord:
 A voice is heard in Ramah,
 lamentation and bitter weeping.
 Rachel is weeping for her children;
 she refuses to be comforted for her children,
 because they are no more.
Thus says the Lord:
 Keep your voice from weeping,
 and your eyes from tears;
 for there is a reward for your work,
 says the Lord:
 they shall come back from the land of the enemy;
 there is hope for your future,
 says the Lord:
 your children shall come back to their own country.

A reading from the Lamentations of Jeremiah. (3.22-26,31-33)
 The steadfast love of the Lord never ceases,
 his mercies never come to an end;
 they are new every morning;
 great is your faithfulness.
 'The Lord is my portion,' says my soul,
 'therefore I will hope in him.'

 The Lord is good to those who wait for him,
 to the soul that seeks him.
 It is good that one should wait quietly
 for the salvation of the Lord.

³¹ For the Lord will not
  reject for ever.
Although he causes grief, he will have compassion
  according to the abundance of his steadfast love;
for he does not willingly afflict
  or grieve anyone.

A reading from the Book of Daniel. (12.1-3,[5-9])
'At the time of the end Michael, the great prince, the protector of your
people, shall arise. There shall be a time of anguish, such as has
never occurred since nations first came into existence. But at that
time your people shall be delivered, everyone who is found written
in the book. Many of those who sleep in the dust of the earth shall
awake, some to everlasting life, and some to shame and everlasting
contempt. Those who are wise shall shine like the brightness of the
sky, and those who lead many to righteousness, like the stars for ever
and ever.'
[⁵ Then I, Daniel, looked, and two others appeared, one standing on
this bank of the stream and one on the other. One of them said to the
man clothed in linen, who was upstream, 'How long shall it be until
the end of these wonders?' The man clothed in linen, who was
upstream, raised his right hand and his left hand toward heaven.
And I heard him swear by the one who lives for ever that it would be
for a time, two times, and half a time, and that when the shattering of
the power of the holy people comes to an end, all these things would
be accomplished. I heard but could not understand; so I said, 'My
lord, what shall be the outcome of these things?' He said, 'Go your
way, Daniel, for the words are to remain secret and sealed until the
time of the end.']

A reading from the Wisdom of Solomon. (3.1-5,9)
  The souls of the righteous are in the hand of God,
  and no torment will ever touch them.
  In the eyes of the foolish they seemed to have died,
  and their departure was thought to be a disaster,
  and their going from us to be their destruction;
  but they are at peace.
  For though in the sight of others they were punished,
  their hope is full of immortality.
  Having been disciplined a little, they will receive great good,
  because God tested them and found them worthy of himself.
⁹ Those who trust in him will understand truth,

and the faithful will abide with him in love,
because grace and mercy are upon his holy ones,
and he watches over his elect.

A reading from the Wisdom of Solomon. *(2.22 – 3.5,9)*
They did not know the secret purposes of God,
nor hoped for the wages of holiness,
nor discerned the prize for blameless souls;
for God created us for incorruption,
and made us in the image of his own eternity,
but through the devil's envy death entered the world,
and those who belong to his company experience it.

But the souls of the righteous are in the hand of God,
and no torment will ever touch them.
In the eyes of the foolish they seemed to have died,
and their departure was thought to be a disaster,
and their going from us to be their destruction;
but they are at peace.
For though in the sight of others they were punished,
their hope is full of immortality.
Having been disciplined a little, they will receive great good,
because God tested them and found them worthy of himself;
9 Those who trust in him will understand truth,
and the faithful will abide with him in love,
because grace and mercy are upon his holy ones,
and he watches over his elect.

A readings from the Wisdom of Solomon. *(4.8-11,13-15)*
Old age is not honoured for length of time,
or measured by number of years;
but understanding is grey hair for anyone,
and a blameless life is ripe old age.

There were some who pleased God and were loved by him,
and while living among sinners were taken up.
They were caught up so that evil
might not change their understanding
or guile deceive their souls.
13 Being perfected in a short time, they fulfilled long years;
for their souls were pleasing to the Lord,
therefore he took them quickly from the midst of wickedness.
Yet the peoples saw and did not understand,

or take such a thing to heart,
that God's grace and mercy are with his elect,
and that he watches over his holy ones.

A reading from the book Ecclesiasticus. (38.16-23)
My child, let your tears fall for the dead,
  and as one in great pain begin the lament.
Lay out the body with due ceremony,
  and do not neglect the burial.
Let your weeping be bitter and your wailing fervent;
  make your mourning worthy of the departed,
for one day, or two, to avoid criticism;
  then be comforted for your grief.
For grief may result in death,
  and a sorrowful heart saps one's strength.
When a person is taken away, sorrow is over;
  but the life of the poor weighs down the heart.
Do not give your heart to grief;
  drive it away, and remember your own end.
Do not forget, there is no coming back;
  you do the dead no good, and you injure yourself.
Remember his fate, for yours is like it;
  yesterday it was his, and today it is yours.
When the dead is at rest, let his remembrance rest too,
  and be comforted for him when his spirit has departed.

Psalm 6; Psalm 23; Psalm 25; Psalm 27; Psalm 32; Psalm 38.9-end; Psalm 42; Psalm 84.1-4; Psalm 90; Psalm 116; Psalm 118.4-end; Psalm 121; Psalm 139

A reading from the Letter of Paul to the Romans. (6.3-8,[9-11])
Do you not know that all of us who have been baptized into Christ Jesus were baptized into his death? Therefore we have been buried with him by baptism into death, so that, just as Christ was raised from the dead by the glory of the Father, so we too might walk in newness of life.

For if we have been united with him in a death like his, we will certainly be united with him in a resurrection like his. We know that our old self was crucified with him so that the body of sin might be destroyed, and we might no longer be enslaved to sin. For whoever has died is freed from sin. But if we have died with Christ, we believe that we will also live with him.

[⁹ We know that Christ, being raised from the dead, will never die again; death no longer has dominion over him. The death he died, he died to sin, once for all; but the life he lives, he lives to God. So you also must consider yourselves dead to sin and alive to God in Christ Jesus.]

A reading from the Letter of Paul to the Romans. (8.18-25,[26-30])
I consider that the sufferings of this present time are not worth comparing with the glory about to be revealed to us. For the creation waits with eager longing for the revealing of the children of God; for the creation was subjected to futility, not of its own will but by the will of the one who subjected it, in hope that the creation itself will be set free from its bondage to decay and will obtain the freedom of the glory of the children of God. We know that the whole creation has been groaning in labour pains until now; and not only the creation, but we ourselves, who have the first fruits of the Spirit, groan inwardly while we wait for adoption, the redemption of our bodies. For in hope we were saved. Now hope that is seen is not hope. For who hopes for what is seen? But if we hope for what we do not see, we wait for it with patience.
[²⁶ Likewise the Spirit helps us in our weakness; for we do not know how to pray as we ought, but that very Spirit intercedes with sighs too deep for words. And God, who searches the heart, knows what is the mind of the Spirit, because the Spirit intercedes for the saints according to the will of God.

We know that all things work together for good for those who love God, who are called according to his purpose. For those whom he foreknew he also predestined to be conformed to the image of his Son, in order that he might be the firstborn within a large family. And those whom he predestined he also called; and those whom he called he also justified; and those whom he justified he also glorified.]

A reading from the Letter of Paul to the Romans. (8.18,28,35,37-end)
I consider that the sufferings of this present time are not worth comparing with the glory about to be revealed to us.
²⁸ We know that all things work together for good for those who love God, who are called according to his purpose.
³⁵ Who will separate us from the love of Christ? Will hardship, or distress, or persecution, or famine, or nakedness, or peril, or sword?
³⁷ No, in all these things we are more than conquerors through him who loved us. For I am convinced that neither death, nor life, nor angels, nor rulers, nor things present, nor things to come, nor pow-

ers, nor height, nor depth, nor anything else in all creation, will be able to separate us from the love of God in Christ Jesus our Lord.

A reading from the Letter of Paul to the Romans. (8.31-end)
What are we to say about these things? If God is for us, who is against us? He who did not withhold his own Son, but gave him up for all of us, will he not with him also give us everything else? Who will bring any charge against God's elect? It is God who justifies. Who is to condemn? It is Christ Jesus, who died, yes, who was raised, who is at the right hand of God, who indeed intercedes for us. Who will separate us from the love of Christ? Will hardship, or distress, or persecution, or famine, or nakedness, or peril, or sword? As it is written,
> 'For your sake we are being killed all day long;
>   we are accounted as sheep to be slaughtered.'

No, in all these things we are more than conquerors through him who loved us. For I am convinced that neither death, nor life, nor angels, nor rulers, nor things present, nor things to come, nor powers, nor height, nor depth, nor anything else in all creation, will be able to separate us from the love of God in Christ Jesus our Lord.

A reading from the Letter of Paul to the Romans. (14.7-12)
We do not live to ourselves, and we do not die to ourselves. If we live, we live to the Lord, and if we die, we die to the Lord; so then, whether we live or whether we die, we are the Lord's. For to this end Christ died and lived again, so that he might be Lord of both the dead and the living.

Why do you pass judgment on your brother or sister? Or you, why do you despise your brother or sister? For we will all stand before the judgment seat of God. For it is written,
> 'As I live, says the Lord, every knee shall bow to me,
>   and every tongue shall give praise to God.'

So then, each of us will be accountable to God.

A reading from the First Letter of Paul to the Corinthians. (Chapter 13)
If I speak in the tongues of mortals and of angels, but do not have love, I am a noisy gong or a clanging cymbal. And if I have prophetic powers, and understand all mysteries and all knowledge, and if I have all faith, so as to remove mountains, but do not have love, I am nothing. If I give away all my possessions, and if I hand over my body so that I may boast, but do not have love, I gain nothing.

Love is patient; love is kind; love is not envious or boastful or arrogant or rude. It does not insist on its own way; it is not irritable or resentful; it does not rejoice in wrongdoing, but rejoices in the truth. It bears all things, believes all things, hopes all things, endures all things.

Love never ends. But as for prophecies, they will come to an end; as for tongues, they will cease; as for knowledge, it will come to an end. For we know only in part, and we prophesy only in part; but when the complete comes, the partial will come to an end. When I was a child, I spoke like a child, I thought like a child, I reasoned like a child; when I became an adult, I put an end to childish ways. For now we see in a mirror, dimly, but then we will see face to face. Now I know only in part; then I will know fully, even as I have been fully known. And now faith, hope, and love abide, these three; and the greatest of these is love.

A reading from the First Letter of Paul to the Corinthians.
(15.1-26,35-38,42-44a,53-end)
I would remind you, brothers and sisters, of the good news that I proclaimed to you, which you in turn received, in which also you stand, through which also you are being saved, if you hold firmly to the message that I proclaimed to you – unless you have come to believe in vain.

For I handed on to you as of first importance what I in turn had received: that Christ died for our sins in accordance with the scriptures, and that he was buried, and that he was raised on the third day in accordance with the scriptures, and that he appeared to Cephas, then to the twelve. Then he appeared to more than five hundred brothers and sisters at one time, most of whom are still alive, though some have died. Then he appeared to James, then to all the apostles. Last of all, as to one untimely born, he appeared also to me. For I am the least of the apostles, unfit to be called an apostle, because I persecuted the church of God. But by the grace of God I am what I am, and his grace toward me has not been in vain. On the contrary, I worked harder than any of them – though it was not I, but the grace of God that is with me. Whether then it was I or they, so we proclaim and so you have come to believe.

Now if Christ is proclaimed as raised from the dead, how can some of you say there is no resurrection of the dead? If there is no resurrection of the dead, then Christ has not been raised; and if Christ has not been raised, then our proclamation has been in vain and your faith has been in vain. We are even found to be misrepresenting God, because we testified of God that he raised Christ – whom he did not raise if it is true that the dead are not raised. For if the dead are not raised, then Christ has not been raised. If Christ has not been raised, your faith is futile and you are still in your sins. Then those also who have died in Christ have perished. If for this life only we have hoped in Christ, we are of all people most to be pitied.

But in fact Christ has been raised from the dead, the first fruits of those who have died. For since death came through a human being, the resurrection of the dead has also come through a human being; for as all die in Adam, so all will be made alive in Christ. But each in his own order: Christ the first fruits, then at his coming those who belong to Christ. Then comes the end, when he hands over the kingdom to God the Father, after he has destroyed every ruler and every authority and power. For he must reign until he has put all his enemies under his feet. The last enemy to be destroyed is death.

[35] But someone will ask, 'How are the dead raised? With what kind of body do they come?' Fool! What you sow does not come to life unless it dies. And as for what you sow, you do not sow the body that is to be, but a bare seed, perhaps of wheat or of some other grain. But God gives it a body as he has chosen, and to each kind of seed its own body.

[42] So it is with the resurrection of the dead. What is sown is perishable, what is raised is imperishable. It is sown in dishonour, it is raised in glory. It is sown in weakness, it is raised in power. It is sown a physical body, it is raised a spiritual body.

[53] For this perishable body must put on imperishability, and this mortal body must put on immortality. When this perishable body puts on imperishability, and this mortal body puts on immortality, then the saying that is written will be fulfilled:

'Death has been swallowed up in victory.'

'Where, O death, is your victory?

Where, O death, is your sting?'

The sting of death is sin, and the power of sin is the law. But thanks be to God, who gives us the victory through our Lord Jesus Christ.

Therefore, my belovèd, be steadfast, immovable, always excelling in the work of the Lord, because you know that in the Lord your labour is not in vain.

A reading from the First Letter of Paul to the Corinthians. (15.20-end)
Christ has been raised from the dead, the first fruits of those who have died. For since death came through a human being, the resurrection of the dead has also come through a human being; for as all die in Adam, so all will be made alive in Christ. But each in his own order: Christ the first fruits, then at his coming those who belong

to Christ. Then comes the end, when he hands over the kingdom to God the Father, after he has destroyed every ruler and every authority and power. For he must reign until he has put all his enemies under his feet. The last enemy to be destroyed is death. For 'God has put all things in subjection under his feet.' But when it says, 'All things are put in subjection,' it is plain that this does not include the one who put all things in subjection under him. When all things are subjected to him, then the Son himself will also be subjected to the one who put all things in subjection under him, so that God may be all in all.

Otherwise, what will those people do who receive baptism on behalf of the dead? If the dead are not raised at all, why are people baptized on their behalf?

And why are we putting ourselves in danger every hour? I die every day! That is as certain, brothers and sisters, as my boasting of you – a boast that I make in Christ Jesus our Lord. If with merely human hopes I fought with wild animals at Ephesus, what would I have gained by it? If the dead are not raised,

'Let us eat and drink,
for tomorrow we die.'

Do not be deceived:

'Bad company ruins good morals.'

Come to a sober and right mind, and sin no more; for some people have no knowledge of God. I say this to your shame.

But someone will ask, 'How are the dead raised? With what kind of body do they come?' Fool! What you sow does not come to life unless it dies. And as for what you sow, you do not sow the body that is to be, but a bare seed, perhaps of wheat or of some other grain. But God gives it a body as he has chosen, and to each kind of seed its own body. Not all flesh is alike, but there is one flesh for human beings, another for animals, another for birds, and another for fish. There are both heavenly bodies and earthly bodies, but the glory of the heavenly is one thing, and that of the earthly is another. There is one glory of the sun, and another glory of the moon, and another glory of the stars; indeed, star differs from star in glory.

So it is with the resurrection of the dead. What is sown is perishable, what is raised is imperishable. It is sown in dishonour, it is raised in glory. It is sown in weakness, it is raised in power. It is sown a physical body, it is raised a spiritual body. If there is a physical body, there is also a spiritual body. Thus it is written, 'The first man, Adam, became a living being'; the last Adam became a life-giving spirit. But it is not the spiritual that is first, but the physical, and then the spiritual. The first man was from the earth, a man of dust; the second man is from heaven. As was the man of dust, so are those who are of the dust; and as is the man of heaven, so are those who are of heaven. Just as we have borne the image of the man of dust, we will also bear the image of the man of heaven.

What I am saying, brothers and sisters, is this: flesh and blood cannot inherit the kingdom of God, nor does the perishable inherit the imperishable. Listen, I will tell you a mystery! We will not all die, but we will all be changed, in a moment, in the twinkling of an eye, at the last trumpet. For the trumpet will sound, and the dead will be raised imperishable, and we will be changed. For this perishable body must put on imperishability, and this mortal body must put on immortality. When this perishable body puts on imperishability, and this mortal body puts on immortality, then the saying that is written will be fulfilled:

'Death has been swallowed up in victory.'

'Where, O death, is your victory?

Where, O death, is your sting?'

The sting of death is sin, and the power of sin is the law. But thanks be to God, who gives us the victory through our Lord Jesus Christ.

Therefore, my belovèd, be steadfast, immovable, always excelling in the work of the Lord, because you know that in the Lord your labour is not in vain.

A reading from the Second Letter of Paul to the Corinthians. (4.7-15)
We have this treasure in clay jars, so that it may be made clear that this extraordinary power belongs to God and does not come from us. We are afflicted in every way, but not crushed; perplexed, but not driven to despair; persecuted, but not forsaken; struck down, but not destroyed; always carrying in the body the death of Jesus, so that the life of Jesus may also be made visible in our bodies. For while we live, we are always being given up to death for Jesus' sake, so that the life of Jesus may be made visible in our mortal flesh. So death is at work in us, but life in you.

But just as we have the same spirit of faith that is in accordance with scripture – 'I believed, and so I spoke' – we also believe, and so we speak, because we know that the one who raised the Lord Jesus will raise us also with Jesus, and will bring us with you into his presence. Yes, everything is for your sake, so that grace, as it extends to more and more people, may increase thanksgiving, to the glory of God.

A reading from the Second Letter of Paul to the Corinthians.

(4.16 – 5.10)

We do not lose heart. Even though our outer nature is wasting away, our inner nature is being renewed day by day. For this slight momentary affliction is preparing us for an eternal weight of glory beyond all measure, because we look not at what can be seen but at what cannot be seen; for what can be seen is temporary, but what cannot be seen is eternal.

For we know that if the earthly tent we live in is destroyed, we have a building from God, a house not made with hands, eternal in the heavens. For in this tent we groan, longing to be clothed with our heavenly dwelling – if indeed, when we have taken it off we will not be found naked. For while we are still in this tent, we groan under our burden, because we wish not to be unclothed but to be further clothed, so that what is mortal may be swallowed up by life. He who has prepared us for this very thing is God, who has given us the Spirit as a guarantee.

So we are always confident; even though we know that while we are at home in the body we are away from the Lord – for we walk by faith, not by sight. Yes, we do have confidence, and we would rather be away from the body and at home with the Lord. So whether we are at home or away, we make it our aim to please him. For all of us must appear before the judgment seat of Christ, so that each may receive recompense for what has been done in the body, whether good or evil.

A reading from the Letter of Paul to the Ephesians. *(3.14-19,[20-end])*
I bow my knees before the Father, from whom every family in heaven and on earth takes its name. I pray that, according to the riches of his glory, he may grant that you may be strengthened in your inner being with power through his Spirit, and that Christ may dwell in your hearts through faith, as you are being rooted and grounded in love. I pray that you may have the power to comprehend, with all the saints, what is the breadth and length and height and depth, and to know the love of Christ that surpasses knowledge, so that you may be filled with all the fullness of God.
[20 Now to him who by the power at work within us is able to accomplish abundantly far more than all we can ask or imagine, to him be glory in the church and in Christ Jesus to all generations, for ever and ever. Amen.]

A reading from the Letter of Paul to the Philippians. (3.10-end)

I want to know Christ and the power of his resurrection and the sharing of his sufferings by becoming like him in his death, if somehow I may attain the resurrection from the dead.

Not that I have already obtained this or have already reached the goal; but I press on to make it my own, because Christ Jesus has made me his own. Belovèd, I do not consider that I have made it my own; but this one thing I do: forgetting what lies behind and straining forward to what lies ahead, I press on toward the goal for the prize of the heavenly call of God in Christ Jesus. Let those of us then who are mature be of the same mind; and if you think differently about anything, this too God will reveal to you. Only let us hold fast to what we have attained.

Brothers and sisters, join in imitating me, and observe those who live according to the example you have in us. For many live as enemies of the cross of Christ; I have often told you of them, and now I tell you even with tears. Their end is destruction; their god is the belly; and their glory is in their shame; their minds are set on earthly things. But our citizenship is in heaven, and it is from there that we are expecting a Saviour, the Lord Jesus Christ. He will transform the body of our humiliation that it may be conformed to the body of his glory, by the power that also enables him to make all things subject to himself.

A reading from the First Letter of Paul to the Thessalonians. (4.13-end)

We do not want you to be uninformed, brothers and sisters, about those who have died, so that you may not grieve as others do who have no hope. For since we believe that Jesus died and rose again, even so, through Jesus, God will bring with him those who have died. For this we declare to you by the word of the Lord, that we who are alive, who are left until the coming of the Lord, will by no means precede those who have died. For the Lord himself, with a cry of command, with the archangel's call and with the sound of God's trumpet, will descend from heaven, and the dead in Christ will rise first. Then we who are alive, who are left, will be caught up in the clouds together with them to meet the Lord in the air; and so we will be with the Lord for ever. Therefore encourage one another with these words.

A reading from the Second Letter of Paul to Timothy. (2.8-13)
Remember Jesus Christ, raised from the dead, a descendant of David
– that is my gospel, for which I suffer hardship, even to the point of
being chained like a criminal. But the word of God is not chained.
Therefore I endure everything for the sake of the elect, so that they
may also obtain the salvation that is in Christ Jesus, with eternal
glory. The saying is sure:
> If we have died with him, we will also live with him;
> if we endure, we will also reign with him;
> if we deny him, he will also deny us;
> if we are faithless, he remains faithful –
> for he cannot deny himself.

A reading from the First Letter of Peter. (1.3-9)
Blessèd be the God and Father of our Lord Jesus Christ! By his great
mercy he has given us a new birth into a living hope through the
resurrection of Jesus Christ from the dead, and into an inheritance
that is imperishable, undefiled, and unfading, kept in heaven for you,
who are being protected by the power of God through faith for a
salvation ready to be revealed in the last time. In this you rejoice,
even if now for a little while you have had to suffer various trials, so
that the genuineness of your faith – being more precious than gold
that, though perishable, is tested by fire – may be found to result in
praise and glory and honour when Jesus Christ is revealed.
Although you have not seen him, you love him; and even though
you do not see him now, you believe in him and rejoice with an
indescribable and glorious joy, for you are receiving the outcome of
your faith, the salvation of your souls.

A reading from the First Letter of John. (3.1-3)
See what love the Father has given us, that we should be called
children of God; and that is what we are. The reason the world
does not know us is that it did not know him. Belovèd, we are God's
children now; what we will be has not yet been revealed. What we
do know is this: when he is revealed, we will be like him, for we
will see him as he is. And all who have this hope in him purify
themselves, just as he is pure.

A reading from the Revelation to John. (7.9-end)
I looked, and there was a great multitude that no one could count,
from every nation, from all tribes and peoples and languages,
standing before the throne and before the Lamb, robed in white, with
palm branches in their hands. They cried out in a loud voice, saying,

'Salvation belongs to our God who is seated on the throne,
 and to the Lamb!'
And all the angels stood around the throne and around the elders
and the four living creatures, and they fell on their faces before the
throne and worshipped God, singing,

'Amen! Blessing and glory and wisdom
and thanksgiving and honour
and power and might
be to our God for ever and ever! Amen.'

Then one of the elders addressed me, saying, 'Who are these, robed
in white, and where have they come from?' I said to him, 'Sir, you
are the one that knows.' Then he said to me, 'These are they who
have come out of the great ordeal; they have washed their robes and
made them white in the blood of the Lamb.

For this reason they are before the throne of God,
 and worship him day and night within his temple,
 and the one who is seated on the throne will shelter them.
They will hunger no more, and thirst no more;
 the sun will not strike them,
 nor any scorching heat;
for the Lamb at the centre of the throne will be their shepherd,
 and he will guide them to springs of the water of life,
 and God will wipe away every tear from their eyes.'

A reading from the Revelation to John. (21.1-7)

I saw a new heaven and a new earth; for the first heaven and the first
earth had passed away, and the sea was no more. And I saw the holy
city, the new Jerusalem, coming down out of heaven from God,
prepared as a bride adorned for her husband. And I heard a loud
voice from the throne saying,

See, the home of God is among mortals.
 He will dwell with them as their God;
they will be his peoples,
 and God himself will be with them;
 he will wipe every tear from their eyes.
Death will be no more;
 mourning and crying and pain will be no more,
 for the first things have passed away.'

And the one who was seated on the throne said, 'See, I am making
all things new.' Also he said, 'Write this, for these words are
trustworthy and true.' Then he said to me, 'It is done! I am the Alpha
and the Omega, the beginning and the end. To the thirsty I will

give water as a gift from the spring of the water of life. Those who conquer will inherit these things, and I will be their God and they will be my children.'

A reading from the Revelation to John. (21.22-end & 22.3b-5)
I saw no temple in the city, for its temple is the Lord God the Almighty and the Lamb. And the city has no need of sun or moon to shine on it, for the glory of God is its light, and its lamp is the Lamb. The nations will walk by its light, and the kings of the earth will bring their glory into it. Its gates will never be shut by day – and there will be no night there. People will bring into it the glory and the honour of the nations. But nothing unclean will enter it, nor anyone who practises abomination or falsehood, but only those who are written in the Lamb's book of life.
22.3b But the throne of God and of the Lamb will be in it, and his servants will worship him; they will see his face, and his name will be on their foreheads. And there will be no more night; they need no light of lamp or sun, for the Lord God will be their light, and they will reign for ever and ever.

A reading from the Gospel according to Matthew. (18.1-5,10)
The disciples came to Jesus and asked, 'Who is the greatest in the kingdom of heaven?' He called a child, whom he put among them, and said, 'Truly I tell you, unless you change and become like children, you will never enter the kingdom of heaven. Whoever becomes humble like this child is the greatest in the kingdom of heaven. Whoever welcomes one such child in my name welcomes me.
10 'Take care that you do not despise one of these little ones; for, I tell you, in heaven their angels continually see the face of my Father in heaven.'

A reading from the Gospel according to Matthew. (25.31-end)
Jesus said to his disciples, 'When the Son of Man comes in his glory, and all the angels with him, then he will sit on the throne of his glory. All the nations will be gathered before him, and he will separate people one from another as a shepherd separates the sheep from the goats, and he will put the sheep at his right hand and the goats at the left.
Then the king will say to those at his right hand, "Come, you that are blessed by my Father, inherit the kingdom prepared for you from the foundation of the world; for I was hungry and you gave me food,

I was thirsty and you gave me something to drink, I was a stranger and you welcomed me, I was naked and you gave me clothing, I was sick and you took care of me, I was in prison and you visited me." Then the righteous will answer him, "Lord, when was it that we saw you hungry and gave you food, or thirsty and gave you something to drink? And when was it that we saw you a stranger and welcomed you, or naked and gave you clothing? And when was it that we saw you sick or in prison and visited you?" And the king will answer them, "Truly I tell you, just as you did it to one of the least of these who are members of my family, you did it to me."

Then he will say to those at his left hand, "You that are accursed, depart from me into the eternal fire prepared for the devil and his angels; for I was hungry and you gave me no food, I was thirsty and you gave me nothing to drink, I was a stranger and you did not welcome me, naked and you did not give me clothing, sick and in prison and you did not visit me." Then they also will answer, "Lord, when was it that we saw you hungry or thirsty or a stranger or naked or sick or in prison, and did not take care of you?" Then he will answer them, "Truly I tell you, just as you did not do it to one of the least of these, you did not do it to me." And these will go away into eternal punishment, but the righteous into eternal life.'

A reading from the Gospel according to Mark. (10.13-16)
People were bringing little children to Jesus in order that he might touch them; and the disciples spoke sternly to them. But when Jesus saw this, he was indignant and said to them, 'Let the little children come to me; do not stop them; for it is to such as these that the kingdom of God belongs. Truly I tell you, whoever does not receive the kingdom of God as a little child will never enter it.' And he took them up in his arms, laid his hands on them, and blessed them.

A reading from the Gospel according to Mark. (15.33-39 & 16.1-6)
When it was noon, darkness came over the whole land until three in the afternoon. At three o'clock Jesus cried out with a loud voice, 'Eloi, Eloi, lema sabachthani?' which means, 'My God, my God, why have you forsaken me?' When some of the bystanders heard it, they said, 'Listen, he is calling for Elijah.' And someone ran, filled a sponge with sour wine, put it on a stick, and gave it to him to drink, saying, 'Wait, let us see whether Elijah will come to take him down.' Then Jesus gave a loud cry and breathed his last.

And the curtain of the temple was torn in two, from top to bottom. Now when the centurion, who stood facing him, saw that in this way he breathed his last, he said, 'Truly this man was God's Son!'

16.1 When the sabbath was over, Mary Magdalene, and Mary the mother of James, and Salome bought spices, so that they might go and anoint him. And very early on the first day of the week, when the sun had risen, they went to the tomb. They had been saying to one another, 'Who will roll away the stone for us from the entrance to the tomb?' When they looked up, they saw that the stone, which was very large, had already been rolled back. As they entered the tomb, they saw a young man, dressed in a white robe, sitting on the right side; and they were alarmed. But he said to them, 'Do not be alarmed; you are looking for Jesus of Nazareth, who was crucified. He has been raised; he is not here. Look, there is the place they laid him.'

A reading from the Gospel according to Luke. (12.35-40)

Jesus said to his disciples, 'Be dressed for action and have your lamps lit; be like those who are waiting for their master to return from the wedding banquet, so that they may open the door for him as soon as he comes and knocks. Blessèd are those slaves whom the master finds alert when he comes; truly I tell you, he will fasten his belt and have them sit down to eat, and he will come and serve them. If he comes during the middle of the night, or near dawn, and finds them so, blessèd are those slaves.

'But know this: if the owner of the house had known at what hour the thief was coming, he would not have let his house be broken into. You also must be ready, for the Son of Man is coming at an unexpected hour.'

A reading from the Gospel according to Luke. (24.1-9,[10-11])

On the first day of the week, at early dawn, the women came to the tomb, taking the spices that they had prepared. They found the stone rolled away from the tomb, but when they went in, they did not find the body. While they were perplexed about this, suddenly two men in dazzling clothes stood beside them. The women were terrified and bowed their faces to the ground, but the men said to them, 'Why do you look for the living among the dead? He is not here, but has risen. Remember how he told you, while he was still in Galilee, that the Son of Man must be handed over to sinners, and be crucified, and on the third day rise again.' Then they remembered his words, and returning from the tomb, they told all this to the eleven and to all the rest.

[10 Now it was Mary Magdalene, Joanna, Mary the mother of James, and the other women with them who told this to the apostles. But these words seemed to them an idle tale, and they did not believe them.]

A reading from the Gospel according to John. *(5.[19-20],21-29)*
[Jesus said to the Jews, 'Very truly, I tell you, the Son can do nothing on his own, but only what he sees the Father doing; for whatever the Father does, the Son does likewise. The Father loves the Son and shows him all that he himself is doing; and he will show him greater works than these, so that you will be astonished.]
21 'Indeed, just as the Father raises the dead and gives them life, so also the Son gives life to whomever he wishes. The Father judges no one but has given all judgment to the Son, so that all may honour the Son just as they honour the Father. Anyone who does not honour the Son does not honour the Father who sent him. Very truly, I tell you, anyone who hears my word and believes him who sent me has eternal life, and does not come under judgment, but has passed from death to life.

'Very truly, I tell you, the hour is coming, and is now here, when the dead will hear the voice of the Son of God, and those who hear will live. For just as the Father has life in himself, so he has granted the Son also to have life in himself; and he has given him authority to execute judgment, because he is the Son of Man. Do not be astonished at this; for the hour is coming when all who are in their graves will hear his voice and will come out – those who have done good, to the resurrection of life, and those who have done evil, to the resurrection of condemnation.'

A reading from the Gospel according to John. *(6.35-40,[53-58])*
Jesus said to the crowd, 'I am the bread of life. Whoever comes to me will never be hungry, and whoever believes in me will never be thirsty. But I said to you that you have seen me and yet do not believe. Everything that the Father gives me will come to me, and anyone who comes to me I will never drive away; for I have come down from heaven, not to do my own will, but the will of him who sent me. And this is the will of him who sent me, that I should lose nothing of all that he has given me, but raise it up on the last day. This is indeed the will of my Father, that all who see the Son and believe in him may have eternal life; and I will raise them up on the last day.'
[53 'Very truly, I tell you, unless you eat the flesh of the Son of Man and drink his blood, you have no life in you. Those who eat my flesh and drink my blood have eternal life, and I will raise them up on the

last day; for my flesh is true food and my blood is true drink. Those who eat my flesh and drink my blood abide in me, and I in them. Just as the living Father sent me, and I live because of the Father, so whoever eats me will live because of me. This is the bread that came down from heaven, not like that which your ancestors ate, and they died. But the one who eats this bread will live for ever.']

A reading from the Gospel according to John. (10.27-28)
Jesus said to the Jews, 'My sheep hear my voice. I know them, and they follow me. I give them eternal life, and they will never perish. No one will snatch them out of my hand.'

A reading from the Gospel according to John. (11.17-27)
When Jesus arrived in Bethany, he found that Lazarus had already been in the tomb four days. Now Bethany was near Jerusalem, some two miles away, and many of the Jews had come to Martha and Mary to console them about their brother. When Martha heard that Jesus was coming, she went and met him, while Mary stayed at home. Martha said to Jesus, 'Lord, if you had been here, my brother would not have died. But even now I know that God will give you whatever you ask of him.' Jesus said to her, 'Your brother will rise again.' Martha said to him, 'I know that he will rise again in the resurrection on the last day.' Jesus said to her, 'I am the resurrection and the life. Those who believe in me, even though they die, will live, and everyone who lives and believes in me will never die. Do you believe this?' She said to him, 'Yes, Lord, I believe that you are the Messiah, the Son of God, the one coming into the world.'

A reading from the Gospel according to John. (14.1-6)
Jesus said to his disciples, 'Do not let your hearts be troubled. Believe in God, believe also in me. In my Father's house there are many dwelling places. If it were not so, would I have told you that I go to prepare a place for you? And if I go and prepare a place for you, I will come again and will take you to myself, so that where I am, there you may be also. And you know the way to the place where I am going.' Thomas said to him, 'Lord, we do not know where you are going. How can we know the way?' Jesus said to him, 'I am the way, and the truth, and the life. No one comes to the Father except through me.'

A reading from the Gospel according to John. (19.38-end)
Joseph of Arimathea, who was a disciple of Jesus, though a secret one because of his fear of the Jews, asked Pilate to let him take away the body of Jesus. Pilate gave him permission; so he came and removed his body. Nicodemus, who had at first come to Jesus by night, also came, bringing a mixture of myrrh and aloes, weighing about a hundred pounds. They took the body of Jesus and wrapped it with the spices in linen cloths, according to the burial custom of the Jews. Now there was a garden in the place where he was crucified, and in the garden there was a new tomb in which no one had ever been laid. And so, because it was the Jewish day of Preparation, and the tomb was nearby, they laid Jesus there.

A reading from the Gospel according to John. (20.1-11a)
Early on the first day of the week, while it was still dark, Mary Magdalene came to the tomb and saw that the stone had been removed from the tomb. So she ran and went to Simon Peter and the other disciple, the one whom Jesus loved, and said to them, 'They have taken the Lord out of the tomb, and we do not know where they have laid him.' Then Peter and the other disciple set out and went toward the tomb. The two were running together, but the other disciple outran Peter and reached the tomb first. He bent down to look in and saw the linen wrappings lying there, but he did not go in. Then Simon Peter came, following him, and went into the tomb. He saw the linen wrappings lying there, and the cloth that had been on Jesus' head, not lying with the linen wrappings but rolled up in a place by itself. Then the other disciple, who reached the tomb first, also went in, and he saw and believed; for as yet they did not understand the scripture, that he must rise from the dead. Then the disciples returned to their homes.

But Mary stood weeping outside the tomb.

Particularly at the Funeral of a Child

A reading from the Song of Solomon. (2.10-13)
My belovèd speaks and says to me:
   'Arise, my love, my fair one,
     and come away;
   for now the winter is past,
     the rain is over and gone.
   The flowers appear on the earth;
     the time of singing has come,
   and the voice of the turtledove
     is heard in our land.
   The fig tree puts forth its figs,
     and the vines are in blossom;
     they give forth fragrance.
   Arise, my love, my fair one,
     and come away.'

A reading from the prophecy of Isaiah. (49.15-16)
   Can a woman forget her nursing child,
     or show no compassion for the child of her womb?
   Even these may forget,
     yet I will not forget you.
   See, I have inscribed you on the palms of my hands;
     your walls are continually before me.

A reading from the prophecy of Jeremiah. (1.4-8)
   The word of the Lord came to me saying,
   'Before I formed you in the womb I knew you,
   and before you were born I consecrated you;
   I appointed you a prophet to the nations.'
Then I said, 'Ah, Lord God! Truly I do not know how to speak, for
I am only a boy.' But the Lord said to me,
   'Do not say, "I am only a boy";
   for you shall go to all to whom I send you,
   and you shall speak whatever I command you.
   Do not be afraid of them,
   for I am with you to deliver you,' says the Lord.

A reading from the prophecy of Jeremiah. (31.15-17)
Thus says the Lord:

A voice is heard in Ramah,
lamentation and bitter weeping.
Rachel is weeping for her children;
she refuses to be comforted for her children,
because they are no more.

Thus says the Lord:

Keep your voice from weeping,
and your eyes from tears;
for there is a reward for your work,
says the Lord:
they shall come back from the land of the enemy;
there is hope for your future,
says the Lord:
your children shall come back to their own country.

Psalm 23; Psalm 84.1-4

A reading from the Letter of Paul to the Romans. (8.18,28,35,37-end)
I consider that the sufferings of this present time are not worth comparing with the glory about to be revealed to us. [28] We know that all things work together for good for those who love God, who are called according to his purpose. [35] Who will separate us from the love of Christ? Will hardship, or distress, or persecution, or famine, or nakedness, or peril, or sword? [37] No, in all these things we are more than conquerors through him who loved us. For I am convinced that neither death, nor life, nor angels, nor rulers, nor things present, nor things to come, nor powers, nor height, nor depth, nor anything else in all creation, will be able to separate us from the love of God in Christ Jesus our Lord.

A reading from the First Letter of Paul to the Corinthians. (Chapter 13)
If I speak in the tongues of mortals and of angels, but do not have love, I am a noisy gong or a clanging cymbal. And if I have prophetic powers, and understand all mysteries and all knowledge, and if I have all faith, so as to remove mountains, but do not have love, I am nothing. If I give away all my possessions, and if I hand over my body so that I may boast, but do not have love, I gain nothing.

Love is patient; love is kind; love is not envious or boastful or arrogant or rude. It does not insist on its own way; it is not irritable or resentful; it does not rejoice in wrongdoing, but rejoices in the truth. It bears all things, believes all things, hopes all things, endures

Funeral of a Child

all things.

Love never ends. But as for prophecies, they will come to an end; as for tongues, they will cease; as for knowledge, it will come to an end. For we know only in part, and we prophesy only in part; but when the complete comes, the partial will come to an end. When I was a child, I spoke like a child, I thought like a child, I reasoned like a child; when I became an adult, I put an end to childish ways. For now we see in a mirror, dimly, but then we will see face to face. Now I know only in part; then I will know fully, even as I have been fully known. And now faith, hope, and love abide, these three; and the greatest of these is love.

A reading from the Letter of Paul to the Ephesians. *(3.14-19)*
I bow my knees before the Father, from whom every family in heaven and on earth takes its name. I pray that, according to the riches of his glory, he may grant that you may be strengthened in your inner being with power through his Spirit, and that Christ may dwell in your hearts through faith, as you are being rooted and grounded in love. I pray that you may have the power to comprehend, with all the saints, what is the breadth and length and height and depth, and to know the love of Christ that surpasses knowledge, so that you may be filled with all the fullness of God.

A reading from the Gospel according to Matthew. *(18.1-5,10)*
The disciples came to Jesus and asked, 'Who is the greatest in the kingdom of heaven?' He called a child, whom he put among them, and said, 'Truly I tell you, unless you change and become like children, you will never enter the kingdom of heaven. Whoever becomes humble like this child is the greatest in the kingdom of heaven. Whoever welcomes one such child in my name welcomes me.
[10] 'Take care that you do not despise one of these little ones; for, I tell you, in heaven their angels continually see the face of my Father in heaven.'

A reading from the Gospel according to Mark. *(10.13-16)*
People were bringing little children to Jesus in order that he might touch them; and the disciples spoke sternly to them. But when Jesus saw this, he was indignant and said to them, 'Let the little children come to me; do not stop them; for it is to such as these that the kingdom of God belongs. Truly I tell you, whoever does not receive the kingdom of God as a little child will never enter it.' And he took them up in his arms, laid his hands on them, and blessed them.

A reading from the Gospel according to John. (6.37-40)
Jesus said to the crowd, 'Everything that the Father gives me will come to me, and anyone who comes to me I will never drive away; for I have come down from heaven, not to do my own will, but the will of him who sent me. And this is the will of him who sent me, that I should lose nothing of all that he has given me, but raise it up on the last day. This is indeed the will of my Father, that all who see the Son and believe in him may have eternal life; and I will raise them up on the last day.'

A reading from the Gospel according to John. (10.27-28)
Jesus said to the Jews, 'My sheep hear my voice. I know them, and they follow me. I give them eternal life, and they will never perish. No one will snatch them out of my hand.'

After the Funeral

A reading from the Song of Solomon. *(2.10-13)*
My belovèd speaks and says to me:
 'Arise, my love, my fair one,
  and come away;
 for now the winter is past,
  the rain is over and gone.
 The flowers appear on the earth;
  the time of singing has come,
 and the voice of the turtledove
  is heard in our land.
 The fig tree puts forth its figs,
  and the vines are in blossom;
  they give forth fragrance.
 Arise, my love, my fair one,
  and come away.

Psalm 71.1-6,17-18; Psalm 121; Psalm 126.5-6; Psalm 139.6-11

A reading from the Letter of Paul to the Philippians. *(3.20 – 4.1)*
Our citizenship is in heaven, and it is from there that we are
expecting a Saviour, the Lord Jesus Christ. He will transform the
body of our humiliation that it may be conformed to the body of his
glory, by the power that also enables him to make all things subject
to himself. Therefore, my brothers and sisters, whom I love and long
for, my joy and crown, stand firm in the Lord in this way, my
belovèd.

A reading from the Gospel according to Matthew. *(11.28-end)*
Jesus said, 'Come to me, all you that are weary and are carrying
heavy burdens, and I will give you rest. Take my yoke upon you,
and learn from me; for I am gentle and humble in heart, and you will
find rest for your souls. For my yoke is easy, and my burden is light.'

A reading from the Gospel according to John. *(14.1-3)*
Jesus said to his disciples, 'Do not let your hearts be troubled. Believe
in God, believe also in me. In my Father's house there are many
dwelling places. If it were not so, would I have told you that I go to
prepare a place for you? And if I go and prepare a place for you, I
will come again and will take you to myself, so that where I am, there
you may be also.'

The Burial of Ashes

A reading from the Book of Job. *(19.23-27)*
Job said:
'O that my words were written down!
O that they were inscribed in a book!
O that with an iron pen and with lead
they were engraved on a rock for ever!
For I know that my Redeemer lives,
and that at the last he will stand upon the earth;
and after my skin has been thus destroyed,
then in my flesh I shall see God,
whom I shall see on my side,
and my eyes shall behold, and not another.
My heart faints within me!'

Psalm 16.4-10; Psalm 139.1-11,13

A reading from the First Letter of Paul to the Corinthians.
(15.35-38,42-44a)
Someone will ask, 'How are the dead raised? With what kind of body do they come?' Fool! What you sow does not come to life unless it dies. And as for what you sow, you do not sow the body that is to be, but a bare seed, perhaps of wheat or of some other grain. But God gives it a body as he has chosen, and to each kind of seed its own body.

So it is with the resurrection of the dead. What is sown is perishable, what is raised is imperishable. It is sown in dishonour, it is raised in glory. It is sown in weakness, it is raised in power. It is sown a physical body, it is raised a spiritual body.

A reading from the Revelation to John. *(21.22-end;22.3b-5)*
I saw no temple in the city, for its temple is the Lord God the Almighty and the Lamb. And the city has no need of sun or moon to shine on it, for the glory of God is its light, and its lamp is the Lamb. The nations will walk by its light, and the kings of the earth will bring their glory into it. Its gates will never be shut by day – and there will be no night there. People will bring into it the glory and the honour of the nations. But nothing unclean will enter it, nor anyone who practises abomination or falsehood, but only those who are written in the Lamb's book of life.

²²·³ᵇ But the throne of God and of the Lamb will be in it, and his servants will worship him; they will see his face, and his name will be on their foreheads. And there will be no more night; they need no light of lamp or sun, for the Lord God will be their light, and they will reign for ever and ever.

A reading from the Gospel according to John. (19.38-end)
Joseph of Arimathea, who was a disciple of Jesus, though a secret one because of his fear of the Jews, asked Pilate to let him take away the body of Jesus. Pilate gave him permission; so he came and removed his body. Nicodemus, who had at first come to Jesus by night, also came, bringing a mixture of myrrh and aloes, weighing about a hundred pounds. They took the body of Jesus and wrapped it with the spices in linen cloths, according to the burial custom of the Jews. Now there was a garden in the place where he was crucified, and in the garden there was a new tomb in which no one had ever been laid. And so, because it was the Jewish day of Preparation, and the tomb was nearby, they laid Jesus there.

The Church

The Church

Thanksgiving for the Institution of Holy Baptism

Collect
Eternal Father,
who at the baptism of Jesus
revealed him to be your Son,
anointing him with the Holy Spirit:
grant to us, who are born again by water and the Spirit,
that we may be faithful to our calling as your adopted children;
through Jesus Christ your Son our Lord,
who is alive and reigns with you
in the unity of the Holy Spirit,
one God, now and for ever.

Post Communion
Lord of all time and eternity,
you opened the heavens and revealed yourself as Father
in the baptism of Jesus your belovèd Son:
by the power of your Spirit
complete the heavenly work of our rebirth
through the waters of the new creation;
through Jesus Christ our Lord.

A reading from the prophecy of Ezekiel. (36.24-28)
I will take you from the nations, and gather you from all the countries, and bring you into your own land. I will sprinkle clean water upon you, and you shall be clean from all your uncleannesses, and from all your idols I will cleanse you. A new heart I will give you, and a new spirit I will put within you; and I will remove from your body the heart of stone and give you a heart of flesh. I will put my spirit within you, and make you follow my statutes and be careful to observe my ordinances. Then you shall live in the land that I gave to your ancestors; and you shall be my people, and I will be your God.

Psalm 42.1-7; Psalm 34.1-8

A reading from the Letter of Paul to the Romans. (6.3-11)
Do you not know that all of us who have been baptized into Christ Jesus were baptized into his death? Therefore we have been buried with him by baptism into death, so that, just as Christ was raised from the dead by the glory of the Father, so we too might walk in newness of life.

For if we have been united with him in a death like his, we will certainly be united with him in a resurrection like his. We know that our old self was crucified with him so that the body of sin might be destroyed, and we might no longer be enslaved to sin. For whoever has died is freed from sin. But if we have died with Christ, we believe that we will also live with him. We know that Christ, being raised from the dead, will never die again; death no longer has dominion over him. The death he died, he died to sin, once for all; but the life he lives, he lives to God. So you also must consider yourselves dead to sin and alive to God in Christ Jesus.

A reading from the Gospel according to Matthew. (28.16-end)
The eleven disciples went to Galilee, to the mountain to which Jesus had directed them. When they saw him, they worshipped him; but some doubted. And Jesus came and said to them, 'All authority in heaven and on earth has been given to me. Go therefore and make disciples of all nations, baptizing them in the name of the Father and of the Son and of the Holy Spirit, and teaching them to obey everything that I have commanded you. And remember, I am with you always, to the end of the age.'

Thanksgiving for Baptism

Thanksgiving for the Institution of Holy Communion

Collect
Lord Jesus Christ,
we thank you that in this wonderful sacrament
you have given us the memorial of your passion:
grant us so to reverence the sacred mysteries
   of your body and blood
that we may know within ourselves
and show forth in our lives
the fruits of your redemption;
for you are alive and reign with the Father
in the unity of the Holy Spirit,
one God, now and for ever.

Post Communion
All praise to you, our God and Father,
for you have fed us with the bread of heaven
and quenched our thirst from the true vine:
hear our prayer that, being grafted into Christ,
we may grow together in unity
and feast with him in his kingdom;
through Jesus Christ our Lord.

A reading from the book of Genesis. *(14.18-20)*
King Melchizedek of Salem brought out bread and wine; he was
priest of God Most High. He blessed God and said,
   'Blessed be Abram by God Most High,
      maker of heaven and earth;
   and blessed be God Most High,
      who has delivered your enemies into your hand!'

Psalm 116.10-end

A reading from the First Letter of Paul to the Corinthians. *(11.23-26)*
I received from the Lord what I also handed on to you, that the Lord
Jesus on the night when he was betrayed took a loaf of bread, and
when he had given thanks, he broke it and said, 'This is my body that
is for you. Do this in remembrance of me.' In the same way he took
the cup also, after supper, saying, 'This cup is the new covenant in

my blood. Do this, as often as you drink it, in remembrance of me.'
For as often as you eat this bread and drink the cup, you proclaim the
Lord's death until he comes.

A reading from the Gospel according to John. (6.51-58)
Jesus said to the Jews, 'I am the living bread that came down from
heaven. Whoever eats of this bread will live forever; and the bread
that I will give for the life of the world is my flesh.'

   The Jews then disputed among themselves, saying, 'How can this
man give us his flesh to eat?' So Jesus said to them, 'Very truly, I tell
you, unless you eat the flesh of the Son of Man and drink his blood,
you have no life in you. Those who eat my flesh and drink my blood
have eternal life, and I will raise them up on the last day; for my flesh
is true food and my blood is true drink. Those who eat my flesh and
drink my blood abide in me, and I in them. Just as the living Father
sent me, and I live because of the Father, so whoever eats me will live
because of me. This is the bread that came down from heaven, not
like that which your ancestors ate, and they died. But the one who
eats this bread will live for ever.'

Mission & Evangelism

Collect
Almighty God,
who called your Church to witness
that you were in Christ reconciling the world to yourself:
help us to proclaim the good news of your love,
that all who hear it may be drawn to you;
through him who was lifted up on the cross,
and reigns with you
in the unity of the Holy Spirit,
one God, now and for ever.

Post Communion
Eternal God, giver of love and power,
your Son Jesus Christ has sent us into all the world
to preach the gospel of his kingdom:
confirm us in this mission,
and help us to live the good news we proclaim;
through Jesus Christ our Lord.

A reading from the prophecy of Isaiah. (49.1-6)
Listen to me, O coastlands,
   pay attention, you peoples from far away!
The Lord called me before I was born,
   while I was in my mother's womb he named me.
He made my mouth like a sharp sword,
   in the shadow of his hand he hid me;
he made me a polished arrow,
   in his quiver he hid me away.
And he said to me, 'You are my servant,
   Israel, in whom I will be glorified.'
But I said, 'I have laboured in vain,
   I have spent my strength for nothing and vanity;
yet surely my cause is with the Lord,
   and my reward with my God.'

And now the Lord says,
   who formed me in the womb to be his servant,
to bring Jacob back to him,
   and that Israel might be gathered to him,
for I am honoured in the sight of the Lord,

and my God has become my strength –
he says,
   'It is too light a thing that you should be my servant
     to raise up the tribes of Jacob
     and to restore the survivors of Israel;
   I will give you as a light to the nations,
     that my salvation may reach to the end of the earth.'

A reading from the prophecy of Isaiah. (52.7-10)
   How beautiful upon the mountains
     are the feet of the messenger who announces peace,
   who brings good news,
     who announces salvation,
     who says to Zion, 'Your God reigns.'
   Listen! Your sentinels lift up their voices,
     together they sing for joy;
   for in plain sight they see
     the return of the Lord to Zion.
   Break forth together into singing,
     you ruins of Jerusalem;
   for the Lord has comforted his people,
     he has redeemed Jerusalem.
   The Lord has bared his holy arm
     before the eyes of all the nations;
   and all the ends of the earth shall see
     the salvation of our God.

A reading from the prophecy of Micah. (4.1-5)
   In days to come
     the mountain of the Lord's house
   shall be established as the highest of the mountains,
     and shall be raised up above the hills.
   Peoples shall stream to it,
   and many nations shall come and say:
   'Come, let us go up to the mountain of the Lord,
     to the house of the God of Jacob;
   that he may teach us his ways
     and that we may walk in his paths.'
   For out of Zion shall go forth instruction,
     and the word of the Lord from Jerusalem.
   He shall judge between many peoples,
     and shall arbitrate between strong nations far away;

they shall beat their swords into ploughshares,
  and their spears into pruning hooks;
nation shall not lift up sword against nation,
  neither shall they learn war any more;
but they shall all sit under their own vines
      and under their own fig trees,
  and no one shall make them afraid;
  for the mouth of the Lord of hosts has spoken.

For all the peoples walk,
  each in the name of its god,
but we will walk in the name of the Lord our God
  for ever and ever.

Psalm 2; Psalm 46; Psalm 67

A reading from the Acts of the Apostles. (17.12-end)
Many of the Jews believed, including not a few Greek women and
men of high standing. But when the Jews of Thessalonica learned
that the word of God had been proclaimed by Paul in Beroea as well,
they came there too, to stir up and incite the crowds. Then the believers
immediately sent Paul away to the coast, but Silas and Timothy
remained behind. Those who conducted Paul brought him as far as
Athens; and after receiving instructions to have Silas and Timothy
join him as soon as possible, they left him.
   While Paul was waiting for them in Athens, he was deeply
distressed to see that the city was full of idols. So he argued in the
synagogue with the Jews and the devout persons, and also in the
market-place every day with those who happened to be there. Also
some Epicurean and Stoic philosophers debated with him. Some
said, 'What does this babbler want to say?' Others said, 'He seems to
be a proclaimer of foreign divinities.' (This was because he was
telling the good news about Jesus and the resurrection.) So they took
him and brought him to the Areopagus and asked him, 'May we
know what this new teaching is that you are presenting? It sounds
rather strange to us, so we would like to know what it means.' Now
all the Athenians and the foreigners living there would spend their
time in nothing but telling or hearing something new.
   Then Paul stood in front of the Areopagus and said, 'Athenians, I
see how extremely religious you are in every way. For as I went
through the city and looked carefully at the objects of your worship,
I found among them an altar with the inscription, "To an unknown
god." What therefore you worship as unknown, this I proclaim to

you. The God who made the world and everything in it, he who is Lord of heaven and earth, does not live in shrines made by human hands, nor is he served by human hands, as though he needed anything, since he himself gives to all mortals life and breath and all things. From one ancestor he made all nations to inhabit the whole earth, and he allotted the times of their existence and the boundaries of the places where they would live, so that they would search for God and perhaps grope for him and find him – though indeed he is not far from each one of us. For "In him we live and move and have our being"; as even some of your own poets have said,

"For we too are his offspring."

Since we are God's offspring, we ought not to think that the deity is like gold, or silver, or stone, an image formed by the art and imagination of mortals. While God has overlooked the times of human ignorance, now he commands all people everywhere to repent, because he has fixed a day on which he will have the world judged in righteousness by a man whom he has appointed, and of this he has given assurance to all by raising him from the dead.'

When they heard of the resurrection of the dead, some scoffed; but others said, 'We will hear you again about this.' At that point Paul left them. But some of them joined him and became believers, including Dionysius the Areopagite and a woman named Damaris, and others with them.

A reading from the Second Letter of Paul to the Corinthians.

(5.14 – 6.2)

The love of Christ urges us on, because we are convinced that one has died for all; therefore all have died. And he died for all, so that those who live might live no longer for themselves, but for him who died and was raised for them.

From now on, therefore, we regard no one from a human point of view; even though we once knew Christ from a human point of view, we know him no longer in that way. So if anyone is in Christ, there is a new creation: everything old has passed away; see, everything has become new! All this is from God, who reconciled us to himself through Christ, and has given us the ministry of reconciliation; that is, in Christ God was reconciling the world to himself, not counting their trespasses against them, and entrusting the message of reconciliation to us. So we are ambassadors for Christ, since God is making his appeal through us; we entreat you on behalf of Christ, be reconciled to God. For our sake he made him to be sin who knew no sin, so that in him we might become the righteousness of God.

As we work together with him, we urge you also not to accept the grace of God in vain. For he says,

'At an acceptable time I have listened to you,
and on a day of salvation I have helped you.'

See, now is the acceptable time; see, now is the day of salvation!

A reading from the Letter of Paul to the Ephesians. (2.13-end)
In Christ Jesus you who once were far off have been brought near by the blood of Christ. For he is our peace; in his flesh he has made both groups into one and has broken down the dividing wall, that is, the hostility between us. He has abolished the law with its commandments and ordinances, that he might create in himself one new humanity in place of the two, thus making peace, and might reconcile both groups to God in one body through the cross, thus putting to death that hostility through it. So he came and proclaimed peace to you who were far off and peace to those who were near; for through him both of us have access in one Spirit to the Father. So then you are no longer strangers and aliens, but you are citizens with the saints and also members of the household of God, built upon the foundation of the apostles and prophets, with Christ Jesus himself as the cornerstone. In him the whole structure is joined together and grows into a holy temple in the Lord; in whom you also are built together spiritually into a dwelling-place for God.

A reading from the Gospel according to Matthew. (5.13-16)
Jesus said to his disciples, 'You are the salt of the earth; but if salt has lost its taste, how can its saltiness be restored? It is no longer good for anything, but is thrown out and trampled under foot.

'You are the light of the world. A city built on a hill cannot be hid. No one after lighting a lamp puts it under the bushel basket, but on the lampstand, and it gives light to all in the house. In the same way, let your light shine before others, so that they may see your good works and give glory to your Father in heaven.'

A reading from the Gospel according to Matthew. (28.16-end)
The eleven disciples went to Galilee, to the mountain to which Jesus had directed them. When they saw him, they worshipped him; but some doubted. And Jesus came and said to them, 'All authority in heaven and on earth has been given to me. Go therefore and make disciples of all nations, baptizing them in the name of the Father and of the Son and of the Holy Spirit, and teaching them to obey everything that I have commanded you. And remember, I am with you always, to the end of the age.'

A reading from the Gospel according to John. (17.20-end)
Jesus looked up to heaven and said, 'Father, I ask not only on behalf of these, but also on behalf of those who will believe in me through their word, that they may all be one. As you, Father, are in me and I am in you, may they also be in us, so that the world may believe that you have sent me. The glory that you have given me I have given them, so that they may be one, as we are one, I in them and you in me, that they may become completely one, so that the world may know that you have sent me and have loved them even as you have loved me. Father, I desire that those also, whom you have given me, may be with me where I am, to see my glory, which you have given me because you loved me before the foundation of the world.

'Righteous Father, the world does not know you, but I know you; and these know that you have sent me. I made your name known to them, and I will make it known, so that the love with which you have loved me may be in them, and I in them.'

The Unity of the Church

Collect
Heavenly Father,
you have called us in the Body of your Son Jesus Christ
to continue his work of reconciliation
and reveal you to the world:
forgive us the sins which tear us apart;
give us the courage to overcome our fears
and to seek that unity which is your gift and your will;
through Jesus Christ your Son our Lord,
who is alive and reigns with you
in the unity of the Holy Spirit,
one God, now and for ever.

Or:

Lord Jesus Christ,
who said to your apostles,
'Peace I leave with you, my peace I give to you':
look not on our sins but on the faith of your Church
and grant it the peace and unity of your kingdom;
where you are alive and reign with the Father
in the unity of the Holy Spirit,
one God, now and for ever.

Post Communion
Eternal God and Father,
whose Son at supper prayed that his disciples might be one,
as he is one with you:
draw us closer to him,
that in common love and obedience to you
we may be united to one another
in the fellowship of the one Spirit,
that the world may believe that he is Lord, to your eternal glory;
through Jesus Christ our Lord.

A reading from the prophecy of Jeremiah. *(33.6-9a)*
I am going to bring Jerusalem recovery and healing; I will heal them
and reveal to them abundance of prosperity and security. I will
restore the fortunes of Judah and the fortunes of Israel, and rebuild
them as they were at first. I will cleanse them from all the guilt of
their sin against me, and I will forgive all the guilt of their sin and

rebellion against me. And this city shall be to me a name of joy, a praise and a glory before all the nations of the earth who shall hear of all the good that I do for them.

A reading from the prophecy of Ezekiel. (36.23-28)
I will sanctify my great name, which has been profaned among the nations, and which you have profaned among them; and the nations shall know that I am the Lord, says the Lord God, when through you I display my holiness before their eyes. I will take you from the nations, and gather you from all the countries, and bring you into your own land. I will sprinkle clean water upon you, and you shall be clean from all your uncleannesses, and from all your idols I will cleanse you. A new heart I will give you, and a new spirit I will put within you; and I will remove from your body the heart of stone and give you a heart of flesh. I will put my spirit within you, and make you follow my statutes and be careful to observe my ordinances. Then you shall live in the land that I gave to your ancestors; and you shall be my people, and I will be your God.

A reading from the prophecy of Zephaniah. (3.16-end)
It shall be said to Jerusalem:
Do not fear, O Zion;
  do not let your hands grow weak.
The Lord, your God, is in your midst,
  a warrior who gives victory;
he will rejoice over you with gladness,
  he will renew you in his love;
he will exult over you with loud singing
  as on a day of festival.
I will remove disaster from you,
  so that you will not bear reproach for it.
I will deal with all your oppressors
  at that time.
And I will save the lame
  and gather the outcast,
and I will change their shame into praise
  and renown in all the earth.
At that time I will bring you home,
at the time when I gather you;
for I will make you renowned and praised
  among all the peoples of the earth,
when I restore your fortunes
  before your eyes, says the Lord.

                                    Unity of the Church

Psalm 100; Psalm 122; Psalm 133

A reading from the Letter of Paul to the Ephesians. (4.1-6)
I, the prisoner in the Lord, beg you to lead a life worthy of the calling to which you have been called, with all humility and gentleness, with patience, bearing with one another in love, making every effort to maintain the unity of the Spirit in the bond of peace. There is one body and one Spirit, just as you were called to the one hope of your calling, one Lord, one faith, one baptism, one God and Father of all, who is above all and through all and in all.

A reading from the Letter of Paul to the Colossians. (3.9-17)
Do not lie to one another, seeing that you have stripped off the old self with its practices and have clothed yourselves with the new self, which is being renewed in knowledge according to the image of its creator. In that renewal there is no longer Greek and Jew, circumcised and uncircumcised, barbarian, Scythian, slave and free; but Christ is all and in all!

As God's chosen ones, holy and belovèd, clothe yourselves with compassion, kindness, humility, meekness, and patience. Bear with one another and, if anyone has a complaint against another, forgive each other; just as the Lord has forgiven you, so you also must forgive. Above all, clothe yourselves with love, which binds everything together in perfect harmony. And let the peace of Christ rule in your hearts, to which indeed you were called in the one body. And be thankful. Let the word of Christ dwell in you richly; teach and admonish one another in all wisdom; and with gratitude in your hearts sing psalms, hymns, and spiritual songs to God. And whatever you do, in word or deed, do everything in the name of the Lord Jesus, giving thanks to God the Father through him.

A reading from the First Letter of John. (4.9-15)
God's love was revealed among us in this way: God sent his only Son into the world so that we might live through him. In this is love, not that we loved God but that he loved us and sent his Son to be the atoning sacrifice for our sins. Belovèd, since God loved us so much, we also ought to love one another. No one has ever seen God; if we love one another, God lives in us, and his love is perfected in us.

By this we know that we abide in him and he in us, because he has given us of his Spirit. And we have seen and do testify that the Father has sent his Son as the Saviour of the world. God abides in those who confess that Jesus is the Son of God, and they abide in God.

A reading from the Gospel according to Matthew. (18.19-22)
Jesus said to his disciples, 'Truly I tell you, if two of you agree on earth about anything you ask, it will be done for you by my Father in heaven. For where two or three are gathered in my name, I am there among them.'

Then Peter came and said to him, 'Lord, if another member of the church sins against me, how often should I forgive? As many as seven times?' Jesus said to him, 'Not seven times, but, I tell you, seventy-seven times.'

A reading from the Gospel according to John. (11.45-52)
Many of the Jews who had come with Mary and had seen what Jesus did believed in him. But some of them went to the Pharisees and told them what he had done. So the chief priests and the Pharisees called a meeting of the council, and said, 'What are we to do? This man is performing many signs. If we let him go on like this, everyone will believe in him, and the Romans will come and destroy both our holy place and our nation.' But one of them, Caiaphas, who was high priest that year, said to them, 'You know nothing at all! You do not understand that it is better for you to have one man die for the people than to have the whole nation destroyed.' He did not say this on his own, but being high priest that year he prophesied that Jesus was about to die for the nation, and not for the nation only, but to gather into one the dispersed children of God.

A reading from the Gospel according to John. (17.11b-23)
Speaking of those whom the Father had given him from the world, Jesus looked up to heaven and said, 'Holy Father, protect them in your name that you have given me, so that they may be one, as we are one. While I was with them, I protected them in your name that you have given me. I guarded them, and not one of them was lost except the one destined to be lost, so that the scripture might be fulfilled. But now I am coming to you, and I speak these things in the world so that they may have my joy made complete in themselves. I have given them your word, and the world has hated them because they do not belong to the world, just as I do not belong to the world. I am not asking you to take them out of the world, but I ask you to protect them from the evil one. They do not belong to the world, just as I do not belong to the world. Sanctify them in the truth; your word is truth. As you have sent me into the world, so I have sent them into the world. And for their sakes I sanctify myself, so that they also may be sanctified in truth.

Unity of the Church

'I ask not only on behalf of these, but also on behalf of those who will believe in me through their word, that they may all be one. As you, Father, are in me and I am in you, may they also be in us, so that the world may believe that you have sent me. The glory that you have given me I have given them, so that they may be one, as we are one, I in them and you in me, that they may become completely one, so that the world may know that you have sent me and have loved them even as you have loved me.'

The Guidance of the Holy Spirit

Collect
God, who from of old
taught the hearts of your faithful people
by sending to them the light of your Holy Spirit:
grant us by the same Spirit
to have a right judgement in all things
and evermore to rejoice in his holy comfort;
through the merits of Christ Jesus our Saviour,
who is alive and reigns with you
in the unity of the Holy Spirit,
one God, now and for ever.

Or:

Almighty God,
you have given your Holy Spirit to the Church
to lead us into all truth:
bless with the Spirit's grace and presence
   the members of *this . . . (synod/PCC/etc.)*;
keep *us/them* steadfast in faith and united in love,
that *we/they* may manifest your glory
and prepare the way of your kingdom;
through Jesus Christ your Son our Lord,
who is alive and reigns with you
in the unity of the Holy Spirit,
one God, now and for ever.

Post Communion
God of power,
whose Holy Spirit renews your people
in the bread and wine we bless and share:
may the boldness of the Spirit transform us,
the gentleness of the Spirit lead us,
and the gifts of the Spirit equip us
   to serve and worship you;
through Jesus Christ our Lord.

A reading from book Proverbs. (24.3-7)

By wisdom a house is built,
   and by understanding it is established;
by knowledge the rooms are filled
   with all precious and pleasant riches.
Wise warriors are mightier than strong ones,
   and those who have knowledge than those who have strength;
for by wise guidance you can wage your war,
   and in abundance of counsellors there is victory.
Wisdom is too high for fools;
   in the gate they do not open their mouths.

A reading from the prophecy of Isaiah. (30.15-21)

Thus said the Lord God, the Holy One of Israel:

In returning and rest you shall be saved;
   in quietness and in trust shall be your strength.
But you refused and said,
'No! We will flee upon horses' –
   therefore you shall flee!
and, 'We will ride upon swift steeds' –
   therefore your pursuers shall be swift!
A thousand shall flee at the threat of one,
   at the threat of five you shall flee,
until you are left
   like a flagstaff on the top of a mountain,
   like a signal on a hill.

Therefore the Lord waits to be gracious to you;
   therefore he will rise up to show mercy to you.
For the Lord is a God of justice;
   blessèd are all those who wait for him.

Truly, O people in Zion, inhabitants of Jerusalem, you shall weep no
more. He will surely be gracious to you at the sound of your cry;
when he hears it, he will answer you. Though the Lord may give you
the bread of adversity and the water of affliction, yet your Teacher
will not hide himself any more, but your eyes shall see your Teacher.
And when you turn to the right or when you turn to the left,
your ears shall hear a word behind you, saying, 'This is the way;
walk in it.'

A reading from the Wisdom of Solomon. (9.13-17)
> Who can learn the counsel of God?
> Or who can discern what the Lord wills?
> For the reasoning of mortals is worthless,
> and our designs are likely to fail;
> for a perishable body weighs down the soul,
> and this earthy tent burdens the thoughtful mind.
> We can hardly guess at what is on earth,
> and what is at hand we find with labour;
> but who has traced out what is in the heavens?
> Who has learned your counsel,
> unless you have given wisdom
> and sent your holy spirit from on high?

Psalm 25.1-9; Psalm 104.26-33; Psalm 143.8-10

A reading from the Acts of the Apostles. (15.22-29)
The apostles and the elders, with the consent of the whole church, decided to choose men from among their members and to send them to Antioch with Paul and Barnabas. They sent Judas called Barsabbas, and Silas, leaders among the brothers, with the following letter: 'The brothers, both the apostles and the elders, to the believers of Gentile origin in Antioch and Syria and Cilicia, greetings. Since we have heard that certain persons who have gone out from us, though with no instructions from us, have said things to disturb you and have unsettled your minds, we have decided unanimously to choose representatives and send them to you, along with our belovèd Barnabas and Paul, who have risked their lives for the sake of our Lord Jesus Christ. We have therefore sent Judas and Silas, who themselves will tell you the same things by word of mouth. For it has seemed good to the Holy Spirit and to us to impose on you no further burden than these essentials: that you abstain from what has been sacrificed to idols and from blood and from what is strangled and from fornication. If you keep yourselves from these, you will do well. Farewell.'

A reading from the Letter of Paul to the Romans. (8.22-27)
 We know that the whole creation has been groaning in labour pains until now; and not only the creation, but we ourselves, who have the first fruits of the Spirit, groan inwardly while we wait for adoption, the redemption of our bodies. For in hope we were saved. Now hope that is seen is not hope. For who hopes for what is seen? But if

we hope for what we do not see, we wait for it with patience.

Likewise the Spirit helps us in our weakness; for we do not know how to pray as we ought, but that very Spirit intercedes with sighs too deep for words. And God, who searches the heart, knows what is the mind of the Spirit, because the Spirit intercedes for the saints according to the will of God.

A reading from the First Letter of Paul to the Corinthians. (12.4-13)
There are varieties of gifts, but the same Spirit; and there are varieties of services, but the same Lord; and there are varieties of activities, but it is the same God who activates all of them in everyone. To each is given the manifestation of the Spirit for the common good. To one is given through the Spirit the utterance of wisdom, and to another the utterance of knowledge according to the same Spirit, to another faith by the same Spirit, to another gifts of healing by the one Spirit, to another the working of miracles, to another prophecy, to another the discernment of spirits, to another various kinds of tongues, to another the interpretation of tongues. All these are activated by one and the same Spirit, who allots to each one individually just as the Spirit chooses.

For just as the body is one and has many members, and all the members of the body, though many, are one body, so it is with Christ. For in the one Spirit we were all baptized into one body – Jews or Greeks, slaves or free – and we were all made to drink of one Spirit.

A reading from the Gospel according to Luke. (14.27-33)
Jesus said to the large crowds following him, 'Whoever does not carry the cross and follow me cannot be my disciple. For which of you, intending to build a tower, does not first sit down and estimate the cost, to see whether he has enough to complete it? Otherwise, when he has laid a foundation and is not able to finish, all who see it will begin to ridicule him, saying, "This fellow began to build and was not able to finish." Or what king, going out to wage war against another king, will not sit down first and consider whether he is able with ten thousand to oppose the one who comes against him with twenty thousand? If he cannot, then, while the other is still far away, he sends a delegation and asks for the terms of peace. So therefore, none of you can become my disciple if you do not give up all your possessions.'

A reading from the Gospel according to John. (14.23-26)
Jesus said, 'Those who love me will keep my word, and my Father will love them, and we will come to them and make our home with them. Whoever does not love me does not keep my words; and the word that you hear is not mine, but is from the Father who sent me.

'I have said these things to you while I am still with you. But the Advocate, the Holy Spirit, whom the Father will send in my name, will teach you everything, and remind you of all that I have said to you.'

A reading from the Gospel according to John. (16.13-15)
Jesus said to his disciples, 'When the Spirit of truth comes, he will guide you into all the truth; for he will not speak on his own, but will speak whatever he hears, and he will declare to you the things that are to come. He will glorify me, because he will take what is mine and declare it to you. All that the Father has is mine. For this reason I said that he will take what is mine and declare it to you.'

Creation

Rogation Days

Collect

Almighty God,
whose will it is that the earth and the sea
  should bear fruit in due season:
bless the labours of those who work on land and sea,
grant us a good harvest
and the grace always to rejoice in your fatherly care;
through Jesus Christ your Son our Lord,
who is alive and reigns with you
in the unity of the Holy Spirit,
one God, now and for ever.

Or:

Almighty God and Father,
you have so ordered our life
  that we are dependent on one another:
prosper those engaged in commerce and industry
and direct their minds and hands
that they may rightly use your gifts in the service of others;
through Jesus Christ your Son our Lord,
who is alive and reigns with you
in the unity of the Holy Spirit,
one God, now and for ever.

Or:

God our Father,
you never cease the work you have begun
and prosper with your blessing all human labour:
make us wise and faithful stewards of your gifts
that we may serve the common good,
maintain the fabric of our world
and seek that justice where all may share
  the good things you pour upon us;
through Jesus Christ your Son our Lord,
who is alive and reigns with you
in the unity of the Holy Spirit,
one God, now and for ever.

Post Communion
God our creator,
you give seed for us to sow and bread for us to eat:
as you have blessed the fruit of our labour in this eucharist,
so we ask you to give all your children their daily bread,
that the world may praise you for your goodness;
through Jesus Christ our Lord.

A reading from the book Deuteronomy. *(8.1-10)*

Moses said to all Israel: This entire commandment that I command
you today you must diligently observe, so that you may live and
increase, and go in and occupy the land that the Lord promised
on oath to your ancestors. Remember the long way that the Lord
your God has led you these forty years in the wilderness, in order to
humble you, testing you to know what was in your heart, whether or
not you would keep his commandments. He humbled you by letting
you hunger, then by feeding you with manna, with which neither
you nor your ancestors were acquainted, in order to make you
understand that one does not live by bread alone, but by every word
that comes from the mouth of the Lord. The clothes on your back did
not wear out and your feet did not swell these forty years. Know
then in your heart that as a parent disciplines a child so the Lord your
God disciplines you. Therefore keep the commandments of the Lord
your God, by walking in his ways and by fearing him. For the Lord
your God is bringing you into a good land, a land with flowing
streams, with springs and underground waters welling up in valleys
and hills, a land of wheat and barley, of vines and fig trees and
pomegranates, a land of olive trees and honey, a land where you may
eat bread without scarcity, where you will lack nothing, a land whose
stones are iron and from whose hills you may mine copper. You
shall eat your fill and bless the Lord your God for the good land that
he has given you.

A reading from the First Book of the Kings. *(8.22-23a,35-40)*

Solomon stood before the altar of the Lord in the presence of all the
assembly of Israel, and spread out his hands to heaven.
   He said, 'O Lord, God of Israel, when heaven is shut up and there is
no rain because your people Israel have sinned against you, and then
they pray toward this place, confess your name, and turn from their
sin, because you punish them, then hear in heaven, and forgive the
sin of your servants, your people Israel, when you teach them the
good way in which they should walk; and grant rain on your land,

which you have given to your people as an inheritance.

'If there is famine in the land, if there is plague, blight, mildew, locust, or caterpillar; if their enemy besieges them in any of their cities; whatever plague, whatever sickness there is; whatever prayer, whatever plea there is from any individual or from all your people Israel, all knowing the afflictions of their own hearts so that they stretch out their hands toward this house; then hear in heaven your dwelling-place, forgive, act, and render to all whose hearts you know – according to all their ways, for only you know what is in every human heart – so that they may fear you all the days that they live in the land that you gave to our ancestors.'

A reading from the Book of Job. (28.1-11)
Job took up his discourse and said:
   'Surely there is a mine for silver,
     and a place for gold to be refined.
Iron is taken out of the earth,
     and copper is smelted from ore.
Miners put an end to darkness,
     and search out to the farthest bound
     the ore in gloom and deep darkness.
They open shafts in a valley away from human habitation;
     they are forgotten by travellers,
     they sway suspended, remote from people.
As for the earth, out of it comes bread;
but underneath it is turned up as by fire.
Its stones are the place of sapphires,
     and its dust contains gold.

'That path no bird of prey knows,
     and the falcon's eye has not seen it.
The proud wild animals have not trodden it;
     the lion has not passed over it.

'They put their hand to the flinty rock,
     and overturn mountains by the roots.
They cut out channels in the rocks,
     and their eyes see every precious thing.
The sources of the rivers they probe;
     hidden things they bring to light.'

Psalm 104.21-30; Psalm 107.1-9; Psalm 121

A reading from the Letter of Paul to the Philippians. (4.4-7)
Rejoice in the Lord always; again I will say, Rejoice. Let your gentleness be known to everyone. The Lord is near. Do not worry about anything, but in everything by prayer and supplication with thanksgiving let your requests be made known to God. And the peace of God, which surpasses all understanding, will guard your hearts and your minds in Christ Jesus.

A reading from the Second Letter of Paul to the Thessalonians. (3.6-13)
We command you, belovèd, in the name of our Lord Jesus Christ, to keep away from believers who are living in idleness and not according to the tradition that they received from us. For you yourselves know how you ought to imitate us; we were not idle when we were with you, and we did not eat anyone's bread without paying for it; but with toil and labour we worked night and day, so that we might not burden any of you. This was not because we do not have that right, but in order to give you an example to imitate. For even when we were with you, we gave you this command: Anyone unwilling to work should not eat. For we hear that some of you are living in idleness, mere busybodies, not doing any work. Now such persons we command and exhort in the Lord Jesus Christ to do their work quietly and to earn their own living. Brothers and sisters, do not be weary in doing what is right.

A reading from the First Letter of John. (5.12-15)
Whoever has the Son has life; whoever does not have the Son of God does not have life.

I write these things to you who believe in the name of the Son of God, so that you may know that you have eternal life.

And this is the boldness we have in him, that if we ask anything according to his will, he hears us. And if we know that he hears us in whatever we ask, we know that we have obtained the requests made of him.

A reading from the Gospel according to Matthew. (6.1-15)
Jesus said to his disciples, 'Beware of practising your piety before others in order to be seen by them; for then you have no reward from your Father in heaven.

'So whenever you give alms, do not sound a trumpet before you, as the hypocrites do in the synagogues and in the streets, so that they may be praised by others. Truly I tell you, they have received their reward. But when you give alms, do not let your left hand know what your right hand is doing, so that your alms may be done in secret; and your Father who sees in secret will reward you.

'And whenever you pray, do not be like the hypocrites; for they love to stand and pray in the synagogues and at the street corners, so that they may be seen by others. Truly I tell you, they have received their reward. But whenever you pray, go into your room and shut the door and pray to your Father who is in secret; and your Father who sees in secret will reward you.

'When you are praying, do not heap up empty phrases as the Gentiles do; for they think that they will be heard because of their many words. Do not be like them, for your Father knows what you need before you ask him.

'Pray then in this way:
Our Father in heaven,
   hallowed be your name.
Your kingdom come.
Your will be done,
   on earth as it is in heaven.
Give us this day our daily bread.
And forgive us our debts,
   as we also have forgiven our debtors.
And do not bring us to the time of trial,
   but rescue us from the evil one.
For if you forgive others their trespasses, your heavenly Father will also forgive you; but if you do not forgive others, neither will your Father forgive your trespasses.'

A reading from the Gospel according to Mark. (11.22-24)
Jesus said to his disciples, 'Have faith in God. Truly I tell you, if you say to this mountain, "Be taken up and thrown into the sea," and if you do not doubt in your heart, but believe that what you say will come to pass, it will be done for you. So I tell you, whatever you ask for in prayer, believe that you have received it, and it will be yours.'

A reading from the Gospel according to Luke. (11.5-13)
Jesus said to his disciples, 'Suppose one of you has a friend, and you go to him at midnight and say to him, "Friend, lend me three loaves of bread; for a friend of mine has arrived, and I have nothing to set before him." And he answers from within, "Do not bother me; the door has already been locked, and my children are with me in bed; I cannot get up and give you anything." I tell you, even though he will not get up and give him anything because he is his friend, at least

because of his persistence he will get up and give him whatever he needs.

'So I say to you, Ask, and it will be given you; search, and you will find; knock, and the door will be opened for you. For everyone who asks receives, and everyone who searches finds, and for everyone who knocks, the door will be opened. Is there anyone among you who, if your child asks for a fish, will give a snake instead of a fish? Or if the child asks for an egg, will give a scorpion? If you then, who are evil, know how to give good gifts to your children, how much more will the heavenly Father give the Holy Spirit to those who ask him!'

Harvest Thanksgiving – Year A

Collect
Eternal God,
you crown the year with your goodness
and you give us the fruits of the earth in their season:
grant that we may use them to your glory,
  for the relief of those in need
  and for our own well-being;
through Jesus Christ your Son our Lord,
who is alive and reigns with you
in the unity of the Holy Spirit,
one God, now and for ever.

Post Communion
Lord of the harvest,
with joy we have offered thanksgiving
  for your love in creation
and have shared in the bread and the wine of the kingdom:
by your grace plant within us a reverence for all that you give us
and make us generous and wise stewards
of the good things we enjoy;
through Jesus Christ our Lord.

A reading from the book Deuteronomy. (8.7-18)

Moses said to all Israel: The Lord your God is bringing you into a
good land, a land with flowing streams, with springs and underground
waters welling up in valleys and hills, a land of wheat and barley, of
vines and fig trees and pomegranates, a land of olive trees and honey,
a land where you may eat bread without scarcity, where you will lack
nothing, a land whose stones are iron and from whose hills you may
mine copper. You shall eat your fill and bless the Lord your God for
the good land that he has given you.

  Take care that you do not forget the Lord your God, by failing to
keep his commandments, his ordinances, and his statutes, which I
am commanding you today. When you have eaten your fill and have
built fine houses and live in them, and when your herds and flocks
have multiplied, and your silver and gold is multiplied, and all that
you have is multiplied, then do not exalt yourself, forgetting the Lord
your God, who brought you out of the land of Egypt, out of the house
of slavery, who led you through the great and terrible wilderness, an
arid waste-land with poisonous snakes and scorpions. He made
water flow for you from flint rock, and fed you in the wilderness with

manna that your ancestors did not know, to humble you and to test you, and in the end to do you good. Do not say to yourself, 'My power and the might of my own hand have gained me this wealth.' But remember the Lord your God, for it is he who gives you power to get wealth, so that he may confirm his covenant that he swore to your ancestors, as he is doing today.

Or:

A reading from the book Deuteronomy. *(28.1-14)*
Moses said to all Israel: If you will only obey the Lord your God, by diligently observing all his commandments that I am commanding you today, the Lord your God will set you high above all the nations of the earth; all these blessings shall come upon you and overtake you, if you obey the Lord your God:

Blessèd shall you be in the city, and blessèd shall you be in the field.

Blessèd shall be the fruit of your womb, the fruit of your ground, and the fruit of your livestock, both the increase of your cattle and the issue of your flock.

Blessèd shall be your basket and your kneading-bowl.

Blessèd shall you be when you come in, and blessèd shall you be when you go out.

The Lord will cause your enemies who rise against you to be defeated before you; they shall come out against you one way, and flee before you seven ways. The Lord will command the blessing upon you in your barns, and in all that you undertake; he will bless you in the land that the Lord your God is giving you. The Lord will establish you as his holy people, as he has sworn to you, if you keep the commandments of the Lord your God and walk in his ways. All the peoples of the earth shall see that you are called by the name of the Lord, and they shall be afraid of you. The Lord will make you abound in prosperity, in the fruit of your womb, in the fruit of your livestock, and in the fruit of your ground in the land that the Lord swore to your ancestors to give you. The Lord will open for you his rich storehouse, the heavens, to give the rain of your land in its season and to bless all your undertakings. You will lend to many nations, but you will not borrow. The Lord will make you the head, and not the tail; you shall be only at the top, and not at the bottom – if you obey the commandments of the Lord your God, which I am commanding you today, by diligently observing them, and if you do not turn aside from any of the words that I am commanding you today, either to the right or to the left, following other gods to serve them.

Psalm 65

A reading from the Second Letter of Paul to the Corinthians. (9.6-15)
The one who sows sparingly will also reap sparingly, and the one who sows bountifully will also reap bountifully. Each of you must give as you have made up your mind, not reluctantly or under compulsion, for God loves a cheerful giver. And God is able to provide you with every blessing in abundance, so that by always having enough of everything, you may share abundantly in every good work. As it is written,
'He scatters abroad, he gives to the poor;
    his righteousness endures for ever.'
He who supplies seed to the sower and bread for food will supply and multiply your seed for sowing and increase the harvest of your righteousness. You will be enriched in every way for your great generosity, which will produce thanksgiving to God through us; for the rendering of this ministry not only supplies the needs of the saints but also overflows with many thanksgivings to God. Through the testing of this ministry you glorify God by your obedience to the confession of the gospel of Christ and by the generosity of your sharing with them and with all others, while they long for you and pray for you because of the surpassing grace of God that he has given you. Thanks be to God for his indescribable gift!

A reading from the Gospel according to Luke. (12.16-30)
Jesus told the people a parable: 'The land of a rich man produced abundantly. And he thought to himself, "What should I do, for I have no place to store my crops?" Then he said, "I will do this: I will pull down my barns and build larger ones, and there I will store all my grain and my goods. And I will say to my soul, Soul, you have ample goods laid up for many years; relax, eat, drink, be merry." But God said to him, "You fool! This very night your life is being demanded of you. And the things you have prepared, whose will they be?" So it is with those who store up treasures for themselves but are not rich towards God.'
Jesus said to his disciples, 'Therefore I tell you, do not worry about your life, what you will eat, or about your body, what you will wear. For life is more than food, and the body more than clothing. Consider the ravens: they neither sow nor reap, they have neither storehouse nor barn, and yet God feeds them. Of how much more value are you than the birds! And can any of you by worrying add a single hour to your span of life? If then you are not able to do so

small a thing as that, why do you worry about the rest? Consider the lilies, how they grow: they neither toil nor spin; yet I tell you, even Solomon in all his glory was not clothed like one of these. But if God so clothes the grass of the field, which is alive today and tomorrow is thrown into the oven, how much more will he clothe you – you of little faith! And do not keep striving for what you are to eat and what you are to drink, and do not keep worrying. For it is the nations of the world that strive after all these things, and your Father knows that you need them.'

Or:

A reading from the Gospel according to Luke. *(17.11-19)*
On the way to Jerusalem Jesus was going through the region between Samaria and Galilee. As he entered a village, ten lepers approached him. Keeping their distance, they called out, saying, 'Jesus, Master, have mercy on us!' When he saw them, he said to them, 'Go and show yourselves to the priests.' And as they went, they were made clean. Then one of them, when he saw that he was healed, turned back, praising God with a loud voice. He prostrated himself at Jesus' feet and thanked him. And he was a Samaritan. Then Jesus asked, 'Were not ten made clean? But the other nine, where are they? Was none of them found to return and give praise to God except this foreigner?' Then he said to him, 'Get up and go on your way; your faith has made you well.'

Harvest Thanksgiving – Year B

For Collect and Post-Communion Prayer, see page 231.

A reading from the prophecy of Joel. (2.21-27)

Do not fear, O soil;
  be glad and rejoice,
  for the Lord has done great things!
Do not fear, you animals of the field,
  for the pastures of the wilderness are green;
the tree bears its fruit,
  the fig tree and vine give their full yield.

O children of Zion, be glad
  and rejoice in the Lord your God;
for he has given the early rain for your vindication,
  he has poured down for you abundant rain,
  the early and the later rain, as before.
The threshing floors shall be full of grain,
  the vats shall overflow with wine and oil.

I will repay you for the years
  that the swarming locust has eaten,
the hopper, the destroyer, and the cutter,
  my great army, which I sent against you.

You shall eat in plenty and be satisfied,
  and praise the name of the Lord your God,
  who has dealt wondrously with you.
And my people shall never again be put to shame.
You shall know that I am in the midst of Israel,
  and that I, the Lord, am your God and there is no other.
And my people shall never again
  be put to shame.

Psalm 126

A reading from the First Letter of Paul to Timothy. (2.1-7)

I urge that supplications, prayers, intercessions, and thanksgivings be made for everyone, for kings and all who are in high positions, so that we may lead a quiet and peaceable life in all godliness and dignity. This is right and is acceptable in the sight of God our Saviour, who desires everyone to be saved and to come to the knowledge of the truth. For
  there is one God;

there is also one mediator between God and humankind,
Christ Jesus, himself human,
who gave himself a ransom for all
– this was attested at the right time. For this I was appointed a
herald and an apostle (I am telling the truth, I am not lying), a teacher
of the Gentiles in faith and truth.

Or:

A reading from the First Letter of Paul to Timothy. (6.6-10)
Of course, there is great gain in godliness combined with contentment;
for we brought nothing into the world, so that we can take nothing
out of it; but if we have food and clothing, we will be content with
these. But those who want to be rich fall into temptation and are
trapped by many senseless and harmful desires that plunge people
into ruin and destruction. For the love of money is a root of all kinds
of evil, and in their eagerness to be rich some have wandered away
from the faith and pierced themselves with many pains.

A reading from the Gospel according to Matthew. (6.25-33)
Jesus said to his disciples, 'I tell you, do not worry about your life,
what you will eat or what you will drink, or about your body, what
you will wear. Is not life more than food, and the body more than
clothing? Look at the birds of the air; they neither sow nor reap nor
gather into barns, and yet your heavenly Father feeds them. Are you
not of more value than they? And can any of you by worrying add
a single hour to your span of life? And why do you worry about
clothing? Consider the lilies of the field, how they grow; they neither
toil nor spin, yet I tell you, even Solomon in all his glory was not
clothed like one of these. But if God so clothes the grass of the field,
which is alive today and tomorrow is thrown into the oven, will he
not much more clothe you – you of little faith? Therefore do not
worry, saying, 'What will we eat?" or "What will we drink?" or
"What will we wear?" For it is the Gentiles who strive for all these
things; and indeed your heavenly Father knows that you need all
these things. But strive first for the kingdom of God and his righteousness, and all these things will be given to you as well.'

Harvest Thanksgiving – Year C

For Collect and Post-Communion Prayer, see page 231.

A reading from the book Deuteronomy. *(26.1-11)*

Moses said to all Israel: When you have come into the land that the Lord your God is giving you as an inheritance to possess, and you possess it, and settle in it, you shall take some of the first of all the fruit of the ground, which you harvest from the land that the Lord your God is giving you, and you shall put it in a basket and go to the place that the Lord your God will choose as a dwelling for his name. You shall go to the priest who is in office at that time, and say to him, 'Today I declare to the Lord your God that I have come into the land that the Lord swore to our ancestors to give us.' When the priest takes the basket from your hand and sets it down before the altar of the Lord your God, you shall make this response before the Lord your God: 'A wandering Aramean was my ancestor; he went down into Egypt and lived there as an alien, few in number, and there he became a great nation, mighty and populous. When the Egyptians treated us harshly and afflicted us, by imposing hard labour on us, we cried to the Lord, the God of our ancestors; the Lord heard our voice and saw our affliction, our toil, and our oppression. The Lord brought us out of Egypt with a mighty hand and an outstretched arm, with a terrifying display of power, and with signs and wonders; and he brought us into this place and gave us this land, a land flowing with milk and honey. So now I bring the first of the fruit of the ground that you, O Lord, have given me.' You shall set it down before the Lord your God and bow down before the Lord your God. Then you, together with the Levites and the aliens who reside among you, shall celebrate with all the bounty that the Lord your God has given to you and to your house.

Psalm 100

A reading from the Letter of Paul to the Philippians. *(4.4-9)*

Rejoice in the Lord always; again I will say, Rejoice. Let your gentleness be known to everyone. The Lord is near. Do not worry about anything, but in everything by prayer and supplication with thanksgiving let your requests be made known to God. And the peace of God, which surpasses all understanding, will guard your hearts and your minds in Christ Jesus.

Finally, belovèd, whatever is true, whatever is honourable, whatever is just, whatever is pure, whatever is pleasing, whatever is commendable, if there is any excellence and if there is anything worthy of praise, think about these things. Keep on doing the things that you have learned and received and heard and seen in me, and the God of peace will be with you.

Or:

A reading from the Revelation to John. *(14.14-18)*
I looked, and there was a white cloud, and seated on the cloud was one like the Son of Man, with a golden crown on his head, and a sharp sickle in his hand! Another angel came out of the temple, calling with a loud voice to the one who sat on the cloud, 'Use your sickle and reap, for the hour to reap has come, because the harvest of the earth is fully ripe.' So the one who sat on the cloud swung his sickle over the earth, and the earth was reaped.

Then another angel came out of the temple in heaven, and he too had a sharp sickle. Then another angel came out from the altar, the angel who has authority over fire, and he called with a loud voice to him who had the sharp sickle, 'Use your sharp sickle and gather the clusters of the vine of the earth, for its grapes are ripe.'

A reading from the Gospel according to John. *(6.25-35)*
When the crowd found Jesus on the other side of the lake, they said to him, 'Rabbi, when did you come here?' Jesus answered them, 'Very truly, I tell you, you are looking for me, not because you saw signs, but because you ate your fill of the loaves. Do not work for the food that perishes, but for the food that endures for eternal life, which the Son of Man will give you. For it is on him that God the Father has set his seal.' Then they said to him, 'What must we do to perform the works of God?' Jesus answered them, 'This is the work of God, that you believe in him whom he has sent.' So they said to him, 'What sign are you going to give us then, so that we may see it and believe you? What work are you performing? Our ancestors ate the manna in the wilderness; as it is written, "He gave them bread from heaven to eat."' Then Jesus said to them, 'Very truly, I tell you, it was not Moses who gave you the bread from heaven, but it is my Father who gives you the true bread from heaven. For the bread of God is that which comes down from heaven and gives life to the world.' They said to him, 'Sir, give us this bread always.'

Jesus said to them, 'I am the bread of life. Whoever comes to me will never be hungry, and whoever believes in me will never be thirsty.'

The World

The World

The Sovereign

Collect
Almighty God,
the fountain of all goodness,
bless our Sovereign Lady, Queen Elizabeth,
and all who are in authority under her;
that they may order all things
    in wisdom and equity, righteousness and peace,
to the honour and glory of your name
and the good of your Church and people;
through Jesus Christ your Son our Lord,
who is alive and reigns with you
in the unity of the Holy Spirit,
one God, now and for ever.

Post Communion
O God, the Father of our Lord Jesus Christ,
our only Saviour, the prince of peace:
give us grace seriously to lay to heart
the great dangers we are in by our unhappy divisions;
take away our hatred and prejudice
and whatever else may hinder us from godly union and concord,
that, as there is but one body, one Spirit
    and one hope of our calling,
one Lord, one faith, one baptism,
one God and Father of us all,
so may we henceforth be all of one heart and of one soul,
united in one holy bond of truth and peace, of faith and charity,
and may with one mind and one mouth glorify you;
through Jesus Christ our Lord.

A reading from the Book of Joshua. (1.1-9)
After the death of Moses, the servant of the Lord, the Lord spoke to
Joshua son of Nun, Moses' assistant, saying, 'My servant Moses is
dead. Now proceed to cross the Jordan, you and all this people, into
the land that I am giving to them, to the Israelites. Every place that
the sole of your foot will tread upon I have given to you, as I
promised to Moses. From the wilderness and the Lebanon as far as

the great river, the river Euphrates, all the land of the Hittites, to the Great Sea in the west shall be your territory. No one shall be able to stand against you all the days of your life. As I was with Moses, so I will be with you; I will not fail you or forsake you. Be strong and courageous; for you shall put this people in possession of the land that I swore to their ancestors to give them. Only be strong and very courageous, being careful to act in accordance with all the law that my servant Moses commanded you; do not turn from it to the right hand or to the left, so that you may be successful wherever you go. This book of the law shall not depart out of your mouth; you shall meditate on it day and night, so that you may be careful to act in accordance with all that is written in it. For then you shall make your way prosperous, and then you shall be successful. I hereby command you: Be strong and courageous; do not be frightened or dismayed, for the Lord your God is with you wherever you go.'

A reading from the book Proverbs. (8.1-16)
Does not wisdom call,
   and does not understanding raise her voice?
On the heights, beside the way,
   at the crossroads she takes her stand;
beside the gates in front of the town,
   at the entrance of the portals she cries out:
'To you, O people, I call,
   and my cry is to all that live.
O simple ones, learn prudence;
   acquire intelligence, you who lack it.
Hear, for I will speak noble things,
   and from my lips will come what is right;
for my mouth will utter truth;
   wickedness is an abomination to my lips.
All the words of my mouth are righteous;
   there is nothing twisted or crooked in them.
They are all straight to one who understands
   and right to those who find knowledge.
Take my instruction instead of silver,
   and knowledge rather than choice gold;
for wisdom is better than jewels,
   and all that you may desire cannot compare with her.
I, wisdom, live with prudence,
   and I attain knowledge and discretion.
The fear of the Lord is hatred of evil.

Pride and arrogance and the way of evil
and perverted speech I hate.
I have good advice and sound wisdom;
I have insight, I have strength.
By me kings reign,
and rulers decree what is just;
by me rulers rule,
and nobles, all who govern rightly.

Psalm 20; Psalm 101; Psalm 121

A reading from the Letter of Paul to the Romans. (13.1-10)
Let every person be subject to the governing authorities; for there is
no authority except from God, and those authorities that exist have
been instituted by God. Therefore whoever resists authority resists
what God has appointed, and those who resist will incur judgment.
For rulers are not a terror to good conduct, but to bad. Do you wish
to have no fear of the authority? Then do what is good, and you will
receive its approval; for it is God's servant for your good. But if you
do what is wrong, you should be afraid, for the authority does not
bear the sword in vain! It is the servant of God to execute wrath on
the wrongdoer. Therefore one must be subject, not only because of
wrath but also because of conscience. For the same reason you also
pay taxes, for the authorities are God's servants, busy with this very
thing. Pay to all what is due them – taxes to whom taxes are due,
revenue to whom revenue is due, respect to whom respect is due,
honour to whom honour is due.

Owe no one anything, except to love one another; for the one who
loves another has fulfilled the law. The commandments, 'You shall
not commit adultery; You shall not murder; You shall not steal; You
shall not covet'; and any other commandment, are summed up in this
word, 'Love your neighbour as yourself.' Love does no wrong to a
neighbour; therefore, love is the fulfilling of the law.

A reading from the Revelation to John. (21.22 – 22.4)
I saw no temple in the city, for its temple is the Lord God the
Almighty and the Lamb. And the city has no need of sun or moon to
shine on it, for the glory of God is its light, and its lamp is the Lamb.
The nations will walk by its light, and the kings of the earth will bring
their glory into it. Its gates will never be shut by day – and there will
be no night there. People will bring into it the glory and the honour
of the nations. But nothing unclean will enter it, nor anyone who

practises abomination or falsehood, but only those who are written in the Lamb's book of life.

Then the angel showed me the river of the water of life, bright as crystal, flowing from the throne of God and of the Lamb through the middle of the street of the city. On either side of the river is the tree of life with its twelve kinds of fruit, producing its fruit each month; and the leaves of the tree are for the healing of the nations. Nothing accursed will be found there any more. But the throne of God and of the Lamb will be in it, and his servants will worship him; they will see his face, and his name will be on their foreheads.

A reading from the Gospel according to Matthew. (22.16-22)
The Pharisees sent their disciples to Jesus, along with the Herodians, saying, 'Teacher, we know that you are sincere, and teach the way of God in accordance with truth, and show deference to no one; for you do not regard people with partiality. Tell us, then, what you think. Is it lawful to pay taxes to the emperor, or not?' But Jesus, aware of their malice, said, 'Why are you putting me to the test, you hypocrites? Show me the coin used for the tax.' And they brought him a denarius. Then he said to them, 'Whose head is this, and whose title?' They answered, 'The emperor's.' Then he said to them, 'Give therefore to the emperor the things that are the emperor's, and to God the things that are God's.' When they heard this, they were amazed; and they left him and went away.

A reading from the Gospel according to Luke. (22.24-30)
A dispute arose among the apostles as to which one of them was to be regarded as the greatest. But Jesus said to them, 'The kings of the Gentiles lord it over them; and those in authority over them are called benefactors. But not so with you; rather the greatest among you must become like the youngest, and the leader like one who serves. For who is greater, the one who is at the table or the one who serves? Is it not the one at the table? But I am among you as one who serves.

'You are those who have stood by me in my trials; and I confer on you, just as my Father has conferred on me, a kingdom, so that you may eat and drink at my table in my kingdom, and you will sit on thrones judging the twelve tribes of Israel.'

The Peace of the World

Collect
Almighty God,
from whom all thoughts of truth and peace proceed:
kindle, we pray, in the hearts of all, the true love of peace
and guide with your pure and peaceable wisdom
those who take counsel for the nations of the earth
that in tranquillity your kingdom may go forward,
till the earth is filled with the knowledge of your love;
through Jesus Christ your Son our Lord,
who is alive and reigns with you
in the unity of the Holy Spirit,
one God, now and for ever.

Post Communion
God our Father,
your Son is our peace
and his cross the sign of reconciliation:
help us, who share the broken bread,
to bring together what is scattered
and to bind up what is wounded,
that Christ may bring in the everlasting kingdom of his peace;
who is alive and reigns, now and for ever.

A reading from the prophecy of Isaiah. *(9.1-6)*

There will be no gloom for those who were in anguish. In the former
time he brought into contempt the land of Zebulun and the land of
Naphtali, but in the latter time he will make glorious the way of the
sea, the land beyond the Jordan, Galilee of the nations.

The people who walked in darkness
 have seen a great light;
those who lived in a land of deep darkness –
 on them light has shined.
You have multiplied the nation,
 you have increased its joy;
they rejoice before you
 as with joy at the harvest,
 as people exult when dividing plunder.
For the yoke of their burden,
 and the bar across their shoulders,
 the rod of their oppressor,

you have broken as on the day of Midian.
For all the boots of the tramping warriors
    and all the garments rolled in blood
    shall be burned as fuel for the fire.
For a child has been born for us,
    a son given to us;
authority rests upon his shoulders;
and he is named
Wonderful Counsellor, Mighty God,
    Everlasting Father, Prince of Peace.

A reading from the prophecy of Isaiah. (57.15-19)
    Thus says the high and lofty one
        who inhabits eternity, whose name is Holy:
    I dwell in the high and holy place,
        and also with those who are contrite and humble in spirit,
    to revive the spirit of the humble,
        and to revive the heart of the contrite.
    For I will not continually accuse,
        nor will I always be angry;
    for then the spirits would grow faint before me,
        even the souls that I have made.
    Because of their wicked covetousness I was angry;
        I struck them, I hid and was angry;
        but they kept turning back to their own ways.
    I have seen their ways, but I will heal them;
        I will lead them and repay them with comfort,
        creating for their mourners the fruit of the lips.
    Peace, peace, to the far and the near, says the Lord;
        and I will heal them.

A reading from the prophecy of Micah. (4.1-5)
    In days to come
        the mountain of the Lord's house
    shall be established as the highest of the mountains,
        and shall be raised up above the hills.
    Peoples shall stream to it,
        and many nations shall come and say:
    'Come, let us go up to the mountain of the Lord,
        to the house of the God of Jacob;
    that he may teach us his ways
        and that we may walk in his paths.'
    For out of Zion shall go forth instruction,

and the word of the Lord from Jerusalem.
He shall judge between many peoples,
    and shall arbitrate between strong nations far away;
they shall beat their swords into ploughshares,
    and their spears into pruning-hooks;
nation shall not lift up sword against nation,
    neither shall they learn war any more;
but they shall all sit under their own vines
            and under their own fig trees,
and no one shall make them afraid;
    for the mouth of the Lord of hosts has spoken.

For all the peoples walk,
    each in the name of its god,
but we will walk in the name of the Lord our God
    for ever and ever.

Psalm 40.14-17; Psalm 72.1-7; Psalm 85.8-13

A reading from the Letter of Paul to the Philippians. (4.6-9)
Do not worry about anything, but in everything by prayer and
supplication with thanksgiving let your requests be made known to
God. And the peace of God, which surpasses all understanding, will
guard your hearts and your minds in Christ Jesus.
  Finally, belovèd, whatever is true, whatever is honourable, whatever
is just, whatever is pure, whatever is pleasing, whatever is commendable, if there is any excellence and if there is anything worthy of
praise, think about these things. Keep on doing the things that you
have learned and received and heard and seen in me, and the God of
peace will be with you.

A reading from the First Letter of Paul to Timothy. (2.1-6)
I urge that supplications, prayers, intercessions, and thanksgivings
be made for everyone, for kings and all who are in high positions,
so that we may lead a quiet and peaceable life in all godliness
and dignity. This is right and is acceptable in the sight of God
our Saviour, who desires everyone to be saved and to come to the
knowledge of the truth. For
    there is one God;
        there is also one mediator between God and humankind,
    Christ Jesus, himself human,
        who gave himself a ransom for all
– this was attested at the right time.

Peace of the World   247

A reading from the Letter of James. *(3.13-end)*

Who is wise and understanding among you? Show by your good life that your works are done with gentleness born of wisdom. But if you have bitter envy and selfish ambition in your hearts, do not be boastful and false to the truth. Such wisdom does not come down from above, but is earthly, unspiritual, devilish. For where there is envy and selfish ambition, there will also be disorder and wickedness of every kind. But the wisdom from above is first pure, then peaceable, gentle, willing to yield, full of mercy and good fruits, without a trace of partiality or hypocrisy. And a harvest of righteousness is sown in peace for those who make peace.

A reading from the Gospel according to Matthew. *(5.43-end)*

Jesus said to his disciples, 'You have heard that it was said, "You shall love your neighbour and hate your enemy." But I say to you, Love your enemies and pray for those who persecute you, so that you may be children of your Father in heaven; for he makes his sun rise on the evil and on the good, and sends rain on the righteous and on the unrighteous. For if you love those who love you, what reward do you have? Do not even the tax collectors do the same? And if you greet only your brothers and sisters, what more are you doing than others? Do not even the Gentiles do the same? Be perfect, therefore, as your heavenly Father is perfect.'

A reading from the Gospel according to John. *(14.23-29)*

Jesus said, 'Those who love me will keep my word, and my Father will love them, and we will come to them and make our home with them. Whoever does not love me does not keep my words; and the word that you hear is not mine, but is from the Father who sent me.

'I have said these things to you while I am still with you. But the Advocate, the Holy Spirit, whom the Father will send in my name, will teach you everything, and remind you of all that I have said to you. Peace I leave with you; my peace I give to you. I do not give to you as the world gives. Do not let your hearts be troubled, and do not let them be afraid. You heard me say to you, "I am going away, and I am coming to you." If you loved me, you would rejoice that I am going to the Father, because the Father is greater than I. And now I have told you this before it occurs, so that when it does occur, you may believe.'

A reading from the Gospel according to John. (15.9-17)

Jesus said to his disciples, 'As the Father has loved me, so I have loved you; abide in my love. If you keep my commandments, you will abide in my love, just as I have kept my Father's commandments and abide in his love. I have said these things to you so that my joy may be in you, and that your joy may be complete.

'This is my commandment, that you love one another as I have loved you. No one has greater love than this, to lay down one's life for one's friends. You are my friends if you do what I command you. I do not call you servants any longer, because the servant does not know what the master is doing; but I have called you friends, because I have made known to you everything that I have heard from my Father. You did not choose me but I chose you. And I appointed you to go and bear fruit, fruit that will last, so that the Father will give you whatever you ask him in my name. I am giving you these commands so that you may love one another.'

Social Justice & Responsibility

Collect
Eternal God,
in whose perfect realm
no sword is drawn but the sword of righteousness,
and no strength known but the strength of love:
so guide and inspire the work of those who seek your kingdom
that all your people may find their security
in that love which casts out fear
and in the fellowship revealed to us
in Jesus Christ our Saviour,
who is alive and reigns with you
in the unity of the Holy Spirit,
one God, now and for ever.

Or:

Almighty and eternal God,
to whom we must all give account:
guide with your Spirit the . . . of this *(city, society, etc.),*
that *we/they* may be faithful to the mind of Christ
and seek in all *our/their* purposes to enrich our common life;
through Jesus Christ your Son our Lord,
who is alive and reigns with you
in the unity of the Holy Spirit,
one God, now and for ever.

Post Communion
Blessèd God,
help us, whom you have fed and satisfied in this eucharist,
to hunger and thirst for what is right;
help us, who here have rejoiced and been glad,
to stand with those who are persecuted and reviled;
help us, who here have glimpsed the life of heaven,
to strive for the cause of right
  and for the coming of the kingdom of Jesus Christ,
who is alive and reigns, now and for ever.

A reading from the book Deuteronomy (5.1-21)

Moses convened all Israel, and said to them:

Hear, O Israel, the statutes and ordinances that I am addressing to you today; you shall learn them and observe them diligently. The Lord our God made a covenant with us at Horeb. Not with our ancestors did the Lord make this covenant, but with us, who are all of us here alive today. The Lord spoke with you face to face at the mountain, out of the fire. (At that time I was standing between the Lord and you to declare to you the words of the Lord; for you were afraid because of the fire and did not go up the mountain.) And he said: I am the Lord your God, who brought you out of the land of Egypt, out of the house of slavery; you shall have no other gods before me.

You shall not make for yourself an idol, whether in the form of anything that is in heaven above, or that is on the earth beneath, or that is in the water under the earth. You shall not bow down to them or worship them; for I the Lord your God am a jealous God, punishing children for the iniquity of parents, to the third and fourth generation of those who reject me, but showing steadfast love to the thousandth generation of those who love me and keep my commandments.

You shall not make wrongful use of the name of the Lord your God, for the Lord will not acquit anyone who misuses his name.

Observe the sabbath day and keep it holy, as the Lord your God commanded you. Six days you shall labour and do all your work. But the seventh day is a sabbath to the Lord your God; you shall not do any work – you, or your son or your daughter, or your male or female slave, or your ox or your donkey, or any of your livestock, or the resident alien in your towns, so that your male and female slave may rest as well as you. Remember that you were a slave in the land of Egypt, and the Lord your God brought you out from there with a mighty hand and an outstretched arm; therefore the Lord your God commanded you to keep the sabbath day.

Honour your father and your mother, as the Lord your God commanded you, so that your days may be long and that it may go well with you in the land that the Lord your God is giving you.

You shall not murder.

Neither shall you commit adultery.

Neither shall you steal.

Neither shall you bear false witness against your neighbour.

Neither shall you covet your neighbour's wife.

Neither shall you desire your neighbour's house, or field, or male or female slave, or ox, or donkey, or anything that belongs to your neighbour.

A reading from the book Deuteronomy (6.1-13)

Moses said to all Israel: Now this is the commandment – the statutes and the ordinances – that the Lord your God charged me to teach you to observe in the land that you are about to cross into and occupy, so that you and your children and your children's children may fear the Lord your God all the days of your life, and keep all his decrees and his commandments that I am commanding you, so that your days may be long. Hear therefore, O Israel, and observe them diligently, so that it may go well with you, and so that you may multiply greatly in a land flowing with milk and honey, as the Lord, the God of your ancestors, has promised you.

Hear, O Israel: The Lord is our God, the Lord alone. You shall love the Lord your God with all your heart, and with all your soul, and with all your might. Keep these words that I am commanding you today in your heart. Recite them to your children and talk about them when you are at home and when you are away, when you lie down and when you rise. Bind them as a sign on your hand, fix them as an emblem on your forehead, and write them on the doorposts of your house and on your gates.

When the Lord your God has brought you into the land that he swore to your ancestors, to Abraham, to Isaac, and to Jacob, to give you – a land with fine, large cities that you did not build, houses filled with all sorts of goods that you did not fill, hewn cisterns that you did not hew, vineyards and olive groves that you did not plant – and when you have eaten your fill, take care that you do not forget the Lord, who brought you out of the land of Egypt, out of the house of slavery. The Lord your God you shall fear; him you shall serve, and by his name alone you shall swear.

A reading from the prophecy of Isaiah. (32.16-20)

Justice will dwell in the wilderness,
   and righteousness abide in the fruitful field.
The effect of righteousness will be peace,
   and the result of righteousness, quietness and trust for ever.
My people will abide in a peaceful habitation,
   in secure dwellings, and in quiet resting places.
The forest will disappear completely,
   and the city will be utterly laid low.
Happy will you be who sow beside every stream,
   who let the ox and the donkey range freely.

A reading from the prophecy of Amos. (5.21-24)

I hate, I despise your festivals,
   and I take no delight in your solemn assemblies.
Even though you offer me your burnt offerings
       and grain-offerings,
   I will not accept them;
and the offerings of well-being of your fatted animals
   I will not look upon.
Take away from me the noise of your songs;
   I will not listen to the melody of your harps.
But let justice roll down like waters,
   and righteousness like an ever-flowing stream.

A reading from the prophecy of Amos. (8.4-7)

Hear this, you that trample on the needy,
   and bring to ruin the poor of the land,
saying, 'When will the new moon be over
   so that we may sell grain;
and the sabbath,
   so that we may offer wheat for sale?
We will make the ephah small and the shekel great,
   and practise deceit with false balances,
buying the poor for silver
   and the needy for a pair of sandals,
   and selling the sweepings of the wheat.'

The Lord has sworn by the pride of Jacob:
Surely I will never forget any of their deeds.

Psalm 20; Psalm 31.21-24; Psalm 67; Psalm 82; Psalm 85.1-7;
Psalm 100; Psalm 146.5-10

A reading from the Acts of the Apostles. (5.1-11)

A man named Ananias, with the consent of his wife Sapphira, sold a
piece of property; with his wife's knowledge, he kept back some of
the proceeds, and brought only a part and laid it at the apostles' feet.
'Ananias,' Peter asked, 'why has Satan filled your heart to lie to the
Holy Spirit and to keep back part of the proceeds of the land? While
it remained unsold, did it not remain your own? And after it was
sold, were not the proceeds at your disposal? How is it that you have
contrived this deed in your heart? You did not lie to us but to God!'
Now when Ananias heard these words, he fell down and died. And
great fear seized all who heard of it. The young men came and

wrapped up his body, then carried him out and buried him.

After an interval of about three hours his wife came in, not knowing what had happened. Peter said to her, 'Tell me whether you and your husband sold the land for such and such a price.' And she said, 'Yes, that was the price.' Then Peter said to her, 'How is it that you have agreed together to put the Spirit of the Lord to the test? Look, the feet of those who have buried your husband are at the door, and they will carry you out.' Immediately she fell down at his feet and died. When the young men came in they found her dead, so they carried her out and buried her beside her husband. And great fear seized the whole church and all who heard of these things.

A reading from the Letter of Paul to the Philippians. (2.1-11)
If there is any encouragement in Christ, any consolation from love, any sharing in the Spirit, any compassion and sympathy, make my joy complete: be of the same mind, having the same love, being in full accord and of one mind. Do nothing from selfish ambition or conceit, but in humility regard others as better than yourselves. Let each of you look not to your own interests, but to the interests of others. Let the same mind be in you that was in Christ Jesus,
> who, though he was in the form of God,
>> did not regard equality with God
>> as something to be exploited,
> but emptied himself,
>> taking the form of a slave,
>> being born in human likeness.
> And being found in human form,
>> he humbled himself
> and became obedient to the point of death –
>> even death on a cross.

> Therefore God also highly exalted him
>> and gave him the name
>> that is above every name,
> so that at the name of Jesus
>> every knee should bend,
>> in heaven and on earth and under the earth,
> and every tongue should confess
>> that Jesus Christ is Lord,
>> to the glory of God the Father.

A reading from the Letter of Paul to the Philippians. (4.8-13)
Belovèd, whatever is true, whatever is honourable, whatever is just, whatever is pure, whatever is pleasing, whatever is commendable, if there is any excellence and if there is anything worthy of praise, think about these things. Keep on doing the things that you have learned and received and heard and seen in me, and the God of peace will be with you.

I rejoice in the Lord greatly that now at last you have revived your concern for me; indeed, you were concerned for me, but had no opportunity to show it. Not that I am referring to being in need; for I have learned to be content with whatever I have. I know what it is to have little, and I know what it is to have plenty. In any and all circumstances I have learned the secret of being well-fed and of going hungry, of having plenty and of being in need. I can do all things through him who strengthens me.

A reading from the Letter of Paul to the Colossians. (3.12-15)
As God's chosen ones, holy and belovèd, clothe yourselves with compassion, kindness, humility, meekness, and patience. Bear with one another and, if anyone has a complaint against another, forgive each other; just as the Lord has forgiven you, so you also must forgive. Above all, clothe yourselves with love, which binds everything together in perfect harmony. And let the peace of Christ rule in your hearts, to which indeed you were called in the one body. And be thankful.

A reading from the Letter of James. (2.1-4)
My brothers and sisters, do you with your acts of favouritism really believe in our glorious Lord Jesus Christ? For if a person with gold rings and in fine clothes comes into your assembly, and if a poor person in dirty clothes also comes in, and if you take notice of the one wearing the fine clothes and say, 'Have a seat here, please,' while to the one who is poor you say, 'Stand there,' or, 'Sit at my feet,' have you not made distinctions among yourselves, and become judges with evil thoughts?

A reading from the Gospel according to Matthew. (5.1-12)
When Jesus saw the crowds, he went up the mountain; and after he sat down, his disciples came to him. Then he began to speak, and taught them, saying:
'Blessèd are the poor in spirit, for theirs is the kingdom of heaven.
'Blessèd are those who mourn, for they will be comforted.
'Blessèd are the meek, for they will inherit the earth.

'Blessèd are those who hunger and thirst for righteousness, for they will be filled.

'Blessèd are the merciful, for they will receive mercy.

'Blessèd are the pure in heart, for they will see God.

'Blessèd are the peacemakers, for they will be called children of God.

'Blessèd are those who are persecuted for righteousness' sake, for theirs is the kingdom of heaven.

'Blessèd are you when people revile you and persecute you and utter all kinds of evil against you falsely on my account. Rejoice and be glad, for your reward is great in heaven, for in the same way they persecuted the prophets who were before you.'

A reading from the Gospel according to Matthew. (25.31-end)
Jesus said to his disciples, 'When the Son of Man comes in his glory, and all the angels with him, then he will sit on the throne of his glory. All the nations will be gathered before him, and he will separate people one from another as a shepherd separates the sheep from the goats, and he will put the sheep at his right hand and the goats at the left. Then the king will say to those at his right hand, "Come, you that are blessed by my Father, inherit the kingdom prepared for you from the foundation of the world; for I was hungry and you gave me food, I was thirsty and you gave me something to drink, I was a stranger and you welcomed me, I was naked and you gave me clothing, I was sick and you took care of me, I was in prison and you visited me." Then the righteous will answer him, "Lord, when was it that we saw you hungry and gave you food, or thirsty and gave you something to drink? And when was it that we saw you a stranger and welcomed you, or naked and gave you clothing? And when was it that we saw you sick or in prison and visited you?" And the king will answer them, "Truly I tell you, just as you did it to one of the least of these who are members of my family, you did it to me."

'Then he will say to those at his left hand, "You that are accursed, depart from me into the eternal fire prepared for the devil and his angels; for I was hungry and you gave me no food, I was thirsty and you gave me nothing to drink, I was a stranger and you did not welcome me, naked and you did not give me clothing, sick and in prison and you did not visit me." Then they also will answer, "Lord, when was it that we saw you hungry or thirsty or a stranger or naked or sick or in prison, and did not take care of you?" Then he will answer them, "Truly I tell you, just as you did not do it to one of the least of these, you did not do it to me." And these will go away into eternal punishment, but the righteous into eternal life.'

Social Justice & Responsibility

A reading from the Gospel according to Mark. (10.42-45)
Jesus called the disciples and said to them, 'You know that among the Gentiles those whom they recognize as their rulers lord it over them, and their great ones are tyrants over them. But it is not so among you; but whoever wishes to become great among you must be your servant, and whoever wishes to be first among you must be slave of all. For the Son of Man came not to be served but to serve, and to give his life a ransom for many.'

A reading from the Gospel according to Luke. (3.7-14)
John said to the crowds that came out to be baptized by him, 'You brood of vipers! Who warned you to flee from the wrath to come? Bear fruits worthy of repentance. Do not begin to say to yourselves, "We have Abraham as our ancestor"; for I tell you, God is able from these stones to raise up children to Abraham. Even now the axe is lying at the root of the trees; every tree therefore that does not bear good fruit is cut down and thrown into the fire.'

And the crowds asked him, 'What then should we do?' In reply he said to them, 'Whoever has two coats must share with anyone who has none; and whoever has food must do likewise.' Even tax collectors came to be baptized, and they asked him, 'Teacher, what should we do?' He said to them, 'Collect no more than the amount prescribed for you.' Soldiers also asked him, 'And we, what should we do?' He said to them, 'Do not extort money from anyone by threats or false accusation, and be satisfied with your wages.'

A reading from the Gospel according to Luke. (16.19-end)
Jesus said to the Pharisees, 'There was a rich man who was dressed in purple and fine linen and who feasted sumptuously every day. And at his gate lay a poor man named Lazarus, covered with sores, who longed to satisfy his hunger with what fell from the rich man's table; even the dogs would come and lick his sores. The poor man died and was carried away by the angels to be with Abraham. The rich man also died and was buried. In Hades, where he was being tormented, he looked up and saw Abraham far away with Lazarus by his side. He called out, "Father Abraham, have mercy on me, and send Lazarus to dip the tip of his finger in water and cool my tongue; for I am in agony in these flames." But Abraham said, "Child, remember that during your lifetime you received your good things, and Lazarus in like manner evil things; but now he is comforted here, and you are in agony. Besides all this, between you and us a great chasm has been fixed, so that those who might want to pass from

here to you cannot do so, and no one can cross from there to us." He said, "Then, father, I beg you to send him to my father's house – for I have five brothers – that he may warn them, so that they will not also come into this place of torment." Abraham replied, "They have Moses and the prophets; they should listen to them." He said, "No, father Abraham; but if someone goes to them from the dead, they will repent." He said to him, "If they do not listen to Moses and the prophets, neither will they be convinced even if someone rises from the dead."'

In Time of Trouble

Collect
Sovereign God,
the defence of those who trust in you
and the strength of those who suffer:
look with mercy on our affliction
and deliver us through our mighty Saviour Jesus Christ,
who is alive and reigns with you
in the unity of the Holy Spirit,
one God, now and for ever.

Post Communion
Almighty God,
whose Son gave us in this meal a pledge of your saving love
and a foretaste of your kingdom of justice and peace:
strengthen your people in their faith
that they may endure the sufferings of this present time
in expectation of the glory to be revealed;
through Jesus Christ our Lord.

A reading from the book Genesis. *(9.8-17)*
God said to Noah and to his sons with him, 'I am establishing my
covenant with you and your descendants after you, and with every
living creature that is with you, the birds, the domestic animals, and
every animal of the earth with you, as many as came out of the ark.
I establish my covenant with you, that never again shall all flesh be
cut off by the waters of a flood, and never again shall there be a flood
to destroy the earth.' God said, 'This is the sign of the covenant that
I make between me and you and every living creature that is with
you, for all future generations: I have set my bow in the clouds, and
it shall be a sign of the covenant between me and the earth. When I
bring clouds over the earth and the bow is seen in the clouds, I will
remember my covenant that is between me and you and every living
creature of all flesh; and the waters shall never again become a flood
to destroy all flesh. When the bow is in the clouds, I will see it and
remember the everlasting covenant between God and every living
creature of all flesh that is on the earth.' God said to Noah, 'This is
the sign of the covenant that I have established between me and all
flesh that is on the earth.'

A reading from the Book of Job. (1.13-22)

One day when Job's sons and daughters were eating and drinking wine in the eldest brother's house, a messenger came to Job and said, 'The oxen were ploughing and the donkeys were feeding beside them, and the Sabeans fell on them and carried them off, and killed the servants with the edge of the sword; I alone have escaped to tell you.' While he was still speaking, another came and said, 'The fire of God fell from heaven and burned up the sheep and the servants, and consumed them; I alone have escaped to tell you.' While he was still speaking, another came and said, 'The Chaldeans formed three columns, made a raid on the camels and carried them off, and killed the servants with the edge of the sword; I alone have escaped to tell you.' While he was still speaking, another came and said, 'Your sons and daughters were eating and drinking wine in their eldest brother's house, and suddenly a great wind came across the desert, struck the four corners of the house, and it fell on the young people, and they are dead; I alone have escaped to tell you.'

Then Job arose, tore his robe, shaved his head, and fell on the ground and worshipped. He said, 'Naked I came from my mother's womb, and naked shall I return there; the Lord gave, and the Lord has taken away; blessèd be the name of the Lord.'

In all this Job did not sin or charge God with wrongdoing.

A reading from the prophecy of Isaiah. (38.6-11)

Thus says the Lord God:

'I will deliver you and this city out of the hand of the king of Assyria, and defend this city.

This is the sign to you from the Lord, that the Lord will do this thing that he has promised: See, I will make the shadow cast by the declining sun on the dial of Ahaz turn back ten steps.' So the sun turned back on the dial the ten steps by which it had declined.

A writing of King Hezekiah of Judah, after he had been sick and had recovered from his sickness:

I said: In the noontide of my days
  I must depart;
I am consigned to the gates of Sheol
  for the rest of my years.
I said, I shall not see the Lord
  in the land of the living;
I shall look upon mortals no more
  among the inhabitants of the world.

In Time of Trouble

Psalm 86.1-7; Psalm 107.4-15; Psalm 142.1-7

A reading from the Letter of Paul to the Romans. (3.21-26)
Irrespective of law, the righteousness of God has been disclosed, and is attested by the law and the prophets, the righteousness of God through faith in Jesus Christ for all who believe. For there is no distinction, since all have sinned and fall short of the glory of God; they are now justified by his grace as a gift, through the redemption that is in Christ Jesus, whom God put forward as a sacrifice of atonement by his blood, effective through faith. He did this to show his righteousness, because in his divine forbearance he had passed over the sins previously committed; it was to prove at the present time that he himself is righteous and that he justifies the one who has faith in Jesus.

A reading from the Letter of Paul to the Romans. (8.18-25)
I consider that the sufferings of this present time are not worth comparing with the glory about to be revealed to us. For the creation waits with eager longing for the revealing of the children of God; for the creation was subjected to futility, not of its own will but by the will of the one who subjected it, in hope that the creation itself will be set free from its bondage to decay and will obtain the freedom of the glory of the children of God. We know that the whole creation has been groaning in labour pains until now; and not only the creation, but we ourselves, who have the first fruits of the Spirit, groan inwardly while we wait for adoption, the redemption of our bodies. For in hope we were saved. Now hope that is seen is not hope. For who hopes for what is seen? But if we hope for what we do not see, we wait for it with patience.

A reading from the Second Letter of Paul to the Corinthians. (8.1-5,9)
We want you to know, brothers and sisters, about the grace of God that has been granted to the churches of Macedonia; for during a severe ordeal of affliction, their abundant joy and their extreme poverty have overflowed in a wealth of generosity on their part. For, as I can testify, they voluntarily gave according to their means, and even beyond their means, begging us earnestly for the privilege of sharing in this ministry to the saints – and this, not merely as we expected; they gave themselves first to the Lord and, by the will of God, to us.
⁹ For you know the generous act of our Lord Jesus Christ, that though he was rich, yet for your sakes he became poor, so that by his poverty you might become rich.

A reading from the Gospel according to Mark. (4.35-41)
When evening had come, Jesus said to his disciples, 'Let us go across to the other side.' And leaving the crowd behind, they took him with them in the boat, just as he was. Other boats were with him. A great gale arose, and the waves beat into the boat, so that the boat was already being swamped. But he was in the stern, asleep on the cushion; and they woke him up and said to him, 'Teacher, do you not care that we are perishing?' He woke up and rebuked the wind, and said to the sea, 'Peace! Be still!' Then the wind ceased, and there was a dead calm. He said to them, 'Why are you afraid? Have you still no faith?' And they were filled with great awe and said to one another, 'Who then is this, that even the wind and the sea obey him?'

A reading from the Gospel according to Luke. (12.1-7)
When the crowd gathered by the thousands, so that they trampled on one another, Jesus began to speak first to his disciples, 'Beware of the yeast of the Pharisees, that is, their hypocrisy. Nothing is covered up that will not be uncovered, and nothing secret that will not become known. Therefore whatever you have said in the dark will be heard in the light, and what you have whispered behind closed doors will be proclaimed from the housetops.

'I tell you, my friends, do not fear those who kill the body, and after that can do nothing more. But I will warn you whom to fear: fear him who, after he has killed, has authority to cast into hell. Yes, I tell you, fear him! Are not five sparrows sold for two pennies? Yet not one of them is forgotten in God's sight. But even the hairs of your head are all counted. Do not be afraid; you are of more value than many sparrows.'

A reading from the Gospel according to John. (16.31-end)
Jesus said to his disciples, 'Do you now believe? The hour is coming, indeed it has come, when you will be scattered, each one to his home, and you will leave me alone. Yet I am not alone because the Father is with me. I have said this to you, so that in me you may have peace. In the world you face persecution. But take courage; I have conquered the world!'

In Time of Trouble